RELIGIOUS LIBERTY IN AMERICA

RELIGIOUS LIBERTY IN AMERICA

The First Amendment in Historical and Contemporary Perspective

Bruce T. Murray

University of Massachusetts Press *Amherst*
in association with
Foundation for American Communications

LC 2007047573
ISBN 978-1-55849-638-5 (paper); 637-8 (library cloth)

Designed by Dennis Anderson
Set in Berthold Walbaum Book by dix!
Printed and bound by The Maple-Vail Book Manufacturing Group

Library of Congress Cataloging-in-Publication Data

Murray, Bruce T.
    Religious liberty in America : the First Amendment in historical and
contemporary perspective / Bruce T. Murray.
        p.   cm.
    Includes bibliographical references and index.
    ISBN 978-1-55849-638-5 (pbk. : alk. paper)—ISBN 978-1-55849-637-8
(library cloth : alk. paper)
    1. Freedom of religion—United States—History.   2. Church and state—United States—
History.   3. Civil religion—United States—History.   4. Freedom of religion—United
States.   5. Church and state—United States.   6. Civil religion—United States.   I. Title.
    KF4783.M87 2008
    342.7308'52—dc22   2007047573

British Library Cataloguing in Publication data are available.

This book is dedicated to Professor Rowland A. "Tony"
Sherrill (1944–2003), longtime Chair and Professor of
Religious Studies at Indiana University–Purdue University
Indianapolis.

Professor Sherrill's lectures on American civil religion and
"Understanding People of Faith" served as the inspiration
for this book.

Congress shall make no law respecting an establishment of religion, or prohibiting the free exercise thereof.

—The Religious Liberty Clauses of the First Amendment

Contents

Preface

Sandwiched between the sprawling city limits of Los Angeles and the city of Pasadena—famous for its annual Tournament of Roses Parade—is the city of South Pasadena, a quiet little burg that has somehow managed to fend off freeways, high rise buildings, and the other encroachments of metropolitan life. Along a quarter-mile stretch of Fremont Avenue, which runs just parallel to a proposed extension of Interstate 710, is the town's "church row." Without breaking a sweat, one can walk by Grace Brethren Church, Calvary Presbyterian Church, St. James Episcopal Church, Holy Family Catholic Church, and South Pasadena Chinese Baptist Church; and just around the corner is a United Methodist Church. South Pasadena looks very much like a small midwestern town transported into the middle of Los Angeles.

What is so remarkable about this seemingly unremarkable scene—repeated in countless small towns across America—is the fact that all these different denominations exist side by side, in peace, and in cooperation. Like Garrison Keillor's semi-mythical Lake Wobegon, it is a place where Lutherans, Catholics, and Presbyterians all rub shoulders at the local "chatterbox cafe"; they are civil to one another, and the local pastors even meet periodically with the priest. It wasn't always this way.

Religious strife was very much a fact of life in seventeenth-century Europe and America. The first colonists in New England came to escape religious persecution in England and on the Continent. Ironically, they themselves often became persecutors of religious dissidents, suspected witches, and especially "Papists," who they feared would undermine the Protestant Reformation and impose the supremacy of Rome upon the shores of America. An early Colonial American would walk down a church row today in amazement or even shock: Where have all the Puritans gone? Why does the Baptist Church have Chinese writing on it? And who let the Catholics in?

One of the early New England colonists, Roger Williams, spoke out loudly for an end to the strife and the "rivers of blood" that had drenched Europe during the Protestant Reformation, the Counter Reformation, and the religious struggles in England that led to its Civil War. Williams called for complete religious freedom—even for Catholics, Muslims, and Jews. Williams' radical ideas resulted in his banishment from the Massachusetts Colony. So he moved next door and founded Rhode Island as a "haven for the cause of conscience." A century and a half later, Williams' aspirations were more fully realized in the First Amendment of the United States Constitution, which states that "Congress shall make no law respecting an establishment of religion, or prohibiting the free exercise thereof. . . ." Broadly speaking, these words translate into religious liberty. But the contours of this liberty—its shape, limits, and boundaries—are still in the process of being defined. Debate over the meaning of the First Amendment has intensified during the past sixty years since the Supreme Court began enforcing a "separation of church and state" doctrine, as discussed in chapter 7.

This book takes a glance at the more than 200-year history of the First Amendment and attempts to distill the volumes of debate, background, and case law into seven chapters. Current issues, such as controversy over the Pledge of Allegiance—with the phrase "under God"—the Ten Commandments, religion in public schools, and Faith-Based Initiatives, are given particular emphasis.

Just two miles away from peaceful church row in South Pasadena, the church district in the city of Pasadena was the center of recent controversy: The All Saints Episcopal Church made national headlines when the Internal Revenue Service launched an investigation into the church because of alleged political content in a sermon given by the Rev. George Regas, the church's rector emeritus. On the eve of the 2004 presidential election, Regas delivered the sermon titled "If Jesus Debated Senator Kerry and President Bush," in which Regas imagines Jesus admonishing Bush: "Mr. President, your doctrine of pre-emptive war is a failed doctrine." In response to publicity regarding the sermon, the IRS sent a letter to the church, warning it that tax-exempt organizations "are expressly prohibited from intervening in any political campaign for public office." More than two years later, in September 2007, the IRS concluded its examination, stating that the church had "intervened in the 2004 presidential election campaign" in violation of IRS code. But, the IRS noted, the incident "appears to be a one-time occurrence," and therefore the church's tax-exempt status would not be revoked. Throughout the controversy, All Saints received broad support from churches across the country—liberal and conservative alike. The story illustrates the potential legal limits of "free exercise." Chapter 1 defines the Free Exercise Clause, and the Supreme Court's continually evolving views of the First Amendment are tracked in chapter 7.

Across town from the All Saints Church, a controversy of another kind arose at the Los Angeles County Board office when the American Civil Liberties Union noticed that the official city seal had a cross on it. The ACLU charged that the cross represented an unconstitutional establishment of religion and called for its removal. Los Angeles County Supervisor Mike Antonovich countered, "The ACLU threat to desecrate the County seal is Orwellian, out-of-control political correctness that has no legal basis." Rather than face a costly lawsuit, the county capitulated and removed the cross. This story exemplifies the sort of challenges that are brought under the Establishment Clause as well as the "culture wars" over religion in the public square. Chapter 1 defines the Establishment Clause, and the culture wars are covered throughout in various contexts. Chapter 2 examines the underlying causes of these conflicts in terms of religious psychology, theology, sociology, and anthropology. In other words, what makes religious people tick, and why are nonreligious people often so perplexed by them?

In the spring of 2006, yet another controversy spilled onto the streets outside the Los Angeles City Hall and in cities across the nation. The mass protests over immigration and the ongoing debate indirectly shed light on another central theme of this book, American civil religion. Broadly speaking, civil religion relates to Americans' sense of national meaning and purpose—a purpose that is sanctified by a higher authority. The early New England colonists were convinced that God was shaping every move they made to create a "new Jerusalem" on America's shores. In 2007, this idea may seem farfetched, but the broader notion of national purpose—sanctioned by a divine authority—is deeply ingrained in the American psyche. Chapter 3 explores the myriad contours of American civil religion, and how it relates to the immigration debate and many other national themes.

From early colonial times, people of "foreign" faiths have come under scrutiny. Quakers and Catholics were the first groups excluded from the mainstream. Over the years the same harsh focus has fallen on other groups. The issue of religion and identity sounded a particularly discordant note in 2007 when U.S. Rep. Keith Ellison (D-Minn.), the first Muslim elected to Congress, swore his oath of office on a Koran. Ellison's gesture was shocking to many. Virginia Congressman Virgil Goode condemned Ellison's act and called for a halt to immigration from Islamic countries. Goode's condemnation prompted many more counter-condemnations against him. How similar conflicts have played out in American history and how Muslims fit into America's religious liberty equation today are covered in chapter 4.

Nowhere are the culture wars more heated than in public schools, where the hearts and minds of children are involved. In 2005, "intelligent design"—a concept that counters Charles Darwin's theory of evolution—took center stage in a Pennsylvania courtroom. The case hearkened back to the infamous 1925 "Scopes Monkey Trial," in which high school biology teacher John Scopes was convicted of illegally teaching evolution. But in the recent case, a federal judge ruled that intelligent design is creationism repackaged, and thus has no constitutionally valid place in a public school science curriculum. Chapter 5 covers this and numerous other issues related to religion and public schools.

An important but often overlooked news story during the George W. Bush administration was Bush's Faith-Based and Community Initiative, which substantially increased the involvement of religious-based organizations in the delivering of social services. The story of Faith-Based Initiatives was largely eclipsed by the September 11 terrorist attacks and the subsequent war in Iraq. The issue resurfaced late in the Bush administration when former White House operative David Kuo released his book *Tempting Faith: An Inside Story of Political Seduction,* in which he describes some of the cynicism and abuses of the Faith-Based Initiative program. Collaboration between government and religious organizations, however, is not a story that begins or ends with the Bush administration. Such partnerships have been going on since America's beginnings. Ronald Reagan ratcheted up church-state collaborations significantly during his administration in the 1980s, and Bill Clinton continued in this direction with "Charitable Choice." Chapter 6 deals with the recent history of faith-based initiatives, and the chapter appendix gives a snapshot of the longer history of church-state partnerships.

Controversies over religion and public life rage at all levels of American society and government—from city halls, statehouses, and school boards to the U.S. Capitol. When the debates can't be settled locally, they end up in federal courts of appeal, some going as far as the Supreme Court, the ultimate arbiter of the First Amendment. This book concludes with an analysis of the Supreme Court's thinking on the Religious Liberty Clauses as the Court has evolved since it was first organized in 1790.

* * *

This project originated in a series of seminars on religion and public life, conducted by the Foundation for American Communications and funded by The Pew Charitable Trusts. The series began on December 4, 2001, with the program "Understanding Religion, Faith, and Terrorism," which sought to make sense of the terrorist attacks of September 11. Subsequent programs covered a wide variety of topics—from religious diversity in America to bioethics and the stem cell debate. I covered most of these seminars and fashioned the content for Web publication. The series provided several possible outlines for the book. As I revised three years' worth of stories on the broad range of topics covered, I found myself guided toward a central theme: the First Amendment—with civil religion a parallel theme.

Frequent program speakers Charles C. Haynes of the First Amendment Center and the late Rowland "Tony" Sherrill of Indiana University–Purdue University Indianapolis lectured on the First Amendment, the history of religious liberty in America, and civil religion. Their presentations were particularly compelling and even inspiring. I felt as if I were hearing something that I had known instinctively for a long time, but had not put into words. I got the same feeling reading Robert Bellah, my primary source on civil religion. From there I turned to the writings of Martin Marty, the leading authority on religious history in America, and William Lee Miller on the First Amendment. And so my interest spiraled and dovetailed.

This book is intended for three different audiences: students, journalists, and general readers. For students, I aim this book for use in journalism, political science, sociology, and religious studies courses. For working journalists, the book is intended as a primer and a reporting tool—a reference to help journalists quickly understand this complex topic. For this purpose, I have relied heavily on primary sources and direct quotes, so that the important players—Supreme Court justices, presidents, and scholars—can be referenced directly without further research when a hurried reporter is on deadline. For a general audience, I hope the book is an easy read on a tough topic. The issues involved with religious liberty are too important to be muddled down in legalese, political double-talk, or even the language of my own profession, the dreaded journalese. My goal was to boil the issues down to the journalist's proverbial "nut graph."

* * *

I am grateful to the following distinguished scholars who assisted with this project:

Rowland A. Sherrill and Philip Goff, both of Indiana University–Purdue University Indianapolis; Charles C. Haynes of the First Amendment Center; Judge Dorothy W. Nelson of the U.S. Court of Appeals; Mark Chaves of the University of Arizona; Robert J. Wineburg of the University of North Carolina, Greensboro; Adam B. Seligman of Boston University; Richard T. Antoun of Binghamton University; Samuel C. Porter of the University of Oregon; Robert V. Kemper of Southern Methodist University; David Howard-Pitney of De Anza College; Gastón Espinosa of Claremont McKenna College; and Angeliki Kanavou of Chapman University.

Special thanks to my mentor in journalism, Steve Devitt, who hired me and gave me a chance when no one else would. I also thank my other editors over the years: R. D. Hohenfeldt (the *Rolla Daily News,* Rolla, Mo.), Bernard Chaillot (*The Daily Advertiser,* Lafayette, La.) and Paul Danison (*The Orange County Register,* Santa Ana, Calif.)

Heartfelt thanks to Randy Reddick, who hired me when I was lying in a hospital bed suffering from a broken hip, a broken shoulder, and blood clots. Randy offered me a new career in the online world. I survived to work under his tutelage for two years.

I am grateful to the two best English teachers I have ever had: Walter Wildung, retired from Rolling Hills High School; and Celeste Pernicone Barber, formerly at the University of California, Santa Barbara, now at Santa Barbara City College. And thanks to Rob Wood, Jeff Cowart, and the FACS Board of Trustees.

A special *danke schön* to Thomas Neukamp, who hired me at Deutscher Paket Dienst in in Munich, Germany, and whose relentless command, "*Auf geht's!*" (Let's go!), still echoes in my mind and shocks me out of any slacking off or procrastinating.

And without the technical help of Tim Capps, I would still be in the basement trying to figure out how to get the router to work.

Last but not least, thanks to my friends who helped either directly or indirectly in the completion of this project: Robert T. Green, Rex McDaniel, Bob Carter, Conrad and Pat von Bibra, John McDonnell, Richard Wilson, Mike Kane, Cheramie Breaux, Jo Ann Jones, Eric Amador; and my family, Pete, Bill, Aurora, Joshua, Valerie, and of course Mom and Dad.

RELIGIOUS LIBERTY IN AMERICA

From Revival to Religious Liberty

When the Press Misses the Story

> The separating of church from state certainly has not meant—despite some shrill cries that it should—the separating of religion from politics. Far from it. Churches and churchgoers have been active in American politics and social policy on explicit religious grounds from the American Revolution through the abolition movement and the Civil War and the Social Gospel and the gospel of wealth and the Prohibition movement and the pacifist movement and the Civil Rights movement. . . .
>
> —William Lee Miller, *The First Liberty: America's Foundation in Religious Freedom*

The media woke up the day after the 2004 election to a collective sigh: "How did we miss the story?" The importance American voters place on religion and moral values had largely escaped the consciousness of political reporters.

"The inescapable verdict is that many of us missed clue after clue to the true arc of Campaign 2004," wrote John McCormick, deputy editor of the *Chicago Tribune*. "Yes, *Fahrenheit 9/11* put a lot of fannies in theater seats—but it grossed less than one-third as much as *The Passion of the Christ*. For many of us in journalism, evangelical America is a parallel and foreign universe—alongside, but apart from, our more secular America." [1]

Many in and outside the media were astonished by the exit polls, in which 22 percent of the voters cited "moral values" as the most important issue in their presidential choice, compared with jobs and the economy at 20 percent, terrorism at 19 percent, and Iraq at 15 percent. [2] "This hit the newsrooms of America with gale force and was reported with breathless amazement," wrote Ron Elving of National Public Radio. "American journalism remains loath to confront the interplay of religion and politics. We'd rather invoke separation of church and state and move on to topics we're more comfortable with." [3]

By the 2006 mid-term elections, the message was sinking in with the media; and Americans began to have a change of heart as to which political party represented moral values. The congressional page scandal involving former Florida Republican Representative Mark Foley; the Jack Abramoff lobbying scandal involving several prominent Republican lawmakers, and an ongoing string of corruption and ethics allegations dogged Republicans and helped bring about their downfall in both the House and the Senate. The Republican royal flush as the party of moral values in 2004 turned up snake eyes in 2006.

The exit polls displayed a subtle shift of faith and politics: In 2004, 58 percent of voters who attend church services weekly voted for George W. Bush, and 41 percent of weekly church-goers voted for John Kerry.[4] In 2006, 55 percent of voters who attend church services weekly voted for Republicans in congressional races, and 43 percent of voters who attend church services weekly voted for Democrats.[5] The shift from 2004 to 2006 is relatively small and still within margin of error; but the races were close, and the disillusionment with the Republicans on moral grounds may have been just enough to tip the scales in the Democrats' favor.

Party politics aside, the election results and exit polls point to the integral connection between religion and politics, a connection that has existed from the early years of the Republic. Politicians can live or die by how they approach religious constituencies, as presidential hopeful John McCain found out the hard way in 2000 when he suggested that the conservative Christian leaders Pat Robertson and Jerry Falwell were "agents of intolerance."[6] McCain's comments helped mobilize evangelical Republicans behind George W. Bush, and McCain has been trying to repair relations with conservative Christian voters ever since.

Discussion of religion and politics can turn an otherwise quiet dinner party into a shouting match.[7] A connection of religion and politics can also destroy an otherwise civil society when church and state become one and the same—fused into a theocracy. The American founders were keenly aware of this danger when they crafted the Constitution and the Bill of Rights. At the forefront of their minds was the separation of church and state, which became the first sixteen words of the First Amendment: "Congress shall make no law respecting an establishment of religion, or prohibiting the free exercise thereof."

Sixteen words with centuries of freight behind them; centuries of *Christendom;* centuries of wars and bloodshed over religion; but in 1789, the first Congress of the new United States took a unique opportunity to change course. A 38-year-old congressman from Virginia named James Madison led the charge for a Bill of Rights to amend the newly minted Constitution.[8]

In the more than two centuries since the passage of the Bill of Rights, libraries of legal opinion and commentaries have been committed to the meaning and application of its first two clauses. Indeed, understanding how these words operate in the real world is no easy task. The United States Supreme Court expends considerable energy interpreting the First Amendment in countless scenarios and challenges ranging from the place of religion in public schools to religious symbols in the public square and the battle over Christmas displays.

Understanding religiosity in America is as complex as the law and the political issues.[9] But America's religious heritage has often gone uncovered in public schools. The litigiousness of the issue has frightened many administrators and school boards out of making any mention *about* religion. Religious studies has become a "black hole" in American public education. By the time journalists end up on their news beats, they are usually on their own when it comes to wading through religious currents in America.

"In our conversation about religion in the United States, we tend to talk about religion as something that happened a long time ago, and what happens today doesn't have much to do with that," said Charles C. Haynes, senior scholar at the First Amendment Center in Arlington, Va. "Religion matters in this country; it has from the beginning, and it still does."[10]

Alone among Nations

Surveys consistently show that religion remains a major force in the lives of Americans. In a 2001 survey by the Pew Research Center for the People and the Press, 64 percent of the respondents said religion is very important in their lives.[11] This number has remained relatively stable over the past two decades, after declining between the mid-1960s and the late 1970s. The Pew figures are corroborated by Gallup polls on religion. (See tables 1.1–1.3).

The Pew study also indicates,

- 90 percent of Americans pray at least once a week, and 59 percent said they pray every day or even several times a day.
- 60 percent attend religious services at least once a month, and 43 percent attend services weekly.

• 38 percent attend prayer group meetings or Bible study groups on a regular or occasional basis.[12]

The United States stands alone among the world's developed nations in its embrace of religion—or reluctance to renounce it. According to a 2002 Pew study, 59 percent of Americans said religion plays a very important role in their lives, compared to Great Britain at 33 percent, Canada at 30 percent, and Germany at 21 percent. France and the Czech Republic reported the lowest levels of religiosity in Europe, both at only 11 percent.[13]

"America is a very religious country, but one of the things that struck me is how little this is discussed and how little it is acknowledged," said Ram A. Cnaan, a native of Israel and a professor at the University of Pennsylvania's School of Social Work. Cnaan says the United States has bucked the theory that as nations modernize and industrialize they will correspondingly decline in religiosity: "It was once predicted that as technology, education and knowledge of the world increased, religion would decrease. In other words, it was assumed that religion would serve people when they don't understand the world around them; and people with rational abilities and the power to control technology would find religion obsolete. In Europe this hypothesis is supported; in Europe, in every generation there is a decrease in religiosity; but in the United States, this theory is totally rejected."[14]

The United States and its European allies share many values in terms of democracy, human rights, and civil society. But Europe and America's stark divergence in religiosity is a major source of misunderstanding and irritation. Understanding these differences is crucial to mending the trans-Atlantic rift, which existed long before the 2003 U.S. invasion of Iraq.

Table 1.1. | America's religious identification

Protestant	50
Catholic	24
Eastern Orthodox	1
Other Christian	8
Jewish	2
Mormon	1
Other non-Christian	3
No religious identification; atheists, agnostics	9
No response	2

Source: Based on 12,043 Gallup Poll interviews conducted in 2004.
Numbers in percentages of U.S. population, with a maximum margin of sampling error of plus or minus 3 percentage points.

Table 1.2. | Personal importance of religion

"How important would you say religion is in your own life—very important, fairly important, or not very important?" (in percentages) (In every case responses of "No opinion" were one percent or less.)

	Very important	Fairly important	Not very important
2004	59	23	17
2003	61	25	14
2001	64	24	12
2000	61	27	12
1995	56	30	13
1990	58	29	13
1985	55	31	13
1980	55	31	13
1965	70	22	7
1952	75	20	5

Table 1.3. | Worship attendance

"How often do you attend church or synagogue—at least once a week, almost every week, about once a month, seldom, or never?" (in percentages)

	Once a week	Almost every week	About once a month	Seldom	Never
2004 December	35	9	14	27	15
2001 December	34	11	15	28	12
2001 June	30	11	12	29	18
2000 March	36	11	13	30	10
1999 September	31	13	14	27	14
1995 September	31	13	14	31	11

Source: Table data courtesy of the Gallup Organization.

"Some nations, like those in Europe, have high political civility and very low religiosity; and other nations have high religiosity but low political civility. The United States is a nation with high religiosity and also high political civility. We are one of the few nations with both," Charles Haynes says. "The place we are in is a very fortunate place, but danger lies ahead if we don't attend to the founding principles of this messy experiment called the United States."

Strangers in Their Own Land

In the hustle and bustle of the newsroom, it was once easy to overlook religion, and leave it relegated to the features section or the Saturday religion page—if the paper had one. This changed with the terrorist attacks of September 11, 2001.

The late Rowland A. Sherrill, longtime chair of the Religious Studies Department at Indiana University–Purdue University Indianapolis, said immediately following the attacks his phone began ringing off the hook with calls from reporters attempting to make sense of what had happened.[15] The media came to realize religion is a topic that touches all news beats—especially education, government, and the courts. Similarly, religion involves all aspects of the humanities—history, literature, sociology, and political science. Ongoing controversies over religion in public schools, Faith-Based Initiatives, and public displays of religious symbols such as the Ten Commandments are hard news stories of considerable complexity that require a depth of understanding to cover adequately.

"How religious people see the world and understand events should be more a part of a wide range of stories," in Charles Haynes's view. "Almost every hot-button issue in public schools has to do with religion. Why are school administrators almost never prepared to deal with religious liberty and the First Amendment? Why are they tone-deaf to religion?" Haynes points out that the terrorist attacks of September 11, 2001, woke up many people—in and outside the newsroom—to the importance of religion in America and the importance of understanding people of different faiths: "Understanding how religious people see and experience the world has an important impact in our lives and should be covered and talked about. If we didn't know this before 9/11, we should know now that it's downright dangerous *not* to know how other people view the world."[16]

Understanding others begins with understanding oneself and one's own biases, says Adam Seligman, a professor of religion at Boston University. In approaching any term paper or news story involving matters of faith and religion, Seligman urges students and journalists to attempt to "get outside of themselves" and see through the eyes of others. No easy task. "Because after all, we are so set in our ways and so imprisoned in our own 'grid' that what do we do? he asks. "We take information reported in the newspaper, radio or television, and filter it through the grid of our pre-existing conceptions of the world, justice, rights and power; and in that way we dull the impact. We don't allow it to upset our preconceptions. That's true in stories about the Middle East; that's true of Iraq; that's true of everything."[17]

Seligman challenges students and journalists to confront issues in such a way that they don't comfortably plug into their "grid" and pander to preconceived notions. For students writing term papers and journalists covering the news, this requires them to first examine their own biases and preconceptions—perhaps the most difficult task of all. "The most important thing for any of us, in the context of journalism and the context of life, is to de-center ourselves—to make ourselves strangers to ourselves; to understand that the world doesn't end, as we say in Yiddish, at our own belly button. That's the first step toward knowledge—to see our own understanding of the world, and realize our own way of living in the world is not the only one. That is a long and difficult process. But to the extent that a little of it is possible, I really think that's the road to good journalism," Seligman says.[18]

Pilgrims in Their Own Land

The French Catholic philosopher Jacques Maritain called America a nation of "pilgrims in their own land"—a people "prodded by a dream, always on the move. They are not settled, installed. . . . In its genuine significance this American mood seems to me to be close to Christian detachment, to the Christian sense of the impermanence of earthly things. Those now with us must fade away if better ones are to appear."[19]

Beginning with the Pilgrims and the first Puritan colonists who landed in New England, and followed by centuries of subsequent waves of immigrants lured to America's shores, new arrivals came as pilgrims from other lands—fleeing persecution and hunger or seeking America's "city on a hill" and all its riches. And "pilgrims they have remained in their new land," wrote religious historian Martin E. Marty, expounding upon Maritain's observation of Americans' sense of impermanence, transience, and spiritual yearning.[20]

The Pilgrims who landed on Plymouth Rock in 1620 were separatists from the Church of England and persecuted by King James. They sought the far shores of America to form a community of worship free from the trappings of the Anglican Church, which they believed had not sufficiently reformed itself from the Catholic Church.[21]

Ten years after the Pilgrims' arrival, a group of Puritans, led by John

Winthrop, launched the Massachusetts Bay Colony. The Puritans, unlike the Pilgrims, did not advocate complete separation from the Church of England, but sought to "purify" it of its Catholic ritual. Although often maligned for their strictness and acts of intolerance against Catholics and dissenters, the Puritans were to have a profound and lasting effect on the American psyche. "Puritan Protestantism forcefully shaped much of early Colonial America and indirectly influences America still, but millions do not recognize the ethos and many reject it," Marty wrote.[22]

The American pilgrimage reached an early high water mark in the 1730s and '40s with the "Great Awakening" that swept across the colonies. The Great Awakening was an extended period of religious revival that involved intense personal religious experiences and conversion. The movement was led by Jonathan Edwards, George Whitfield, and other preachers who traveled up and down the Atlantic Seaboard delivering *the Word*. The Great Awakening marked the beginning of American evangelical Christianity, which would become the dominant force in American religion.[23]

To be "awakened" during a revivalist gathering in 1740 was to be born again in a life-changing religious experience. "It was the idea that you could point to a specific moment in which you could say 'I was changed by an emotional experience of grace,'" said Philip Goff, professor of religious studies at Indiana University–Purdue University Indianapolis. The religious fervor of the time involved "a growing notion that in order for someone to get to heaven, you had to have this experience. That became paramount. Everything else seemed trivial after that."[24]

But the Awakening was not universally heralded. Established clergy often resented the itinerant evangelists who captivated their parishioners and drew away church members. Congregations split. The revivalists came to be known as the "New Lights," and the traditionalists were called the "Old Lights."[25] Churches that embraced the revival—the Presbyterians, Baptists, and Methodists—became the largest American Protestant denominations in the following years. Churches that didn't catch the train—Anglicans, Quakers, and Congregationalists—lost dominance. The Old Light–New Light split carries on to this day, with the evangelical churches in the dominant position and the "mainline" Protestant churches steadily declining in membership.[26] The Great Awakening was a watershed event in Colonial history that Goff and other historians believe laid the groundwork for the American Revolution. The movement crossed denominational lines and drew people together from all walks of life. "This resulted in cooperation among the Protestant groups and helped tie the Colonies together," Goff notes.[27]

More awakenings were to follow in the nineteenth century and beyond. Evangelist Billy Graham brought the "New Light" revivalist spirit into the latter half of the twentieth century, and American-style revivalism continues to renew itself in each successive generation.[28] In Maritain's terms, the great American pilgrimage continues unabated. In Marty's words, "Americans will no doubt continue to express their hunger for wholeness in a fragmented society; will look for simplicity in an ever more complex world, and will find appropriate paths for their sojourns in a world of mazes."[29]

Pluralism and Diversity

The words "diversity" and "pluralism"—so much a part of today's vocabulary—meant something very different in eighteenth-century America. The thirteen colonies were inhabited almost entirely by Protestants, whose origins were in Great Britain and Western Europe.

By today's standards, the colonies would look homogenous. Yet by the standards of the day, Colonial America was diverse, and the American colonists had to find a way to negotiate their differences. The solution at which they arrived in the eighteenth century paved the way for what would become the most diverse nation on earth, religiously and otherwise.[30]

Diversity and pluralism are similar but different. Diversity, at its most basic level, simply means the existence of different types. Bringing those different types into coexistence requires effort, which is where pluralism comes in. Pluralism is a philosophical commitment to diversity, a belief that there is some intrinsic good in difference.[31]

In Colonial America, diversity existed between the different colonies; but within the individual colonies, religious diversity was generally not the order of the day. In most of New England, with the exception of Rhode Island, the Congregationalist Church was the established church; while Virginia and the southern colonies adhered to the "Old Dominion," the Anglican Church.[32]

The idea of established churches followed the traditions of England and Europe, where official churches were endorsed by kings—and their subjects were expected to adhere and support the established church through taxes.[33] Similarly, Colonial governments taxed citizens to support the established churches. In order to serve in public office, one typically had to make a statement of faith in accordance with the established church. For example, in order to hold public office in colonial Massachusetts, one had to be a member of the Congregationalist Church and recite the church's creed. Although Massachusetts was not a theocracy and the laws did not come directly from the church, the church was the gatekeeper of government and exerted control over who would be elected and thus who would make public policy decisions. This arrangement between church and state is sometimes called a "commonwealth."

Religious groups not belonging to the established churches, particularly Baptists, flourished throughout the colonies, but they "flew beneath the radar," and their influence was minimized, Goff said. "In the 1740s, if you were a Baptist in Virginia and you wanted to run for office, you couldn't. You had to be a member of the Anglican Church."

Between the North and South, the middle colonies were incubators of religious diversity.[34] Pennsylvania was founded as a haven for Quakers, a controversial and often disliked group at the time.[35] Pennsylvania also attracted significant numbers of German Lutherans, Scots-Irish Presbyterians, Amish Anabaptists, and Mennonites. Maryland was founded by George Calvert, the first Lord Baltimore, as a haven for Catholics, making it unique among the overwhelmingly Protestant colonies.[36] The Maryland Toleration Act of 1649 codified toleration for many denominations—as long as they were Christian. Rhode Island offered complete free exercise of religion and, along with New York, attracted the first Jews to the colonies.[37]

The growing diversity of religious sects in America would have a critical influence on the advent of the First Amendment, the blueprint for religious freedom in America.[38]

Prelude to the First Amendment

> During almost fifteen centuries has the legal establishment of Christianity been on trial. What have been its fruits? More or less in all places, pride and indolence in the Clergy, ignorance and servility in the laity, in both, superstition, bigotry and persecution.
>
> —James Madison, "Memorial and Remonstrance against Religious Assessments," 1785

The United States is not only one of the most religious nations in the developed world, but it is also the most diverse, with some 3,000 religious groups. This scenario would not be possible but for "The First Liberty," the first sixteen words of the First Amendment.[39]

An important precursor to the First Amendment was the Virginia Statute for Religious Freedom—drafted by Thomas Jefferson in 1777 and adopted by the Virginia Assembly in 1786. Section 2 of the statute, which remains part of the Virginia Constitution, declares, "that no man shall be compelled to frequent or support any religious worship, place, or ministry whatsoever, nor shall be enforced, restrained, molested, or burdened in his body or goods, nor shall otherwise suffer on account of his religious opinions or belief; but that all men shall be free to profess, and by argument to maintain, their opinion in matters of religion, and that the same shall in no wise diminish enlarge, or affect their civil capacities."[40]

Passage of the Virginia statute came on the heels of the defeat of a very different proposal, a law that would have imposed a property tax for the support of "teachers of the Christian religion." Virginia statesman Patrick Henry put forth the proposal, dubbed "General Assessments," as a compromise between a single established church, which in colonial Virginia was the Anglican Church, and complete disassociation of church and state.[41] The General Assessment would instead support a "plural establishment," whereby the state would fund a variety of denominations, according to taxpayer preference.[42] (A similar system of multiple tax-supported churches exists today in Scandinavian countries and Germany—where the government collects taxes to support a variety of churches that have been granted "public law corporation status.")[43]

But even an "establishment-lite" was too much establishment for Madison. The young statesman made the case against the General Assessment bill in his landmark treatise "Memorial and Remonstrance against Religious Assessments." In it, he argued that any government-establishment in religion, even a multiple choice system, constituted an abuse of government power and "spiritual tyranny" against the human conscience.[44] "The Religion of every man must be left to the conviction and conscience of every man; and it is the right of every man to exercise it as these may dictate. This right is in its nature an unalienable right. It is unalienable, because the opinions of men, depending only on the evidence contemplated by their own minds, cannot follow the dictates of other men."[45]

The word "unalienable" should be understood as something that is beyond the powers of government to either grant or retract. Goff explains: "The Founding Fathers looked at liberty as inalienable: It can't be given; it can't be transferred; it can't be taken away. It is a natural right. Religious liberty was a guarantee through the right of nature to choose—to choose to be different or to choose to be the same—whatever the choice might be."[46]

Supporters of the General Assessment came from a broad sector of political life. They included George Washington and future Supreme Court Justice John Marshall.[47] These were hardly religious zealots. They believed, as was the general consensus for centuries past, that religion was necessary for the maintenance of morality and an essential underpinning of civil society. "Let us with caution indulge the supposition that morality can be maintained without religion," Washington would later say in his Farewell Address to the nation.[48] (For a further explanation of Washington's meaning, see the discussion of American civil religion in chapter 3.)

Madison and Jefferson, on the other hand, were deeply suspicious of the influence of the clergy upon institutions of government. Madison would write that "the danger of silent accumulations and encroachments by Ecclesiastical Bodies have not sufficiently engaged attention in the U.S."[49] In the preamble of the Virginia Statute for Religious Freedom, Jefferson stridently declares compulsory state religion as "sinful and tyrannical."[50] He takes the logic to its next step by arguing that state-imposed religion not only tyrannizes the human mind, but it also corrupts religion itself. "The proscribing any citizen as unworthy of the public confidence by laying upon him an incapacity of being called to offices of trust and emolument, unless he profess or renounce this or that religious opinion, is depriving him injuriously of those privileges and advantages to which in common with his fellow-citizens he has a natural right, [and] it tends only to corrupt the principles of that religion it is meant to encourage, by bribing with a monopoly of worldly honors and emoluments, those who will externally profess and conform to it," the statute states.

The political developments in post-Revolutionary Virginia set the stage for the upcoming Constitutional Convention and the drafting of the Bill of Rights. The outcome of these events at the end of the eighteenth century marks a watershed in Western civilization, writes historian William Lee Miller: "These events in Virginia reflect a great historical fork in the river of Western history: For the first time, a responsible government of a 'Christian state' proposed that religion be diverted out of the main current of public things. At this juncture even the conservatives were conceding that free and independent Virginia should not be a 'confessing' state—it should have no official commitment or belief, no collective religious affirmation—and if not Virginia, then probably, as events would unfold, not the other new republican governments, either."[51]

Toleration and Freedom of Conscience

About ten years before the controversy over General Assessments, another key debate on the road to religious liberty took place in Virginia. In 1776, Virginia statesman George Mason drafted the landmark Virginia Declaration of Rights, in which he wrote that "all men should enjoy the fullest toleration in the exercise of religion according to the dictates of conscience."[52]

Mason's draft contains a key word that is *not* present in the First Amendment, but is critical to understanding it: conscience. Freedom of conscience is an underlying philosophical precept behind the First Amendment's Religious Liberty Clauses. Fast forward to 1789, when Madison introduced his first draft of the First Amendment, which read as follows: "The civil rights of none shall be abridged on account of religious belief or worship, nor shall any national religion be established, nor shall the full and equal rights of conscience be in any manner, or on any pretext, infringed."[53]

In the course of revising the amendment, the Senate dropped any mention of conscience, most likely because "conscience" was too broad a concept to codify.[54] With no record of the Senate debates, the exact reason for the wording changes is unknown. Nonetheless, freedom of conscience is still recognized as an important concept behind religious liberty. "As is plain from its text, the First Amendment was adopted to curtail the power of Congress to interfere with the individual's freedom to believe, to worship, and to express himself in accordance with the dictates of his own conscience," Supreme Court Justice John Paul Stevens wrote in *Wallace v. Jaffree* (1985).

Returning to Mason's Declaration of Rights, the document contains another word that is notably absent from the First Amendment: toleration. The word became a sticking point during debates over the Declaration. Madison objected to the wording and successfully pushed through an amendment, replacing Mason's "toleration" clause with the following: "All men are equally entitled to the free exercise of religion, according to the dictates of conscience."[55]

So what's the problem with toleration? It rings nicely to the modern ear, and seems entirely politically correct. Being tolerant is considered an essential personal virtue in a pluralistic society. For Madison, toleration as a personal virtue was fine; but in the hands of government, toleration was another matter.[56] "Mere toleration implied condescension from some institution or belief in the superior position to do the tolerating," according to Miller. "Madison's amendment removed freedom of religion from the purview of what lawyers today call 'legislative grace'—with the implicit assumption that what is thus given can be withdrawn by the power that grants it." [57]

The young Madison's deft maneuverings in Virginia politics were a coup d'état for religious freedom in what was then America's largest and most wealthy state,[58] laying the groundwork for the United States Constitution and the First Amendment—both of which Madison was a principal drafter. The free exercise clause in the Virginia Declaration of Rights would be transferred to the Free Exercise Clause of the First Amendment. Madison's defeat of General Assessments would lead to the formation of the First Amendment's Establishment Clause, "Congress shall make no law respecting an establishment of religion."

No Establishment *and* Free Exercise

> If there is any fixed star in our constitutional constellation, it is that no official, high or petty, can prescribe what shall be orthodox in politics, nationalism, religion, or other matters of opinion or force citizens to confess by word or act their faith therein.
>
> —Justice Robert Jackson, *West Virginia State*
> *Board of Education v. Barnette* (1943)

The first sixteen words of the First Amendment—the Free Exercise Clause and the Establishment Clause—together constitute the Religious Liberty Clauses that guarantee religious liberty in the United States. The 1988 Williamsburg Charter sums them up neatly: "The First Amendment Religious Liberty clauses are mutually reinforcing provisions that act as a double guarantee of religious liberty, one part barring the making of any law 'respecting an establishment of religion' and the other barring any law 'prohibiting the free exercise thereof.'" (More on the Williamsburg Charter below.)

In the real world, the two clauses don't fit together so neatly. First, there is the problem with the language—arcane, overly broad, and seemingly contradictory. "Almost every word is a problem," Miller notes. "No law 'prohibiting' free exercise seems an odd choice of verb. . . . The most dubious phrase is 'no law respecting an establishment of religion.' What does 'respecting' mean? . . . Answers have been proposed, to be sure, but that is the problem: There are multiple answers."[59] Charles Haynes and Oliver Thomas of the First Amendment Center assert the two clauses should be read as one: no establishment *and* free exercise: "The Framers did not intend that the two religion clauses cancel each other out. Any interpretation of the Establishment Clause must take into account the Free Exercise Clause and vice versa." [60]

As the conflict over religious liberty plays itself out in the public square, some try to solve the problem by giving weight to one clause or another, or picking and choosing their favorite interpretation as it suits them. Some might go so far to interpret the Free Exercise Clause to mean their freedom to impose their religious views on society, while ignoring the spirit of the Establishment Clause. [61] On the other side, some might interpret "no establishment" as empowerment to expunge all symbols and expressions of religion from the public square. These are the so-called culture wars, detailed in chapter 3.

The Supreme Court, the ultimate arbiter of the First Amendment, attempts to play the role of the "fixed star in the constitutional constellation," as Justice Robert Jackson so eloquently stated in 1943. [62] But the star is a moving target: The High Court has defined and redefined the meaning of the Religious Liberty Clauses over and over again throughout the centuries. Some of the Court's definitions of no establishment and free exercise have remained constant, while others have evolved over time.

In 1988, marking the bicentennial of the United States Constitution and Virginia's call for the Bill of Rights, a conference of leaders from a broad cross-section of American life attempted to form a "fixed star" with the Williamsburg Charter, which reaffirmed the principles of the First Amendment and defines the meaning of the Religious Liberty Clauses: "The two clauses are essentially one provision for preserving religious liberty. Both parts, No establishment and free exercise, are to be comprehensively understood as being in the service of religious liberty as a positive good. At the heart of the Establishment Clause is the prohibition of state sponsorship of religion and at the heart of Free Exercise Clause is the prohibition of state interference with religious liberty." [63]

No Religious Tests

> No religious test shall ever be required as a qualification to any office or public trust under the United States.
>
> —Article VI of the United States Constitution

Religious tests were another time-honored device used to ensure social conformity and to exclude religious minorities, especially Catholics, from public office. In colonial Virginia, for example, before the Virginia Statute for Religious Freedom, potential office-holders were required to swear disbelief in transubstantiation—a tenet of Catholicism. All of the colonies, with the notable exception of Rhode Island, had some sort of religious test for office-holders. It is therefore no minor footnote that Article VI of the Constitution prohibits requiring anyone to swear a religious oath as a prerequisite for holding public office.[64] "The significance of this often-forgotten provision cannot be exaggerated," Charles Haynes writes.[65] "At the time of the Constitutional Convention in 1787, most of the Colonies still had religious establishments or religious tests for office. It was unimaginable to many Americans that non-Protestants—Catholics, Jews, atheists, and others—could be trusted with public office."

Article VI, the First Amendment, and the rest of the Bill of Rights initially applied only to the federal government. In fact, the First Amendment, as it was massaged by committee into its present wording, was designed *to protect* state establishments from federal interference. In the early Republic, state governments could—and did—keep their established churches. Massachusetts did not do away with its Congregational establishment until 1833; Connecticut disestablished in 1818.[66]

After the Civil War, the Fourteenth Amendment was enacted, primarily to guarantee rights to former slaves. The Fourteenth Amendment had many further ramifications, among them making the Bill of Rights apply to states.[67] Philip Goff explains the logic: "If the federal government is going to establish certain rights, including the free exercise of religion, then a state cannot be allowed to prohibit free exercise."

Some states still required religious tests beyond 1868, when the Fourteenth Amendment was adopted. State tests were gradually litigated away, all the way up to 1961, when Maryland's oath was finally struck down by the U.S. Supreme Court. Coincidentally, John F. Kennedy, the first Catholic president of the United States, was elected the preceding year. That breakthrough event, like the Virginia Statute of Religious Freedom and the First Amendment, may now seem *passé*, but it marks a critical moment in the history of religious liberty in America. "It is one of the familiar effects of a thoroughgoing social achievement that those who come afterward, and live their lives taking its benefits for granted, have a hard time believing that it ever was much of an issue," Miller notes. "Yesterday's battle cry has become today's commonplace. The issue of religious liberty had been of great moment, and still was, and still is, elsewhere in the world."[68]

Some might like to roll back the clock and re-establish the practices of earlier times. At least two members of the U.S. Supreme Court consider themselves "strict constructionists," "textualists," or "originalists." Justices

Clarence Thomas and Antonin Scalia and former Chief Justice William Rehnquist believe modern interpretations of the First Amendment have strayed from the original intent. Justice Thomas, for example, believes that the Establishment Clause should not be "incorporated" by the states via the Fourteenth Amendment.[69]

"I would take this opportunity to begin the process of rethinking the Establishment Clause," Thomas wrote in *Elk Grove Unified School District v. Newdow*, a case challenging the Pledge of Allegiance. "I accept that the Free Exercise Clause, which clearly protects an individual right, applies against the States through the Fourteenth Amendment. But the Establishment Clause is another matter. The text and history of the Establishment Clause strongly suggest that it is a federalism provision intended to prevent Congress from interfering with state establishments. Thus, unlike the Free Exercise Clause, which does protect an individual right, it makes little sense to incorporate the Establishment Clause."[70]

Thus, under this logic, states would be free to re-establish their own churches and require religious oaths. This is clearly not what Madison had in mind in his *Remonstrance*—"because the establishment in question is not necessary for the support of civil government."[71] And since the precedent of Virginia's disestablishment, the nation has clearly evolved along Madisonian lines.

The Joy of Sects

> If one religion only were allowed in England, the Government would very possibly become arbitrary; if there were but two, the people would cut one another's throats; but as there are such a multitude, they all live happy and in peace.
>
> —Voltaire, "Letters on England"

Crucial to Madison's successes in securing religious liberty was the already diverse religious landscape America. By the time of the Revolution, the Anglican Church, formerly the established church of Virginia, had to share space with Presbyterians, Baptists, Methodists, and other smaller religious groups. It was in the interest of each group to have religious liberty for their own empowerment. Madison worked this fact to his advantage, playing one "sect" against another so that no one particular group, or coalition of groups, would gain dominance and attempt to impose their sect as the state church.[72] He was fond of quoting Voltaire's quip: If only one religion were allowed, the government would become despotic; but if there were many, they would all live happy and in peace.[73] Madison expounded upon this philosophy in the Federalist Papers: "In a free government, the security for civil rights must be the same as that for religious rights. It consists in the one case in the multiplicity of interests, and in the other in the multiplicity of sects. The degree of security in both cases will depend on the number of interests and sects."[74]

In drafting the U.S. Constitution, Madison applied this same theory to republican government: The different branches of government, like different religious sects, would provide a "check and balance" on one another and prevent one single entity from gaining an overabundance of power. The American system of federalism—the allotment of powers among the states and the federal government—is based on the same principle of the diffusion of powers among competing interests. "Ambition must be made to counteract ambition," Madison wrote in *The Federalist,* No. 51. "It may be a reflection on human nature, that such devices [checks and balances] should be necessary to control the abuses of government. But what is government itself, but the greatest of all reflections on human nature? If men were angels, no government would be necessary. If angels were to govern men, neither external nor internal controls on government would be necessary. In framing a government which is to be administered by men over men, the great difficulty lies in this: you must first enable the government to control the governed; and in the next place oblige it to control itself."

Thus, the balance of political powers enumerated in the U.S. Constitution corresponds with the balance of cultural powers upon which the First Amendment is predicated. "The multiplicity of mutually balancing sects furnished Madison his sample and analogy for these larger claims about the realistic foundation of republican government in the nature of man and the balancing of ambitions and of interests, which is the contribution to political thinking for which he is best known, and which reverberates to this day," Miller writes.[75]

From Protestant to "Judeo-Christian" America

> In the case of Virginia, it is impossible to deny that religion prevails with more zeal, and a more exemplary priesthood than it ever did when established and patronized by public authority. We are teaching the world the great truth that governments do better without kings and nobles than with them. The merit will be doubled by the other lesson that religion flourishes in greater purity, without than with the aid of government.
>
> —James Madison, from a letter to Edward Livingston, 1822

Separating church from state had unintended consequences. Jefferson and Madison were most concerned about keeping established religion out of government; but in the process they also liberated religion from the hands of government control. Thus, perhaps inadvertently, they created the formula that would allow religion—in multiple forms—to flourish in the United States to an unprecedented degree.

"Under the 'voluntary way' in religion, the new nation developed a revivalist and pietist Protestantism, permeating the culture, that was not what Jefferson and Madison had in mind, and which generated multitudes of sects, splits and new religions," Miller says. "Moreover, all the religious groups of Europe crossed the Atlantic to become a part of the new nation. Into this most 'Christian' country there came the largest Jewish population in Christendom. Into this most Protestant country there came successive waves of Catholics, making the Puritans' ancient 'papist' enemy the largest religious group in the country."[76]

Jefferson believed that America would eventually become Unitarian or deistic, as he was, but this was not to be.[77] Protestant Christianity was to remain the dominant force. Following the founding period, America was to see another Great Awakening, the expansion of revivalistic Christianity into the western territories, and the dramatic proliferation of sects—Protestant and otherwise. These developments were enabled, ironically, by the secular-minded Founders who fought to keep an established church out of American government. "By enacting the First Amendment and ending established churches in the state, the early American leaders 'deregulated' the religion market," Miller notes. "The resulting 'free market,' was not neutral among the competitors; it favored those in a position to take advantage of its particular conditions. These well-positioned entrepreneurs were the evangelicals, the revivalists, the pietists, the free-churches—the churches of the common man."[78]

Into the nineteenth century, the American Protestant majority developed a de facto Protestant establishment in government institutions and public schools, simply by virtue of their majority status. The majority ruled. Or, continuing the free market metaphor, "at the level of the national culture, one might say these Protestant competitors were an oligopoly engaging in price fixing. They cooperated in an attempt to make a 'Christian America.'. . . By Christian, they always meant Protestant," Miller writes.[79]

Then with the onset of massive waves of immigration—particularly Irish and German Catholics in the mid-1800s, and Eastern European Catholics and Jews in the early 1900s—Protestants increasingly had to share their place in America. The increasing diversity often met with strong resistance and backlash, such as the nativist "Know-Nothing" movement before the Civil War, the Ku Klux Klan after the Civil War, and the temperance movement—which eventually succeeded in instituting Prohibition with the passage of the Eighteenth Amendment in 1919. But these movements came and went, and diversity marched forward.[80] "Protestant pluralism grew into a 'Christian pluralism' with more cooperation between Protestants and Catholics, part of which arose during World War II when Protestants served alongside Catholics; services at the front were conducted by Catholic priests; and oftentimes the only Christian minister was a Catholic minister," Goff said.

Following World War II and the horror of the Holocaust, Jews were embraced by the American mainstream. The Cold War struggle against atheistic communism provided a rallying point for Protestants, Catholics and Jews. "You had to present a united front against godless communism," Goff said. "And popular culture helped mainstream Judaism through movies like *The Ten Commandments*. What began as Protestant pluralism, over time becomes Christian pluralism, to 'Judeo-Christian.'"[81] The balance tilted further away from the old Protestant order with the Immigration Act of 1965, which abolished country-of-origin quotas and opened the United States to a more diverse group of immigrants than ever, especially Asians and Hispanics. The new arrivals brought with them their culture and their religion, thus redefining and re-infusing America's religious character.

But amidst all of the diversity, evangelical Protestantism still remains the most influential religious and political force in America—spanning from the Second Great Awakening of the 1820s and '30s all the way to the election of Ronald Reagan in 1980 and the elections of George W. Bush in 2000 and 2004, both outcomes strongly influenced by religious conservatives.

The United States in 2007, although dizzyingly diverse and becoming ever more so, still has a distinctive religious and political heritage that continues to shape its development. Or, as Miller describes it, "America did not drop down on this planet out of pure air of abstract possibility; it arose out of a specific history. We came not from reason but from Europe. America was born not from Walt Whitman's imagination but from Western Christendom. The United States is the distinct product of the modernizing and democratizing movements of Europe, especially the Reformation and the Enlightenment. We have a history and a tradition that has shaped our mind, our nation, our institutions."[82]

A New Covenant with an Old Covenant

> Ye States of America, which retain in your constitutions or codes, any
> aberration from the sacred principle of religious liberty, by giving to
> Caesar what belongs to God, or joining together what God has put asun-
> der, hasten to revise and purify your systems, and make the example of
> your Country as pure and complete, in what relates to the freedom of the
> mind and its allegiance to its maker, as in what belongs to the legitimate
> objects of political and civil institutions.
>
> —James Madison, Detached Memoranda, 1817

> In sum, as much if not more than any other single provision in the entire
> Constitution, the Religious Liberty provisions hold the key to American
> distinctiveness and American destiny. Far from being settled by the inter-
> pretations of judges and historians, the last word on the First Amendment
> likely rests in a chapter yet to be written, documenting the unfolding
> drama of America. If religious liberty is neglected, all civil liberties will
> suffer. If it is guarded and sustained, the American experiment will be the
> more secure.
>
> —Williamsburg Charter, 1988

What does the ever-increasing diversity mean to Americans' national identity and religious notions of their country? What will America become?
How can Americans manage their religious differences and negotiate
conflicts as the nation becomes more and more ethnically and religiously
diverse?

The First Amendment—and the philosophy behind it—is the core
framework for dealing with these issues, Charles Haynes believes. "It is, in
fact, what we do share across our differences," he said.[83]

The United States is unique among nations in that it was founded not on
kinship, blood lines, or ethnicity, but on an idea—liberty—as espoused by
the Founders and embodied in the Constitution, the Declaration of Independence, and the Bill of Rights. Haynes believes this philosophy is the key
to maintaining national unity in an increasingly diverse landscape. "At our
best, Americans are defined by the principles and ideals that we share and
hold in the framing documents," he said. "As we move into the 21st century
and as we become more and more diverse, if we don't define ourselves along
principles and ideals—and instead define ourselves along race, religion and
other ways—we are going to have a difficult time as a nation."

In 1988, more than 200 prominent representatives of government, business, academia, and religious groups signed the Williamsburg Charter, which calls for a national reaffirmation of religious liberty and a renewed commitment to the values of the First Amendment. The Charter is also a plea for civility at a time when public discourse seems to grow ever more ugly and contentious. "The First Amendment's meaning is too often debated in ways that ignore the genuine grievances or justifiable fears of opposing points of view. This happens when the logic of opposing arguments favors either an unwarranted intrusion of religion into public life or an unwarranted exclusion of religion from it. History plainly shows that with religious control over government, political freedom dies; with political control over religion, religious freedom dies," the Charter states.

Madison's assertion of religious liberty as an "unalienable" right remains as valid today as it did during Revolutionary times, the Charter affirms: "Two hundred years later . . . this right to religious liberty based upon freedom of conscience remains fundamental and inalienable. While particular beliefs may be true or false, better or worse, the right to reach, hold, exercise them freely, or change them, is basic and non-negotiable."

Haynes asserts that all Americans need to either discover or renew their commitment to America's principles of religious liberty, and do so in terms of the present reality: "We have to think about the First Amendment in light of who we have become. That is very challenging. This requires moving from a model of unity at the expense of diversity, to a model that expresses unity in the interest of diversity."

In other words, every ethnic and religious group must be able to identify with the common civic ideas and principles of the nation. And they will be able to do so only if the laws are applied equally and fairly. "The atheist, the Sikh, the Hindu, the Jew—they respond to that American part of their identity if they understand that it is not weighted for or against them, but is in their interest," Haynes said.

Behind these sixteen words—"Congress shall make no law respecting an establishment of religion, or prohibiting the free exercise thereof"—is a set of core values that Americans of all backgrounds can seize onto. The Founders set out to create a lasting republic that could be governed by people of any religious creed. For Madison and Jefferson, religious liberty and freedom of conscience were beyond the powers of government; they were unalienable and untouchable by the state. And so they should remain.

"Religious liberty is something this country recognizes people have by birthright," Haynes said. "Many of the framers believed there was a higher authority in their lives than the state, and the state's role is to protect the rights of individuals to follow the dictates of their conscience as far as possible. This may be the greatest contribution the United States has made to civilization."

2

Understanding
People of Faith

Challenging Bias

> Religious insanity is very common in the United States.
> —Alexis de Tocqueville, *Democracy in America* (1835)

Typecasting people of faith is as easy from the living room armchair as it is from the newsroom or the classroom, especially when religious people in the news are shown saying or doing unreasonable things in the name of their religion.

The image of religious people in America is often shaped by their responses to the most polarizing issues like abortion, homosexuality, and evolution. The most extreme views get the most press. Not surprisingly, opinions of religious people are often polarized.

"Let's not beat around the bush: Our first response to people who are religious in ways other than we are is to be irritated," said Religious Studies Professor Rowland A. Sherrill.[1] He lectured journalists on the issue shortly after the September 11, 2001, terrorist attacks, and began his presentation by challenging those in the room on their own biases toward religion and religious people. "What is it about religious people that mystifies you, or you think is wrong, or just generally annoys you?" he asked.

Among the answers:

- Religious people are intolerant.
- Religious people believe heaven is reserved only for a narrow, select group of people.
- Religious people believe they have a monopoly on morality and spirituality.
- Many religious believers are blind adherents of their religion; they accept certainty of faith without empirical knowledge; and they are unwilling to question things.
- Religious people turn mythology and metaphor into literal truth.

Sherrill said he poses the same question to his freshmen students and gets similar responses, among them:

- Religious people sacrifice reason and rationality for faith.
- Religious people misunderstand the church-state issue.
- Religious people believe religion belongs only to organized institutions and don't make allowances for private spirituality and personal faith.
- Religious people are homogenous—they think and act exactly alike.

There are many sub-levels to these perceptions, Sherrill said. "The corollaries are that religious people are superstitious, stupid, exhibit deep dependency traits to a neurotic level; they belong to an archaic world, are anti-intellectual, are absolutist and dogmatic, brainwashed, or are under some kind of mind control." He said these perceptions often echo Karl Marx's definition of religion as "the opiate of the masses"—the idea that religion numbs the mind and allows people to avoid reality—and Sigmund Freud's theory that religion is really a projection of a person's deep neuroses.[2]

Even at the academic level, Sherrill said, religion and religious people are still subject to similar perceptions. "It's the idea that religion is reducible to some other thing; or to say, whenever you find religion, what you're really dealing with is some kind of neurosis, a political ideology, or a quest for self-interest," he said. "At the university level, like the public, one is inclined to think that there is no such thing as religion; and that religion is just a camouflage for some other thing."

What Is Religion?

> Religion is a system of symbols which acts to establish powerful,
> pervasive and long-lasting moods and motivations in men by formulating
> conceptions of a general order of existence, and clothing these concep-
> tions with such an aura of factuality that the moods and motivations seem
> uniquely realistic.
>
> —Clifford Geertz, *The Interpretation of Cultures*, 1973

Religion is at once impossible to define because it is so all-encompassing yet so personal; and it comes in as many varieties as there are people. Broadly speaking, religion is deeply concerned about life's ultimate meaning, morality, and transcendence, and it is expressed in symbolic actions, scriptures, and rituals.

Robert Bellah, professor emeritus at the University of California, Berkeley, defines religion as "a set of symbolic forms and acts that relate man to the ultimate conditions of his existence." Religion, he writes, is "the most general mechanism for integrating meaning and motivation" in human action and the interaction with society.[3]

Religion scholar Martin E. Marty describes five basic elements of religion: "ultimate concern," community, myth and symbol, rite and ceremony, and "behavioral correlates."[4]

In terms of ultimate concern, Marty asks, "What do you finally live by? For what would you be willing to die? For you, what is the Big Deal . . . ? What guiding principle organizes and infuses your life with meaning? The answer is your *ultimate concern.*[5] It may or may not relate to God or gods. By itself it is not necessarily religion, but all religions will make metaphysical claims about the nature and purpose of reality."

The outcome in Marty's equation is behavior and action—how a religion compels and motivates people. "Most religions map out for followers what virtues are most important and what actions are or are not acceptable. These behaviors, like rites and ceremonies, further clarify the core identity of religious groups," he writes.[6]

In the past four centuries, the study of Western religion has crossed two major schools of thought: the "rationalist" and "non-rationalist" views. The rationalist idea, which arose in the "Age of Enlightenment" during the seventeenth and eighteenth centuries, held that religion could be brought within the bounds of rational analysis and human understanding. The non-rationalist view, which emerged in Germany during the nineteenth century, held that religion was primarily a personal feeling and thus "irreducible and insoluble in purely scientific terms," as Bellah puts it. "The non-rationalist tradition continues to our own day in relatively pure form. . . . The utilitarian rationalist position also continues, strengthened by its gradual fusion with a Marxian understanding of religion as essentially an ideological cover, either for the defense of the status quo or for protests against it."[7]

The rationalist approach, if taken to certain extremes, can explain religion completely out of existence, or as a cover for some other thing. Princeton anthropologist Clifford Geertz devised an oft-quoted definition of religion, which he calls a system of symbols "clothed with such an aura of factuality that they seem uniquely realistic."[8] Extending the logic of Geertz's definition, although sensible from an anthropological point of view, when one removes that "clothing," what *seems* realistic is, in fact, illusion; and religion is once again reduced to some other thing.[9]

Marty offered another way to look at myth and symbol: "Myth here does not indicate something false; rather it refers to modes of communicating and believing through stylized narratives. Symbol does not mean that one 'merely' finds an image, metaphor or sign to stand for something else. It does mean that the religious person does not like flat, reductive matter-of-fact communications when more memorable, evocative forms are present. Myths and symbols relate religious truths in creative, often artistic ways." [10]

Even those who believe religion is nothing but myth or a false cover are not exempt from the need to understand religious people and their motivations, Sherrill said. This is an important task of not only students and journalists, but all of society. "Maybe isn't any such thing as religion, but there is such a thing as religious people," he said.

Social scientists who study religion and religious people are oddly similar to forensic scientists, Sherrill observed: "At university departments of religion, the 'creature' we study is the religious person. It's as if we were in a biology lab with a specimen."

The September 11 terrorist attacks spurred a sudden public interest in religion—Islam and Christianity alike. The media suddenly discovered university religious studies departments. Sherrill's phone was ringing off the hook. Many general assignment reporters stumbled upon a dumbfounding subject they hadn't before encountered: people of faith.

So just who are these "creatures?" Sherrill's quick definition: "Religious people live in a world in which they are fundamentally oriented toward something larger than themselves. Non-religious people live in a world without that." The long answer requires time and effort to develop an understanding of people who are different from ourselves. This process also involves understanding our own biases and motivations. Cultivating such an understanding is crucial to the functioning of civil society in America. In Sherrill's view: "If the media can educate the public, then you can give people the intellectual grounds to say, 'I'm never going to agree with you, but I can talk to you in a way that is respectful; and you permit me to live and I permit you to live.'"

Varieties of Religion

A particular problem in understanding the "religious creature" is the sheer variety of different religious expressions in America. Aside from the growing number of non-Christian faiths in the United States, within Christianity there are three main branches: Protestant, Catholic, and Eastern Orthodox.

Within Protestantism, the liberal "mainline" churches are distinguished from the evangelical and fundamentalist streams. In the evangelical realm, Pentecostals' focus on the embodiment of the Holy Spirit differs substantially from that of all other Protestant churches. The denominational puzzle could continue to unfold in many different directions. Similarly, non-Christian religions such as Judaism and Islam have various branches, reformed varieties, and fundamentalists. Mormons occupy a unique place of their own in America's religious panoply.[11]

Table 2.1. | Largest Christian denominations in the United States, as a percentage of the population

Catholic	24
Other Baptist	10
Southern Baptist	7
Methodist	7
Lutheran	5
Presbyterian	4
Church of Christ	3
Pentecostal	2
Episcopal	2

Source: Data from the Gallup Organization, 2004

Collectively, Protestants represent about half the U.S. population, with evangelical denominations the majority among them. Baptists are the largest Protestant group, with the various Baptist groups representing about 17 percent of the U.S. population. The Southern Baptist Convention is the largest Protestant denomination, with 20 million adherents, or slightly more than 7 percent of the population. Catholics are the single largest congregation in the United States, with more than 60 million adherents, or about 24 percent of the U.S. population.[12]

In the broadest terms, Christianity in America breaks down, like politics, into liberal, moderate, and conservative camps. American Protestantism follows three major streams: liberal, evangelical, and fundamentalist. American Catholicism has similar wings beneath its large umbrella, ranging from liberals, Catholic charismatics, to the ultra-conservative Opus Dei, which gained notoriety recently in Dan Brown's novel *The Da Vinci Code.*

Although Catholics are the single largest denomination in the United States, Protestants collectively represent the largest group and thus have the greatest influence on American society. Within Protestantism, evangelicals have captured the greatest influence at this point in history, scholar Walter Russell Mead argues in his article "God's Country?"[13] The longstanding decline of liberal mainline Protestant churches, coupled with the limited popular appeal of fundamentalism, has allowed evangelicals to capture the "middle ground" of the American religious mind, according to Mead.

"In a nutshell, fundamentalists are deeply pessimistic about the prospects for world order and see an unbridgeable divide between believers and nonbelievers. Liberals are optimistic about the prospects for world order and see little difference between Christians and nonbelievers. And evangelicals stand somewhere in between these extremes," Mead writes. "Evangelicals' core beliefs share common roots with fundamentalism, but their ideas about the world have been heavily influenced by the optimism endemic to U.S. society."

The dominant forms of American Protestantism are informed, in varying degrees, by the Calvinist Puritan forbears of early colonial America. Derived from the teachings of church reformer John Calvin (1509–1564), Calvinism upholds the total supremacy of God, and the idea that grace comes from God alone, rather than being earned through one's earthly deeds.[14] The early Puritans believed that their destiny had been predetermined by God, and that the world was divided between those chosen to receive God's grace and those who were not.[15]

"Like the Puritans, many fundamentalists hold the bleak view that there is an absolute gap between those few souls God has chosen to redeem and the many he has predestined to end up in hell," Mead says. "Evangelicals tend to act under the influence of a cheerier form of Calvinism. The strict position is that Christ's sacrifice on the cross was only intended for the small number of souls God intended to save; the others have no chance for salvation. Psychologically and doctrinally, American evangelicals generally have a less bleak outlook. They believe that the benefits of salvation are potentially available to everyone, and that God gives everyone just enough grace to be able to choose salvation if he wishes."[16]

Liberal Christianity places a greater emphasis on the ethical teachings of Jesus and the contextual meaning of the Bible, rather than absolutist doctrines. But within the mainline Christian churches—which include the Methodist, Presbyterian, Congregational, Episcopal, and Lutheran churches—there is broad disagreement on theological issues. Fundamentalist and evangelical denominations also encompass a wide variety of positions. "It would be wrong to read too much precision into these labels," according to Mead. "Most American Christians mix and match theological and social ideas from these and other strands of Protestant and Christian thought with little concern for consistency."

Indeed, Americans not only freely pick and choose within their core religious faiths, but increasingly mix them with completely different religious traditions. Eastern practices such as yoga and Zen Buddhism, as well as cabala (an offshoot of Judaism) have become popular in recent years, especially on the West Coast. Many people follow these practices in addition to their traditional faiths.[17] Most famously—or infamously—pop star Madonna embraced cabala, seemingly without any concern about contradicting her Catholic upbringing. Her much publicized move was met with both delight and dismay among Jewish and Catholic observers. But then everyone got over it—characteristic of American pluralism. "The pragmatism of U.S. culture combines with the somewhat anti-intellectual cast of evangelical religion to create a very broad public tolerance for what, to some, might seem an intolerable level of cognitive dissonance," Mead says.

Public and Private Religion

Beyond the liberal-conservative paradigm, Bellah observes religion in terms of its public and private expression. The public expression of religion seeks active intervention in the world, social or political change. The private, internal expression focuses on the inner spiritual world. These expressions exist in both liberal and conservative faiths. "For some, religion is primarily a private matter, having to do with family and congregations. For others, it is private in one sense but also a primary vehicle for expression of national and even global concerns," Bellah writes.[18]

Outward-looking religious expressions in America reached their high points during the Abolitionist movement before the Civil War, and later during the Civil Rights movement of the 1950s and '60s. Both of these movements were incubated in churches. The biblical basis for social justice served as a catalyst for emancipation from slavery and the end of segregation.[19]

But for many, religion is primarily an expression of personal faith and devotion. For those who follow longstanding faith traditions such as Catholicism, Eastern Orthodoxy, and Orthodox Judaism, religion serves to preserve the memory of a common heritage and a way to share tradition and communion. These traditions also have strong mystical and monastic expressions.[20]

The religious revivalists in eighteenth- and nineteenth-century America took the idea of personalized religion to new levels, with the emphasis on conversion—the personal encounter with Jesus Christ, being "born again." This personal expression of faith often leads in the seemingly opposite direction: In order to gain true validity, many believe a personal experience with Jesus Christ must be recounted in the form of testimony before a community of faith, turning the private experience into a public one.[21]

The personal expression of faith can cut in still other directions. Bellah speaks of a "religious individualism" in which the traditional structures of church are replaced by one's personal inclinations. This form of religious individualism is often expressed in the creed, "I'm spiritual, but not religious." This strain, while having a modern ring to it, has a long tradition in America, going back to Thomas Jefferson, who famously said, "I am a sect to myself"; and Thomas Paine, who said "My mind is my church."[22]

Religious individualism, when taken to its logical conclusion, can border on narcissism, with the individual self as the center of the universe. Bellah describes radically individualistic religion as the "belief in a cosmic selfhood," in which "God is simply the self magnified; one seeks a self that is finally identical with the world." Traditional Christian teaching about sin and redemption is replaced by an emphasis on what Bellah calls "therapeutic self-realization."[23] Again, although having a seemingly modern ring to it, this notion has a long tradition in America, as when poet Walt Whitman proclaimed in 1855, "I celebrate myself and sing myself," in the opening lines of his poem "Song of Myself."[24]

In contrast to this personal stylized spirituality, conservative religious believers seek "an external God who will provide order in the world," Bellah writes. For conservative Christians, biblical Christianity provides clear answers in a complex, sometimes threatening modern world. "The Bible provides unambiguous moral answers about 'the essential issues'—love, obedience, faith and hope," he writes. "To follow the scriptures and the words of Jesus provides a clear, but narrow, morality centered on family and personal life."[25]

For many serious believers, this "external God" issues a call to action: Go out into the world to offer healing and assistance, and deliver *The Word*. According to this philosophy, God works "horizontally" through his followers, rather than directly willing outcomes "vertically." (See the chapter 6 appendix on the "Social Gospel.") In contemporary America, evangelical Christians are the most visible in putting their faith into action and influencing public policy and the political agenda. Evangelicals are credited with giving George W. Bush about 40 percent of the votes in the 2004 election.[26] But the evangelical call to action is far from limited to conservative political causes: images of former President Jimmy Carter building homes for Habitat for Humanity;[27] megachurch pastor Rick Warren's worldwide campaign to combat AIDS and assist AIDS orphans in Africa—these are widely visible examples of external "faith in action."

"Evangelicals constantly reinforce the message of Christian responsibility to the world," Mead writes. "Partly as a result, evangelicals are often open to, and even eager for, social action and cooperation with nonbelievers in projects to improve human welfare. . . . For evangelicals, the example Christians set in their daily lives, the help they give the needy, and the effectiveness of their proclamation of the gospel—these can bring lost souls to Christ and help fulfill the divine plan."

The external expression of faith has still yet another face: "public religion" or "civil religion," the subject of the next chapter. American thinkers from Benjamin Franklin to Robert Bellah have advocated a "public church" or civil religion, which fuses the broad moral themes of the American religious tradition with America's destiny and development. Most Americans believe in some form of civil religion, even though they may not know it or even know what the term means. Almost half of all Americans believe faith is important in upholding moral values, according to a 2002 survey by the Pew Research Center for the People and the Press. About 61 percent say that children are more likely to grow up to be moral adults when they are raised in a religious faith. This idea is an important factor in the functioning of civil society in America.[28]

Irritating Religion

In observing his students' perceptions about religion and religious people, Professor Sherrill noted how strongly and personally they react to the subject. Generally, when people feel irritated by religion or religious people, it is not just a minor irritation. The issues tend to cut to the core. As with politics, disagreement over religious issues has a way of sucking the oxygen out of a room, or igniting flames.

Sherrill said some of the negative stereotypes about religion and religious people may in fact be true. "Religious people may be religious in ways that are nonsensical even to people of the same faith," he said.

Generally, the more conservative and "fundamental" the religion is, the more irritating it is to those outside the faith. Christian fundamentalists and evangelicals both possess particular tendencies that can be irritating to the outsider: Evangelicals' persistent proselytizing sends many running in the opposite direction; and the harsh theology of fundamentalists is off-putting to many.

In Mead's analysis, American fundamentalism possesses three primary characteristics: "a high view of biblical authority and inspiration; a strong determination to defend the historical Protestant faith against Roman Catholic and modernist, secular, and non-Christian influence; and the conviction that believers should separate themselves from the non-Christian world." Fundamentalists place a high importance on the difference between believers and nonbelievers, between those who are "saved" and those who are not. This notion hearkens back to the Calvinist theology of the early Puritans—that God had chosen a special "elect" group of people to receive salvation, while the rest are damned.[29] "For evangelicals and fundamentalists, liberals' emphasis on ethics translates into a belief that good works and the fulfillment of moral law are the road to God—a betrayal of Christ's message, in their view," Mead writes. "Because of original sin, they argue, humanity is utterly incapable of fulfilling any moral law whatsoever. The fundamental message of Christianity is that human efforts to please God by observing high ethical standards must fail; only Christ's crucifixion and resurrection can redeem man."[30]

Fundamentalism is also associated with a rejection of many aspects of the modern world such as stem-cell research, abortion, and the teaching of evolution in public schools. The anti-intellectual and emotional streak of some fundamentalists is alienating and infuriating to many—especially scientific academia and intellectuals who are threatened by these views.[31]

Conservative and fundamentalist Christians in America can be annoying not only to their next-door neighbors and fellow citizens, but to the rest of the world. The stark difference in religiosity between Europe and America has long been the source of trans-Atlantic tension, as Alexis de Tocqueville noted as far back as 1835. "Here and there in the midst of American society you meet with men full of a fanatical and almost wild spiritualism, which hardly exists in Europe," he wrote in *Democracy in America*. "If their social condition, their present circumstances, and their laws did not confine the minds of the Americans so closely to the pursuit of worldly welfare, it is probable that they would display more reserve and more experience whenever their attention is turned to things immaterial, and that they would check themselves without difficulty. But they feel imprisoned within bounds, which they will apparently never be allowed to pass. As soon as they have passed these bounds, their minds do not know

---

Sidebar 2.1. | Characteristics of Fundamentalism

Richard Antoun, a professor of anthropology at Binghamton University, defines fundamentalism as a particular world-view and ethos (an emotional attitude toward the world) characterized by the following attributes:

• The quest for purity in an impure world.
• A struggle of good against evil.
• Protest, outrage, certainty, and fear.
• Rigorous adherence to traditions.
• Taking a stand against the rapid change of the 21st century.
• Opposition to the ideology of modernism.
• Opposition to the secularization of society.
• Infusion of everyday activities with religious meaning.

Source: Richard Antoun, "Making Sense of Fundamentalists" (lecture presented at the FACS/Pew Journalism, Religion and Public Life seminar entitled, "Understanding Faith and Terrorism" Dec. 4, 2001, at the Scripps Howard Newspapers Board Room, Cincinnati, Ohio), http://www.facsnet.org/issues/faith/antoun.php3.

---

where to fix themselves and they often rush unrestrained beyond the range of common sense."[32]

Beyond the various manifestations of religion that can be socially divisive or otherwise irritating, religion can involve problematic psychological characteristics—among them, its "totalizing" tendency, according to Sherrill. "When you are religious, it affects everything you are," he said.

In psychological terms, religious practice can become dysfunctional, or even pathological, bringing the source of simple annoyance to something more critical. Pathological religious beliefs can manifest themselves as crippling guilt, doubt, self-righteousness, or excessive religiosity, which can lead to social isolation, according to Bellah.[33]

"Religious doubt can concentrate and summarize meaninglessness in an almost overwhelming way," he wrote. "The other pathological outcome is over-commitment, that is, dogmatism that may take such a form that it is felt that not only does religious faith meet the problem of religious meaning, but it should close all significant problems in the realm of science, technology and so on." Individuals can become religiously pathological in an otherwise normal church or other religious setting. "If, however, not merely random individuals are showing pathological symptoms but the religious system has shifted its balance or is impaired in its function so that large numbers of people are being impelled in a pathological direction, then the religious system itself has become pathological," Bellah writes.[34] Such a situation could have serious consequences for society, and in the worst case scenario, produce religious radicals who commit crimes in the name of their religion.[35]

Tearing Down the Idols

In the spring of 2001, much of the world watched in horror as the Taliban militia in Afghanistan blasted away gigantic ancient sandstone statues of Buddha in an effort to purge the country of false religious "idols."[36] At the same time in Alabama, a legal storm was brewing over a monument to the Ten Commandments that former chief justice of the state Supreme Court Roy Moore had placed in the state courthouse. The American Civil Liberties Union and Americans United for Separation of Church and State sued Moore, eventually resulting in the removal of both the monument from the courthouse and Moore from office. (See more on Roy Moore in chapters 3 and 4.)

The destruction of the Buddha statues by a fanatical Islamist regime bears an ironic similarity to the removal of religious symbols like the Ten Commandments from the American public square by secularist groups, Sherrill said. If taken too far, the drive toward secularism alters history and robs society of its heritage. "For the Taliban to take down those statues was to rob Afghanistan of a rich part of its cultural heritage," he said. "In a civil society, you don't expunge the history just because you don't happen to care for it; or because you are not religious; or you are religious in some other shape."

Sherrill emphasized that America needs to strike a balance between its religious and secular identities that does not involve obliterating religion from the public square, while at the same time respecting the separation of church and state: "A civil society has to understand how certain long-standing religious traditions have played in the cultural and historical experience of the society and to honor and respect that without privileging it. Like it or not, America does have a religious history and culture; and to refuse to honor that—not to privilege it—is absurd. It would be like tearing down the Jefferson Memorial because you lately found out Jefferson wasn't such a good guy."

Sidebar 2.2. | Six Shapes of Religion and Culture

Professor Rowland Sherrill offered six scenarios of how religion interacts with society:

- The religion of culture: When *the religion* is *the culture,* as in a theocratic state.
- Religion above culture: When religious people incorporate certain parts of the culture of larger society, but the religious element is paramount.
- Religion against culture: When religious people or groups withdraw from the world, for example, retreating to monasticism or home-schooling in reaction to the worldly culture.
- Religion and culture in tension: The clash of the liberal, secular identity of a society with its religious consciousness, as is the situation in the United States.
- Culture above and against religion: When the aspiration is for a totally secular culture. The hyper-secular French state is an example of this scenario.
- "Religion in the form of a fist": When religion becomes a transformer of culture through revolutions, reformation, and holy wars.

Source: Sherrill, "Understanding People of Faith."

The battles over the Ten Commandments, the Pledge of Allegiance—with the phrase "under God"—and other disputed religious symbols in the public square are emblematic of a deep conflict between America's religious identity and its secular character. Poor dialogue and a lack of understanding on either side of these "culture wars" further aggravate the dispute. The secular partisans in the ongoing conflict have gained the upper hand in the courts in recent years. The outcome of the Alabama Ten Commandments case in 2003 marked a decisive defeat for the religious side. A case involving the Pledge of Allegiance, further discussed in the next chapter, is pending. The religious reactions to these developments are predictably hostile. Religious people are particularly annoyed—and thus become annoying—when they are made to feel marginalized and their faith diminished, Sherrill points out: "Religious people don't like it when their religion is regarded as just another aspect of life—something without great importance."

Removing religion and religious symbols from society removes important cultural markers for many people and thereby forces them to confront the prospect of nihilism, emptiness, and a world without God. "When action approaches meaninglessness, the organization of the system of action, whether personality or social system, is seriously threatened," Bellah said.[37] When secular society dominates and triumphs over religious culture, the religious side may respond in a pathological manner, "taking the form of irrational attachment and hostile reaction to any threat."[38] At that point, civil society begins to break down.

Just like Satan, Just like Hitler

> The several sides have pursued their objectives in ways which contradict their own best ideals. Too often, for example, religious believers have been uncharitable, liberals have been illiberal, conservatives have been insensitive to tradition, champions of tolerance have been intolerant, defenders of free speech have been censorious, and citizens of a republic based on democratic accommodation have succumbed to a habit of relentless confrontation.
>
> —The Williamsburg Charter

People who oppose a particular religious group or viewpoint often point to certain events in history where religious people have behaved badly, such as the Crusades, the Inquisition, or the murdering of doctors who perform abortions. "Waving the bloody flag" is a time-honored tradition not bound to any political party or any century. James Madison, in his arguments against a general assessment to support churches in Virginia, found it convenient to leverage the Inquisition. "A Bill establishing a provision for 'teachers of the Christian religion'. . . degrades from the equal rank of citizens all those whose opinions in religion do not bend to those of the Legislative authority. Distant as it may be in its present form from the Inquisition, it differs from it only in degree," Madison wrote in his landmark "Memorial and Remonstrance against Religious Assessments."[39]

In modern times, Adolf Hitler has replaced the perpetrators of the Inquisition as the ultimate incarnation of evil on earth. The shrill tone of the current culture wars often ends up *reductio ad Hitlerum:* "He's just like Hitler," or "They're just like the Nazis." Sherrill said using a historical parallel, such as the Inquisition or the Third Reich, as representative of all people or all religion falls under the category of the "fallacy of misplaced concreteness," which involves thinking something is a "concrete" reality when in fact it is an abstract belief, opinion, or concept about the way things are.[40] In this case, the fallacy involves characterizing a whole thing by one instance of it, as if all of Christianity were represented by the Salem witch trials. "It is a historical fact that much mayhem, viciousness, meanness and violence has occurred in the name of religion," Sherrill agrees. "But on the other hand, it is not fair to any group of people to characterize them on the basis of one thing. The Inquisition is no more representative of Christianity at large than televangelism."

The Williamsburg Charter makes a plea for civility in the face of increasingly polarized public discourse. "The role of religion in American public life is too often devalued or dismissed in public debate, as though the American people's historically vital religious traditions were at best a purely private matter and at worst essentially sectarian and divisive," the Charter states.[41] "Too often in recent disputes over religion and public affairs, some have insisted that any evidence of religious influence on public policy represents an establishment of religion and is therefore precluded as an improper imposition. Overreacting to an improper veto on religion in public life, many have used religious language and images not for the legitimate influencing of policies but to inflame. . . . As a result, they bring to politics a misplaced absoluteness that idolizes politics, 'Satanizes' their enemies and politicizes their own faith." Civility, therefore, is a two-way street that requires give-and-take on either side. "Those who claim the right to criticize should assume the responsibility to comprehend. . . . Genuine tolerance considers contrary views fairly and judges them on merit. . . . Genuine tolerance honestly weighs honest differences and promotes both impartiality and pluralism," the Charter states.

A Bit of Slack

> Our history is pervaded by expressions of religious beliefs. . . . Equally pervasive is the evidence of accommodation of all faiths and all forms of religious expression, and hostility toward none.
> — U.S. Supreme Court Chief Justice Warren Burger, *Lynch v. Donnelly* (1984)

Sherrill's study of the "religious creature" moves to the study of the multitude of religious creatures—in all of their different varieties. Understanding them, from a nonreligious perspective or from the standpoints of people with differing religious views, is critical to the maintenance of civil society in America, as Sherrill said.

"A little sympathy goes a long way in dealing with religious people," he suggested. "What may appear to outsiders as misguided motivation or a failure of intelligence may be some deeply religious person trying to make sense of things. . . . On the other hand, just because people are religious doesn't mean they're right."

Sherrill offered some points to keep in mind:

- Religion is not just institutional, or something that only happens in churches, temples, or mosques. It is also a very personal and individual experience.
- Religion is not one-dimensional. "Religion is multi-expressive," as Sherrill put it. "Religious people tend to express themselves according to the adherence to a particular religious institution, but others are motivated by a commitment to scripture, ritual activities, or ideas about their own realities."
- Recognize the importance of tradition: "Religion—even liberal versions of it—always has one eye on the past."
- Religion is not always as rigid as it seems. "You can never catch religion standing still. It is adaptable; it shifts, moves and dodges. Religious people prove time and time again how capable they are of thinking things through in a way to allow refined interpretation."
- Beware of "reductionism"—the idea that religion can always be reduced to some other thing like neurosis, ignorance, or an instrument of social control.[42]

In *Education, Religion, and the Common Good,* Martin Marty offers techniques for transitioning from argument to conversation. Americans often communicate with one another as if they were in a courtroom litigating. Instead of using the adversarial technique, Marty suggests a kind of "civil Socratic method" that involves listening, questions, answers, and dialogue.

"When contentious issues are in the air, citizens naturally choose sides. They line up the armament of their arguments and fire away. Often their shooting is so noisy that they cannot hear one another. But some combatants may tire of such a battle, lay down arms and begin to listen to what opponents have to say," Marty writes. "Opponents can step back a bit and, without tossing away their arsenal of answers, start making more of questions. This is the essence of conversation: Participants allow the question to guide them. . . . Combatants can let down their guard, meet the other, and begin to listen. Constructive responses often follow."[43]

America's diverse society—with its multitude of religious communities competing for recognition—presents a challenge for both religious and nonreligious citizens alike. For the nonreligious, Sherrill stressed that the most important thing to understand is how compelling religion is to religious people, and not to belittle them or their beliefs. At the same time, "religious groups need to understand that people of other religions and secular people are as fully compelled by their outlooks as they are."

Religious people, Sherrill said, need to recognize the following challenges:

- The meaning of separation of church and state—"Religious groups need to understand how civil law and order underpins religious freedom, without which some of these religious groups would not exist."
- The value of the secular state—"The establishment of a state religion is the end of cosmopolitanism and the end of tolerance."
- The dangers of tribalism and fundamentalism—"Religious people in a civil society need to learn how to treat the religious 'other' respectfully. The biggest danger I see in fundamentalism is the tendency to go tribal— pulling the wagons into a circle, reducing life to that kinship network or blood brother network and to admit no other."
- The virtue of cosmopolitanism—"We live in a society of irretrievable pluralism. Religious groups need to understand that they live in a world replete with strangers. Cosmopolitanism requires people to continually negotiate with strangers. A new kind of cosmopolitanism among religious groups will be required for all of us to flourish."

It is unlikely all of these challenges will be met, but they are worthy goals to work toward. "We'll never live in a world where everyone agrees; but if we can disagree respectfully, we've made it," Sherrill said.

With "God on Our Side"?

American Civil Religion

What's God Got to Do with It?

> The same revolutionary beliefs for which our forebears fought are still at issue around the globe—the belief that the rights of man come not from the generosity of the state, but from the hand of God.
>
> —John F. Kennedy, Inaugural Address, January 20, 1961

> I've spoken of the shining city all my political life, but I don't know if I ever quite communicated what I saw when I said it. But in my mind it was a tall, proud city built on rocks stronger than oceans, wind-swept, God-blessed, and teeming with people of all kinds living in harmony and peace.
>
> —Ronald Reagan, Farewell Address to the Nation, January 11, 1989

> It is through the truthful exercising of the best of human qualities—respect for others, honesty about ourselves, faith in our ideals—that we come to life in God's eyes. It is how our soul, as a nation and as individuals, is revealed.
>
> —Bruce Springsteen, "Chords for Change," August 5, 2004

A convergence of current events has shed light on an elusive but pervasive phenomenon in America known as civil religion—a belief system that binds the nation's deepest-held values with transcendent meaning.

The public outpouring following the September 11, 2001, terrorist attacks; the searing debate over immigration; the response to lawsuits challenging the Pledge of Allegiance, with the phrase "under God"; and an American president who liberally invokes his faith in the context of national mission—all of these elements have come together to create a kind of "perfect storm" that has stirred civil religion to the surface.

"The Sept. 11 attacks have produced a great revitalization, for a time, of the American civil religion, that strain of American piety that bestows many of the elements of religious sentiment and faith upon the fundamental political and social institutions of the United States," wrote historian Wilfred McClay.[1]

The words "civil" and "religion" don't often fit together in everyday conversation. Indeed, the term is often disputed and misunderstood even among academics who study the subject. So just what is this civil religion? Religious Studies Professor Rowland A. Sherrill provided a succinct definition: "American civil religion is a form of devotion, outlook and commitment that deeply and widely binds the citizens of the nation together with ideas they possess and express about the sacred nature, the sacred ideals, the sacred character, and sacred meanings of their country. Civil religion is the mysterious way that religion, politics, ideas of nationhood, patriotism, etc.—energized by faith outlooks—represent a national force. Civil religion gets very little careful thought. But we live in it, and we appeal to it all of the time."[2]

Perhaps nowhere is civil religion more clearly defined—and disputed—than in the Pledge of Allegiance, with the phrase "under God." California atheist Michael Newdow has challenged the Pledge in a series of lawsuits, most recently *Roe v. Rio Linda Union School District,* currently on appeal in the United States Court of Appeals, Ninth Circuit. In an earlier lawsuit, the Ninth Circuit Court in San Francisco ruled that the Pledge of Allegiance, with the phrase "under God," represents an unconstitutional endorsement of religion in the context of public schools. Outraged, the Senate passed a unanimous resolution in the summer of 2002 condemning the court's decision. In solidarity, about 100 congressmen gathered on the steps of the Capitol and recited the pledge—"under God"—and immediately thereafter sang "God Bless America."[3]

Public displays and disputes of civil religion boiled over again in the spring of 2006, when hundreds of thousands of Latino activists and their supporters took to the streets to protest proposed legislation that would make illegal immigrants felons. The immigration debate has raised the core questions: What does it mean to be an American? What are American values? Does God bless America, or *que Dios bendiga los Estados Unidos?* On the eve of the immigration street protests, a group of various Latino and hip-hop artists released *Nuestro Himno* (Our Anthem), a Spanish adaptation of the "Star Spangled Banner," which elicited strong rebukes, including one from President George W. Bush, who asserted that the National Anthem should be sung in English.[4]

California Governor Arnold Schwarzenegger, himself an immigrant from Austria, chimed in with his own take on American civil religion (although not specifically identified as such): "Immigration is about our values. Above all, we owe it to our country and our immigrants to share our values. We should talk about our history, our institutions and our beliefs. As a river gains strength and momentum from joining waters, so America is blessed and enriched by new people and new energy. But we still need a new immigration law to properly channel the flow."[5]

Civil religion, so it seems, is most often defined under duress, in times of trial and under challenge. Most Americans don't think about civil religion every day, if at all; but when the nation is under stress, at war, or when the courts attempt to chip away at cherished national symbols, notions of God and country emerge and take a definite shape. "We go through periods when civil religion lies dormant, especially during times of economic prosperity; and then when we get something like a war, it flames back up again," Sherrill said. "In America, we don't just have material wealth, but also a 'supply side' of spiritual wealth. It's there; you just have to tap it."

The Nature of American Civil Religion

What we have, from the earliest years of the republic, is a collection of beliefs, symbols and rituals with respect to sacred things and institutionalized in a collectivity. . . . American civil religion has its own prophets and its own martyrs, its own sacred events and sacred places, its own solemn rituals and symbols. It is concerned that America be a society as perfectly in accord with the will of God as men can make it, and a light to all the nations.

—Robert Bellah, "Civil Religion in America," 1967

Civil religion goes by many different monikers: civic faith, public piety, republican religion (small "r"). Benjamin Franklin called it "public religion"; Abraham Lincoln called it "political religion."[6] Alexis de Tocqueville, the great nineteenth-century political scientist, described what he observed in America as a "republican religion": "In the United States even the religion of most of the citizens is republican, since it submits the truths of the other world to private judgment, as in politics the care of their temporal interests is abandoned to the good sense of the people. Thus every man is allowed freely to take that road which he thinks will lead him to heaven, just as the law permits every citizen to have the right of choosing his own government," Tocqueville wrote in his landmark study, *Democracy in America*. Tocqueville observed that the United States had achieved a unique balance between religion and government, whereby the two were disconnected in the Constitution but connected on a broader level through "the prevailing habits and ideas of the people."

"These partisans of liberty [Americans] know that liberty cannot be established without morality, nor morality without faith," he wrote. "That Providence has given to every human being the degree of reason necessary to direct himself in the affairs that interest him exclusively is the grand maxim upon which civil and political society rests in the United States."[7]

The binding of national conception with sacred meaning and purpose are the critical ingredients of civil religion. From the early years of the republic to the present, Americans have viewed their country in such terms, according to Sherrill. "There is a religious aura and coloration in the ways many Americans think about, live within and operate in relation to their ideas of their country as sacred entity," he noted. "People believe the country has been specially blessed by God, and that means they, the Americans, have been blessed. America and Americans, therefore, have a special place and role in the world and in human history."

A survey by the Pew Research Center for the People and the Press bears out this notion: Nearly half of Americans (48 percent) think that the United States has had special protection from God for most of its history. But this view is not unanimous: One quarter of the respondents say America has had no special divine protection.[8] (Both of these ideas have a theological basis, which is discussed in chapter 4.)

Civil religion is to be distinguished from patriotism and its various negative exponents—nationalism, jingoism, and chauvinism. Civil religion does involve patriotism—when it is taken to mean the love of and commitment to one's country. But only when the religious significance and character of the country are added does the equation add up to civil religion. "Civil religion adds to the idea [of patriotism] that the governing authority and civil order are sanctified in some way with spiritual or religious significance," Sherrill said.

The public response to the September 11 attacks was, at face value, a simple patriotic expression: waving flags, singing songs, and commiserating. But in addition, millions of Americans sought refuge and meaning in churches, impromptu neighborhood prayer meetings, and candlelight vigils. Attendance in churches and synagogues spiked the week after the attacks, according to the Gallup poll. The injection of religious meaning elevated the response to something more than patriotism and flag-waving.[9]

If taken too far, these sentiments can fall off the cliff and into the black hole of national chauvinism; and God becomes a steamroller for nationalistic triumph—what Bob Dylan so poignantly critiqued in his 1964 song, "With God on Our Side."[10]

"I's taught and brought up there
The laws to abide;
And that land that I live in
Has God on its side."

Sociologist Robert Bellah cautions against the corruption of civil religion he calls "the idolatrous worship of the state": "American civil religion is not the worship of the American nation but an understanding of the American experience in the light of ultimate and universal reality," he wrote. "Civil religion at its best is a genuine apprehension of universal and transcendent religious reality as seen in or, one could almost say, as revealed through the experience of the American people."[11]

Origins of Civil Religion

There is, therefore, a purely civil profession of faith of which the Sovereign should fix the articles, not exactly as religious dogmas, but as social sentiments without which a man cannot be a good citizen or a faithful subject. . . . Now that there is and can be no longer an exclusive national religion, tolerance should be given to all religions that tolerate others, so long as their dogmas contain nothing contrary to the duties of citizenship.
—Jean Jacques Rousseau, *On the Social Contract*

The phenomenon of civil religion has an important historical prototype in the ancient Greek city states. The philosophers Plato and Aristotle discussed at length the importance of civic piety, and each envisioned the ideal "polis" (city). Each city-state had a patron deity, such as Athena, who watched over Athens but did not rule it. At a time when the political order of the day was usually theocratic, or as in Egypt, where the pharaohs were monarch and deity fused into one, the Hellenic world managed a level of separation between church and state that allowed civil religion to emerge as a distinct form of piety.

"In Greece, you could say there was a 'divine right of the citizen,' especially in the Athenian democracy," says Angeliki Kanavou, a professor of political science at Chapman University in Orange, California. "Democracy was seen as a gift from Athena to the deserving polis. As long as people did not play god, invoke gods in their decisions and cross the line into hubris, then citizens and the gods were in harmony."[12]

The term "civil religion" was coined by Jean Jacques Rousseau in his treatise *On the Social Contract* (1762), which was widely influential among

America's founders. Rousseau analyzed the many different arrangements between government and religion: theocracy, divine-right monarchy, and the emperor-deities of Rome and Egypt. He frowned on his contemporary model of absolutist monarchies, which claimed a "divine right" to rule, and he took a negative view of Christianity itself, because he believed it divided citizens' loyalties between their civic and spiritual obligations. His solution was to create a "purely civil profession of faith" that would be promoted by a nation's leaders. "The dogmas of civil religion ought to be few, simple, and exactly worded, without explanation or commentary," he wrote. "The existence of a mighty, intelligent and beneficent Divinity, possessed of foresight and providence, the life to come, the happiness of the just, the punishment of the wicked, the sanctity of the social contract and the laws: These are its positive dogmas."[13]

The philosophers of antiquity and the Enlightenment were highly influential among the Founding Fathers, particularly Thomas Jefferson and Benjamin Franklin, who were great proponents of civil religion. After the Revolutionary period in America, the subject went without much examination or commentary until University of California, Berkeley, professor Robert Bellah revived the subject in his 1967 essay "Civil Religion in America."

"In American political theory, sovereignty rests, of course, with the people; but implicitly, and often explicitly, the ultimate sovereignty has been attributed to God," Bellah wrote. "This is the meaning of the motto, 'In God we trust,' as well as the inclusion of the phrase 'under God' in the pledge to the flag."[14] Bellah's piece generated discussion and controversy that has continued ever since. Does this civil religion really exist? If so, is it good or bad? Would we be better off without it? Should it be called something different?[15]

The Genesis of American Civil Religion

> Thus stands the cause between God and us. We are entered into covenant with Him for this work. We have taken out a commission. . . . For we must consider that we shall be as a city upon a hill. The eyes of all people are upon us.
>
> —John Winthrop, "A Model of Christian Charity," 1630

John Winthrop, a devout Puritan and leader of the Massachusetts Bay Colony, delivered his sermon "A Model of Christian Charity" on board the *Arbella* en route to Massachusetts.[16] Winthrop's landmark sermon, made familiar in modern times by Ronald Reagan, marks the genesis of American civil religion.

"The people set to come here were thinking about themselves in biblical language, especially the language of the Hebrew Bible. They referred to this place before they even got here as 'God's new Israel' and 'God's new Zion,'" Sherrill said.[17] Winthrop's Puritan followers looked upon him as a Moses-like figure, leading them to the promised land. The crossing of the Atlantic became a metaphor for crossing the Red Sea and the Jordan River, and Massachusetts would be the new Israel. The "city on a hill" echoes Jesus' "Sermon on the Mount."[18]

"These early settlers thought they were people who had been specially picked out to complete the Protestant Reformation on these shores, to create a 'city upon a hill' that would be a model to the European world. They thought of themselves as the next chapter in biblical history," Sherrill said.

This idea has carried forward from colonial times, through the American Revolution, the Civil War, and right up to the present. The language of civil religion invariably invokes the themes spelled out by Winthrop. Ronald Reagan based his presidency on the image of the "city on a hill." Bill Clinton, trying to follow up Reagan's show and fashion himself after John F. Kennedy, launched his "New Covenant" at his 1992 Democratic Nomination. Although Clinton wasn't as convincing as Reagan in preaching civil religion, he knew which language to reach for to get elected.

"Americans want to feel, 'This is our special mission, and we are a special people,'" said First Amendment scholar Charles C. Haynes. "Covenant language is a very powerful way of enunciating what the nation is about. It has to do with our special mission, which has motivated us in some powerful and important ways. It has been secularized, but it begins here."[19] (Winthrop and the beginnings of religious liberty in America are discussed further in the next chapter.)

Revolution and Civil Religion

> We hold these truths to be self-evident, that all men are created equal, that they are endowed by their Creator with certain unalienable rights. . . . And for the support of this declaration, with a firm reliance on the protection of Divine Providence, we mutually pledge to each other our lives, our fortunes, and our sacred honor.
>
> —Declaration of Independence

The Declaration of Independence marks the "establishment" of American civil religion. It is the gospel of American civil religion. In a nation that would prohibit a government establishment of religion, it simultaneously created a new public religion, under the "Creator" of "Divine Providence."

How is the Declaration of Independence to be understood in relation to American society and governance? The Declaration is not a binding document of law, like the U.S. Constitution. Bellah calls the Declaration part of the nation's "superstructure," a zone that exists apart from and above the structure of government—which is spelled out in the Constitution, which is the nation's "infrastructure."

"The Declaration of Independence points to the sovereignty of God over the collective political society," according to Bellah. "It is significant that the reference to a supra-political sovereignty—to a God who stands above the nation and whose ends are standards by which to judge the nation, and indeed only in terms of which the nation's existence is justified—becomes a permanent feature of American political life ever after." [20]

So just who is this "Creator" who is invoked in the Declaration? Thomas Jefferson, the Declaration's author, was a product of the Age of Enlightenment, which stressed the importance of reason, individualism, and a natural understanding of the world through the new breakthroughs in science. Out of the Enlightenment arose counter-religious beliefs known as universalism and *deism*. Deism rejected the prophecy and miracles of the Bible and instead focused on application of reason to understand God's truths. This mode of thought is reflected in the Declaration's opening paragraph, which describes the "separate and equal station to which the laws of nature and of nature's God entitle them." [21]

The preeminent American religious historian Martin E. Marty explained the origins of American civil religion this way: "The enlightened founders were eager to produce a universal creed that they could throw like a tent over the diverse church religions. The public religionists tore the old drama of heaven and hell from the sky and the netherworld and instead anchored religion in earthly behavior. Reason for them counted more than faith, and morals more than grace. This was the chief idea of the Enlightenment in Europe and America alike. They created the climate and language that made possible acceptance of key ideas in the Declaration of Independence, much of the Constitution and the Bill of Rights, and many freedoms that the churches had not assured for each other." [22]

In the nation's formative years, Benjamin Franklin was a major promoter of public religion, as he called it. In his "Proposals Relating to the Education of Youth in Philadelphia," Franklin proposed making public religion required school curriculum. He argued that public religion was necessary both to promote morality and to "counter the mischiefs of superstition."[23]

Jefferson went a step further, proposing a public school and state college system that would include moral instruction and civic responsibility—along the lines of what Tocqueville later described as "republican religion." Jefferson's *Bill for the More General Diffusion of Knowledge* to establish public education in Virginia was not to pass, but the idea was grafted on to America's public school system in the following century.[24]

When the time came to devise a constitution for the new republic, Jefferson was instrumental in laying the groundwork for a nation disconnected from an established state church.[25] Ironically, the man who envisioned a "wall of separation" between church and state had also devised the unofficial "church of America" in the Declaration of Independence. The U.S. Constitution prohibited the establishment of an official religion, but the public religion of America had already been "extra-established" in 1776. "Nature's God," the ideas of the Enlightenment, and the great minds of America came together in a unique way that would create the public religion—or whatever one wants to call it—that continues today.[26]

The Language of Civil Religion

> May that Being who is supreme over all, the Patron of Order, the Fountain of Justice, and the Protector in all ages of the world of virtuous liberty, continue His blessing upon this nation and its Government and give it all possible success and duration consistent with the ends of His providence.
> —John Adams, Inaugural Address, 1797

Civil religion is more easily defined in its direct expression than analytical definition. It very often comes from the mouths of politicians in formal settings and inaugural speeches, but civil religion is not the sole dominion of elected leaders. It can also be heard from veterans consecrating Memorial Day ceremonies, recitations of the Pledge of Allegiance at sports events, and even rock star Bruce Springsteen invokes civil religion, while Bob Dylan critiques it.[27]

The early American presidents were instrumental in laying the foundation of civil religion, which has been carried on in presidential language ever since. Inaugural and farewell addresses are always imbued with the language of civil religion. The early American presidents referred often to God—but usually in other symbolic terms. In his First Inaugural Address,

George Washington talks about the "Almighty Being who rules over the universe" and the "Great Author of every public and private good."[28] Thomas Jefferson refers to the "Infinite Power which rules the destinies of the universe."[29] James Monroe cut to the chase with "Almighty God"[30] in his Second Inaugural Address in 1821. John F. Kennedy, in his 1961 Inaugural Address, carried the theme through more than a century later: "I have sworn before you and the Almighty God the same solemn oath our forebears prescribed nearly a century and three quarters ago. Let us go forth to lead the land we love, asking His blessing and His help, but knowing that here on earth God's work must truly be our own."[31]

It is crucial that presidents never mention "Jesus" or "Christ" in this context, which would cross the line from civil religion into sectarian religion.[32] American civil religion transcends denomination and religious affiliation. The "Almighty" of civil religion could be Christian, Jewish, or Muslim. Even Wiccans might feel kinship with "Nature's God" of which Jefferson speaks. Strict atheists, however, would still be alienated by any mention of a deity. "While sharing much in common with Christianity, civil religion was [in the early years of the republic] neither sectarian nor in any specific sense Christian," Bellah points out. "There was an implicit but quite clear division of function between the civil religion and Christianity."[33]

Civil religion, most importantly in this context, is entirely voluntary and has no formal requirements. It is incumbent on no one. Any attempt to codify civil religion would fall on its face both legally and practically. Civil religion is reflected in free expression, not in formalized dogma.[34] The Supreme Court generally categorizes invocations of such language not as civil religion but "ceremonial deism"—formal language reserved for inaugurals, farewell addresses, and other such ceremonies. In one of Michael Newdow's challenges to the Pledge of Allegiance, Justice Sandra Day O'Connor said the phrase "under God" fell under the category of ceremonial deism, and therefore carries no religious currency that would violate the First Amendment: "Even if taken literally, the phrase ["under God"] is merely descriptive; it purports only to identify the United States as a Nation subject to divine authority. That cannot be seen as a serious invocation of God or as an expression of individual submission to divine authority," O'Connor wrote.[35]

Extending this line of reasoning, however, strips civil religious language of its meaning and reduces it to a few empty words, regurgitated in a kind of Pavlovian response.[36] But the fact that the language of civil religion still pervades presidential addresses and beyond reveals meaning beyond the mere ceremonial deism. "Using the vocabulary of civil religion is very effective," Sherrill said. "It has the effect of drawing people in the way they wish to be drawn in and identified. Speechwriters know how civil religion works."

Republican Virtue

> A government is like everything else: to preserve it we must love it. . . .
> Everything, therefore, depends on establishing this love in a republic; and
> to inspire it ought to be the principal business of education; but the surest
> way of instilling it into children is for parents to set them an example.
> —Thomas Jefferson, commenting on Montesquieu

Entrance to Winthrop's "city on a hill" was not without conditions, obligations, and duties. Those arriving in the new land were expected to be faithful followers of God *and* faithful citizens in the public sphere. Winthrop spelled out the conditions in his conclusion to "A Model of Christian Charity": "We are commanded this day to love the Lord our God, and to love one another, to walk in his ways and to keep his Commandments and his ordinance and his laws, and the articles of our Covenant with Him, that we may live and be multiplied, and that the Lord our God may bless us in the land whither we go to possess it. But if our hearts shall turn away, so that we will not obey, but shall be seduced, and worship other gods, our pleasure and profits, and serve them; it is propounded unto us this day, we shall surely perish out of the good land whither we pass over this vast sea to possess it." [37]

Individual piety and public virtue went hand in hand. In other words, the colony could not survive and function without the virtue of the people. Failure to live up to these standards would mean failure of the colony. "Our ancestors . . . were certain that if we should decline in piety and public virtue, we would meet the inexorable fate of the nations, which are but dust in the hands of God," Bellah wrote. [38]

The Puritan colonists were part of the Reformed Christian tradition, which was inspired by the teachings of Protestant reformer John Calvin. In the sixteenth century, Calvin established a Christian commonwealth in the Swiss city of Geneva, which served as a model for Christian reformers in Scotland, England, and New England. Calvin sought to create a well-ordered Christian citizenry that would function symbiotically with the government of the city-state. The Geneva government was structured in such a way that the church maintained separation from the state, but the state was infused with the people and principles of the church.[39] Calvin's Swiss commonwealth was no model of religious liberty: Citizens were required to swear confessions of faith; nonconformers were excommunicated, and suspected witches and heretics were executed. But by the standards of the day, Geneva was widely admired for its civic order, political innovations, and the University of Geneva, which was founded by Calvin and became a model for universities throughout Europe.

"John Calvin, the great European predecessor of the New England Puritans, managed to restore much of the dignity of the classical conception of political order and to combine Christian charity with civic virtue," Bellah writes. "Calvin created a city that was Christian and republican in an organic way that had few precedents."[40]

The idea of republican virtue was later expounded upon by the French political philosopher Montesquieu, according to whom the basis of social life is virtue, and a republic cannot survive without it.[41] "Virtue in a republic is a most simple thing: It is a love of the republic; it is a sensation, and not a consequence of acquired knowledge: a sensation that may be felt by the lowest as well as by the highest person in the state," Montesquieu wrote. "The love of our country is conducive to a purity of morals, and the latter is again conducive to the former."[42]

Jefferson quoted Montesquieu often on the subject of virtue—which Jefferson believed was essential to maintain America's democracy. Toward this aim, Jefferson proposed the creation of a public school system to imbue young Americans with these core values. Without careful cultivation of its citizenry, the republic would become corrupt and "perverted into tyranny," Jefferson wrote in the preamble for his *Bill for the More General Diffusion of Knowledge*. "Laws will be wisely formed and honestly administered in proportion as those who form and administer them are wise and honest; whence it becomes expedient for promoting the public happiness that those persons whom nature has endowed with genius and virtue should be rendered by liberal education worthy to receive and able to guard the sacred deposit of the rights and liberties of their fellow citizens."[43]

George Washington, also a strong promoter of republican virtue, added the civil religious element by connecting "providence" with virtue and morality. (Providence, frequently invoked in the language of civil religion, means "God's plan," or "the dynamic process of God," which is rooted in Calvin's theology of predestination.)[44] "Can it be that Providence has not connected the permanent felicity of a nation with its virtue?" Washington said in his Farewell Address in 1796. "It is substantially true that virtue or morality is a necessary spring of popular government. The rule, indeed, extends with more or less force to every species of free government. Who that is a sincere friend to it can look with indifference upon attempts to shake the foundation of the fabric?"[45]

City of Gold on a Hill

> Every individual . . . generally, indeed, neither intends to promote the public interest, nor knows how much he is promoting it. . . . He intends only his own security; and by directing industry in such a manner as its produce may be of the greatest value, he intends only his own gain. He is in this, as in many other cases, led by an invisible hand to promote an end which was no part of his intention. Nor is it always the worse for the society that it was no part of it. By pursuing his own interest he frequently promotes that of the society more effectually than when he really intends to promote it.
>
> —Adam Smith, *An Inquiry into the Nature and Causes of the Wealth of Nations*

The principle of public virtue came into conflict with the economic philosophy of the new nation, which was based on the notion of self-interest, as defined in Adam Smith's treatise on capitalism, *The Wealth of Nations* (1776).[46] The tension between these two philosophies remains until the present day, and was especially evident during the corporate scandals of the early 2000s.[47]

Unlike civil religion, Smith's "invisible hand" has no deistic associations; it is not the hand of Providence, but purely an economic impulse based on self-interest—which by happy coincidence leads to the betterment of society. Industrialist and philanthropist Andrew Carnegie (1835–1919) later attempted to merge capitalistic self-interest with social conscience, creating an "enlightened self-interest."[48]

The conflict between capitalism, the social good, and biblical values was well under way in Colonial America. In the early 1700s, the influential Puritan minister and pamphleteer Cotton Mather preached against the evils of Mammon and land grabs. The Puritans placed utmost value on work—the necessary labor to build God's city on a hill. But when hard work led to material success, dutiful caution was required, Mather preached. "A Christian should with piety follow his occupation. . . . Let every Christian walk with God when he works at his calling, and act in his occupation with an eye to God; act under the eye of God," Mather said in his sermon *A Christian at His Calling.* "But now, let these things call for your attention: Let not the business of your personal calling swallow up the business of your general calling. . . . Be not so foolish and unwise as to neglect Christ, the only savior of thy soul, in whatever thou doest." [49]

As time went by, and especially in the nineteenth century, many Americans came to associate material success with God's blessing. In other words, to be rich and successful meant that one was blessed by God. This notion wove in seamlessly with the Calvinistic idea that God has chosen a special "elect" to receive His grace. [50] "The boundless energy that characterized the early Americans undoubtedly stems in part from this feeling which is similar to that of a child who has been especially favored by its parents," Bellah writes. "And in this simple and harmonious view of human existence, worldly success is clear evidence of moral virtue and religious salvation." [51]

As the intensity of the Protestant Reformation and the Great Awakenings of the eighteenth and nineteenth centuries waned, the American dream evolved from building God's city on a hill to transforming oneself "from rags to riches." This materialistic and utilitarian dream of America was hardly new; it was present even on board the *Arbella* among Winthrop's colonists. While the first settlers were motivated by the desire to purify their religion and their souls, many came for land and opportunity. Some came for both. [52]

The industrial revolution of the nineteenth century gave rise to a class of so-called robber baron capitalists, who accumulated massive sums of wealth by exploiting America's natural resources and labor. Jefferson's vision of an agrarian society of "yeoman farmers" had given way to an urban society of laborers, managers, and owners—haves and have-nots. "Social Darwinism" became a popular philosophy among the industrialists. The fittest of society prospered—not because of divine Providence, but a result of their own ingenuity. [53]

Andrew Carnegie, an immigrant from Scotland who made a fortune in steel, railroads, and oil, defined his own version of Social Darwinism in his essay "The Gospel of Wealth" (1889), which laid out the new laws of competition that had replaced the old theology of his Presbyterian ancestors. [54] "Not evil, but good, has come to the [human] race from the accumulation of wealth by those who have the ability and energy that produce it," he wrote. "The price which society pays for the law of competition, like the price it pays for cheap comforts and luxuries, is also great; but the advantages of this law are also greater still, for it is to this law that we owe our wonderful material development, which brings improved conditions in its train." [55]

Carnegie's philosophy, although utilitarian and non-theistic, also incorporated a strong philanthropic element. According to Carnegie, those who had the facility to acquire great wealth also had the best knowledge as to how to distribute it for the general good of society. Carnegie meant what he said: by the time of his death, he had given away most of his fortune for philanthropic causes.

Both the utilitarian and the civil religious versions of the American dream remain, singularly or in combination, to this day. Many hailed the elections of Ronald Reagan and George W. Bush as the triumph of traditional American values, while opponents criticized their elections, in part, as the triumph of cynical business interests. Bellah fears that the values—or lack thereof—of corporate America have become the dominant force and supplanted the civil religious version of America. "Now our cultural crisis is deeper," he writes. "The transcendent vision is not absent in America, but it is harder than ever to integrate with the dominant cultural mood. The established structures of economic and political power seem perversely set on maximizing wealth and power regardless of the cost to society or the natural environment." This breach in the covenant—the focus on individual wealth instead of the greater good—has its own built-in retribution, according to Bellah: "Ironically, our punishment lies in our 'success.' . . . If our economic and technological advance has placed power in the hands of those who are not answerable to any democratic process; weakened our families and neighborhoods as it turned individuals into mobile, competitive achievers; undermined our morality and stripped us of tradition, as I think it has, then we must consider somewhere else to turn."[56]

This anxiety has existed throughout American history, even during Carnegie's "Gilded Age." Carnegie himself rejected what he called the "idolatry of amassing wealth. . . . No idol is more debasing than the worship of money."[57]

In 1831, Tocqueville observed America's material success with caution: "The prosperity of the United States is the source of their most serious dangers, since it tends to create in some of the federated states that intoxication which accompanies a rapid increase of fortune, and to awaken in others those feelings of envy, mistrust, and regret which usually attend the loss of it. The Americans contemplate this extraordinary progress with exultation; but they would be wiser to consider it with sorrow and alarm," he wrote in *Democracy in America*.[58]

Civil Religion and Civil War

> If we shall suppose that American slavery is one of those offenses which,
> in the providence of God, must needs come, but which, having continued
> through His appointed time, He now wills to remove, and that He gives to
> both North and South this terrible war as the woe due to those by whom
> the offense came, shall we discern therein any departure from those divine
> attributes which the believers in a living God always ascribe to Him?
> Fondly do we hope, fervently do we pray, that this mighty scourge of war
> may speedily pass away.
>
> —Abraham Lincoln, Second Inaugural Address, 1865

The impulse behind civil religion helped propel the colonists successfully
through the Revolution, and later fueled America's "manifest destiny" to
expand across the western plains and beyond. Americans were a chosen
people, and their success proved it.[59] "The success of the Revolution reinforced the idea that the American form of government must be sanctified,
and Americans must be special because they emerged victorious," Sherrill
said.

The underpinnings of the new republic were challenged and eventually unglued by the institution of slavery, which was often wrongly given
biblical justification, but simultaneously unjustified by civil religion. The
outspoken opponents of slavery, going back to the early abolitionists at the
time of the Revolution, feared that divine judgment and retribution hung
over the nation for the sin of slavery.[60] "I am assured the common Father
of all men will severely plead a controversy against these colonies for en-
slaving negroes . . . and possibly for this wickedness God threatens us with
slavery," wrote the Rev. Francis Alison, a prominent Presbyterian minister
from Pennsylvania, in 1768.[61]

Abraham Lincoln, regarded by many as the greatest American civil
theologian, cast the Civil War as a trial of the nation's soul. In his Second
Inaugural Address, Lincoln used the language of civil religion to call the
nation to account for the offense of slavery—an offense against humanity
and an offense against God, who had wrought the retribution the earlier
Americans had feared. In the Gettysburg Address, Lincoln called for the
rebirth of the nation under a new covenant, purified in the blood of the
fallen soldiers: "We here highly resolve that these dead shall not have died
in vain; that the nation shall, under God, have a new birth of freedom, and
that government of the people, by the people, for the people, shall not perish from the earth."[62]

Many viewed Lincoln's death as a parallel biblical event: as Jesus had died for the sins of mankind so that man might live, Lincoln died for America's sins so that the nation could be reborn. "With the Christian archetype in the background, Lincoln, 'our martyred president,' was linked to the war dead—those who 'gave the last full measure of devotion' [language from the Gettysburg Address]," Bellah writes. "The theme of sacrifice was indelibly written into civil religion."[63] Lincoln emerges as "the absolute central exemplar" of American civil religion—"of calling the nation to account as responsible to an authority higher than the nation, of insisting that the nation is not absolute and making that part of our public life. It's there in the Declaration of Independence. We exist under the rule of the laws of God, which are above the laws of men."[64]

Civil Religion and War

> Oh the First World War, boys,
> It closed out its fate.
> The reason for fighting,
> I never got straight.
> But I learned to accept it;
> Accept it with pride,
> For you don't count the dead,
> When God's on your side.
>
> —Bob Dylan, "With God on Our Side" (1964)

President Woodrow Wilson cast America's entry into World War I as a moral imperative to "make the world safe for democracy";[65] Franklin D. Roosevelt declared the war on Germany the mortal struggle of the "forces of justice and of righteousness" against Nazi "paganism";[66] and George W. Bush cast the war in Iraq as part of a broader plan to bring the blessings of liberty to the Middle East. "We are led, by events and common sense, to one conclusion: The survival of liberty in our land increasingly depends on the success of liberty in other lands. The best hope for peace in our world is the expansion of freedom in all the world," Bush said in his 2005 Inaugural Address. "History has an ebb and flow of justice, but history also has a visible direction, set by liberty and the Author of Liberty."[67]

In this context, the "Author of Liberty" is the same "Creator" and "Almighty"—substitute words for God that American presidents have conjured for centuries. More directly stated, in Bush's philosophy, liberty is God-given. God bestowed liberty upon America, and now it is America's duty and destiny to spread it around the world. Liberty is on the move. It is expansionist and imperialistic. Liberty is God's empire.[68]

But God also has ways of dealing with hubris—for which many have criticized Bush. Even the Christian televangelist Pat Robertson chastised Bush for his certainty and seemingly lackadaisical attitude toward the risks of war. "You remember Mark Twain said, 'He looks like a contented Christian with four aces.' I mean he [Bush] was just sitting there like, 'I'm on top of the world,'" Robertson said. "And I warned him about this war. I had deep misgivings about this war, deep misgivings. And I was trying to say, 'Mr. President, you had better prepare the American people for casualties.'"[69]

The issue of God and war raises a central conundrum of American civil religion: How can you tell if God is on your side? How can you be sure? Even in Winthrop's time, God's blessing on the Massachusetts colonists was based on a conditional covenant, which the Puritans had to live up to or end up "but dust in the hands of God."

In the Civil War, civil religion collided into its ultimate dilemma, with both sides claiming that God was on their side. Confederate chaplains led religious revivals to inspire the troops of the rightness of their cause, while the Northern ministers connected the fate of the Union with the will of God. The dilemma put Lincoln in the excruciating position of trying to sort out just how God's will was operating when both sides claimed God's favor.[70] "Neither party expected for the war the magnitude or the duration which it has already attained," Lincoln said in his Second Inaugural Address. "Each looked for an easier triumph. . . . Both read the same Bible and pray to the same God, and each invokes His aid against the other. It may seem strange that any men should dare to ask a just God's assistance in wringing their bread from the sweat of other men's faces, but let us judge not, that we be not judged." Pressing on the issue, Lincoln solved the conundrum by splitting it down the middle: "The prayers of both could not be answered. That of neither has been answered fully. The Almighty has His own purposes."[71]

Ultimately, God's providence is known only by God and is left a mystery to those on earth. Even the president of the United States is left uninformed about God's will, Lincoln lamented. "I am approached with the most opposite opinions and advice, and that by religious men, who are equally certain that they represent the Divine will. I am sure that either the one or the other class is mistaken in that belief, and perhaps in some respects both," Lincoln said a speech to an assembly of clergymen in 1862. "I hope it will not be irreverent for me to say that if it is probable that God would reveal his will to others, on a point so connected with my duty, it might be supposed he would reveal it directly to me; for, unless I am more deceived in myself than I often am, it is my earnest desire to know the will of Providence in this matter. And if I can learn what it is I will do it!"[72]

No other American president has faced such an existential question as to the nation's continuance, and no other president has applied such rigorous examination to American civil religion. "The words of Lincoln condense American political religion into its classic statement," Marty writes. "They affirm the worth of the land and its people and then go on to judge all sections, all parties, all churches."[73]

Civil Religion and Civil Rights

> And so even though we face the difficulties of today and tomorrow, I still have a dream. It is a dream deeply rooted in the American dream. I have a dream that one day this nation will rise up and live out the true meaning of its creed: We hold these truths to be self-evident that all men are created equal.
>
> —Martin Luther King, August 28, 1963

The early American experience and Winthrop's covenant contained flaws and omissions—most glaringly the failure to acknowledge and affirm the existence of people of other races and religions.[74]

"The early experiment was problematic because the colonists didn't build into it the fact that there were strangers in their midst," Charles Haynes said.[75] Native Americans, Africans, and Catholics were not included in the initial covenant. When Bellah speaks of the "broken covenant," he refers to the exclusion of others from the shining city on a hill: "On the one hand, being Christian meant a deep commitment to the oneness of man; on the other it meant the right of Christian Europeans to enslave or destroy any who differed radically from them in belief, custom and complexion. The covenant was broken almost as soon as it was made. For a long time, Americans were able to hide from that fact, to deny the brokenness."[76]

In the years between the end of Reconstruction (1877) and the Civil Rights Movement in the 1950s and '60s, mainstream America largely ignored the unfinished business of emancipation, while the country followed its pursuit of economic development with unparalleled vigor.[77] In the early 1900s, black leaders such as W. E. B. Du Bois and William Trotter made vigorous pleas for civil rights, but progress would have to wait another 50 to 60 years. Historian Lewis Baldwin wrote that civil rights failed during this era, in part, because it did not get strong support from the masses of black churchpersons. Later in his life, Du Bois espoused Marxism—a taboo in the canon of American civil religion.[78]

In the 1960s, the Rev. Martin Luther King Jr. invoked the full power of American civil religion in a way not heard since Lincoln. In the summer of 1963, on the steps of the Lincoln Memorial, King delivered his landmark "I Have a Dream" speech: "When the architects of our republic wrote the magnificent words of the Constitution and the Declaration of Independence, they were signing a promissory note to which every American was to fall heir. This note was a promise that all men, yes, black men as well as white men, would be guaranteed the unalienable rights of life, liberty and the pursuit of happiness. It is obvious today that America has defaulted on this promissory note, insofar as her citizens of color are concerned. Instead of honoring this sacred obligation, America has given the Negro people a bad check, a check which has come back marked 'insufficient funds.' Now is the time to make real the promises of democracy. . . . Now is the time to make justice a reality for all of God's children."[79]

King used the language of civil religion to show how the nation had fallen short of its covenant. Equally effectively, King employed the language of business and finance—the "bad check" and "defaulted promissory note"—striking a chord with America's parallel religion of laissez-faire capitalism. Jim Crow segregation could not withstand such a withering assault on two fronts. "Martin Luther King Jr. criticized the country in its own religious terms—using the country's own religious rhetoric to lodge a critique," Sherrill said.

King's language was intended not only to "convert" white America, but also to touch the hearts and minds of the black masses he was rallying. Historian David Howard-Pitney argues that African Americans are fully vested in American civil religion, particularly as it supports America "under God," a "prophetic America," and progressive reform. The prophetic element fuses the early Calvinistic notion of divine providence with the call to protest and reform—reform for the nation's future, rather than an affirmation of its current level of "perfection," Howard-Pitney writes.[80] "African American civil religion critically judges contemporary society in light of the sacred ideal, finds society wanting, and urges reform. Prophetic civil religion's 'divine discontent' serves the purposes of social protest and reform movements by providing them ideological tenets and rhetorical weapons."

While some African American leaders reject civil religion as the tool of an oppressive white society, black leaders across the political spectrum—

including those as divergent as presidential aspirants Jesse Jackson, Alan Keyes, and Barack Obama—liberally infuse the language of civil religion into their speeches. As savvy politicians, they are keenly aware that winning the hearts and minds of voters is difficult if not impossible if one ignores civil religion. "Imagine Lincoln's Second Inaugural Address without reference to 'the judgments of the Lord,' or King's 'I Have a Dream' speech without reference to 'all of God's children,'" Obama challenges his readers. "Their summoning of a higher truth helped inspire what had seemed impossible and move the nation to embrace a common destiny. Of course organized religion doesn't have a monopoly on virtue, and one need not be religious to make moral claims or appeal to a common good. But we should not avoid making such claims or appeals—or abandon any reference to our rich religious traditions—in order to avoid giving offense."[81]

Civil Religion and Immigration

> Mexicans, Filipinos, Africans and others, our ancestors were among those who founded this land and tamed its natural wilderness. But we are still pilgrims on this land, and we are pioneers who blaze a trail out of the wilderness of hunger and deprivation that we have suffered even as our ancestors did.
>
> —César Chávez, 1969

In the spring of 2006, hundreds of thousands of immigrants and their supporters took to the streets in cities across the United States to protest proposed legislation that would make illegal immigrants felons. The mass protests occurred on a level unseen since the time of Martin Luther King and Chicano activist César Chávez in the late 1960s.[82]

The boiling immigration debate has raised core questions of what it means to be an American—and what is not an American. The issue has often been cast in ugly terms. On one side, some argue that the nation's current crop of immigrants—mostly from Mexico, Latin America, and Asia—are too numerous and too "different" to assimilate into American culture.[83] On the other side, many argue that the immigrants of today are no different from the immigrants of the turn of the last century, who eventually assimilated into mainstream American society.[84]

In the early twentieth century, when the nation was experiencing an unprecedented wave of immigration, the debate was very similar to today's. Theodore Roosevelt, who served as U.S. president from 1901 to 1909, was a staunch advocate of assimilation and what he termed *Americanization*.

Roosevelt argued that immigrants should not only wrap themselves in the flag and learn English, but learn the English of the nation's seminal civil religious documents: "We have room but for one loyalty, loyalty to the United States. We have room but for one language, the language of Washington and Lincoln, the language of the Declaration of Independence and the Gettysburg speech; the English language," Roosevelt wrote in 1917.[85]

But for Roosevelt, the door was open to all regardless of race, religion, or ethnicity, so long as one pledged loyalty to America alone: "We care not where the man's parents are from or where he himself was born, or what religion he professes, so long as he is in good faith and without reservation an American and nothing else. But if he tries to be half American and half something else, it is proof that he isn't an American at all."[86]

During Roosevelt's administration, immigration reached its highest point ever in U.S. history, when the foreign-born are measured as a percentage of the overall population. In 1910, nearly 15 percent of the U.S. population was foreign born. In 2006, more than 12 percent of the U.S. population was foreign born. When measured in raw numbers, rather than a percentage of the population, the current level of immigration is the highest ever, with 35.2 million foreign-born residents in the United States, compared to 13.5 million in 1910.[87]

At the turn of the last century, the immigrant pool had shifted from northern Europe and Britain to eastern and southern Europe. In the current century, immigration has shifted from the western and northern hemispheres to the southern hemisphere and Asia. In 2003, more than 53 percent of the foreign-born population in the United States was from Mexico and Latin America, and 25 percent from Asia. The approximately 11–12 million illegal immigrants in the United States are overwhelmingly—at 78 percent—from Mexico and Latin America.[88]

Harvard Professor Samuel Huntington argues that Mexican and Latin American immigrants are so numerous that they have little incentive to assimilate and adopt American values, unlike previous, more diverse waves of immigrants. Hispanic cultural identity, he says, is distinct, assertive, and resistant to adopting the American "creed," a term Huntington uses, rather than civil religion, to define American national self-identity: "Thomas Jefferson set forth this creed in the Declaration of Independence, and ever since, its principles have been reiterated by statesmen and espoused by the public as an essential component of U.S. identity. Most Americans see the creed as the crucial element of their national identity. The creed, however, was the product of the distinct Anglo-Protestant culture of the founding settlers. Key elements of that culture include the English language; Christianity; religious commitment; English concepts of the rule of law, including the responsibility of rulers and the rights of individuals; and dissenting Protestant values of individualism, the work ethic, and the belief that humans have the ability and the duty to try to create a heaven on earth, a 'city on a hill.'" Huntington contends there is a fundamental clash between American self-conception and Hispanic identity that threatens the United States' cultural and political integrity. "Persistent flow of this massive influx of immigrants, without improved assimilation, could divide the United States into a country of two languages and two cultures," he warns.[89]

Luis D. León of the University of California, Berkeley, argues that Latinos have long appropriated American values and civil religion in the spirit of Martin Luther King. In a case study on Chicano leader César Chávez, Leon documents how Chávez modeled himself after King in both method and spirit. "Chávez created a public political space for *Mexicanos* and other Latinos in the United States by holding America to its promises of justice and equality," Leon writes. "America's deepest values and commitments, those that underpin democracy and unfold policy, are held as religious doctrines for our nation with the soul of a church."[90]

In this light, the 2006 protests are seen not as anti-American, but very American in the long tradition of the struggle for civil rights. In the spirit of Rousseau, California journalist Gustavo Arellano writes that Latinos are seeking to vest themselves in the American "social contract."

"Those Latino multitudes who marched waving the Stars and Stripes sought the right to remain here and enter the American social contract. They want the responsibilities and burdens of citizenship," Arellano wrote. "By protesting, the marchers pledged allegiance to their future and ours, not the past. The U.S. will benefit from these newly conscious illegals, just as it has when it put other minority groups through the fires of nativism and bigotry. The undocumented yearning to be legal should not worry us. Most will turn out like my father. He still loves his Mexico, but he realizes that the best future for him and his family is in *los Estados Unidos*."[91]

Civil Religion, Diversity, and Multiculturalism

In the final decades of the 20th century, the United States' Anglo-Protestant culture and the creed that it produced came under assault by the popularity in intellectual and political circles of the doctrines of multiculturalism and diversity; the rise of group identities based on race, ethnicity, and gender over national identity; the impact of transnational cultural diasporas; the expanding number of immigrants with dual nationalities and dual loyalties.

—Samuel P. Huntington, "The Hispanic Challenge" *(2004)*

In recent decades, American civil religion has found itself in competition with a new civic ideal: diversity and multiculturalism. Some might say diversity and multiculturalism are *the* creed, and civil religion is the relic of a bygone era of white Anglo-Saxon Protestants, who are now dead—and the deader the better.[92]

During the civil rights era, Martin Luther King stressed the importance of bonding black and white interests together, and he effectively applied the broad rubric of civil religion to achieve his goals. On the other side, black nationalist movements, Marxists, and many white intellectuals rejected American civil religion as the corrupt invention of the white man and thus intolerably tainted. The Vietnam War crystallized this cynicism and gave strength to reactionary ideologies. Author Susan Sontag summed up these sentiments in an oft-quoted screed: "America was founded on a genocide, on the unquestioned assumption of the right of white Europeans to exterminate a resident, technologically backward, colored population in order to take over the continent," she wrote. "The white race is the cancer of human history; it is the white race and it alone—its ideologies and inventions— which eradicates autonomous civilizations wherever it spreads, which has upset the ecological balance of the planet, which now threatens the very existence of life itself."[93]

Bellah traces the decline of the "Anglo-Saxons" and their creed to the decline of mainline Protestant churches and to a long-fermenting hostility among American intellectuals to white Protestant culture. "The rejection of the Anglo-Saxon image of the American goes very deep, and there is a great effort to retrieve the experience and history of all the repressed cultures that 'Americanization' tried to obliterate," he writes.[94]

Early in the last century, Theodore Roosevelt was a forceful proponent of "Americanism," and he effectively used the bully pulpit of the presidency to beat down any nascent diversity and multiculturalism (not yet termed as such), which he said would reduce Americans to "dwellers in a polyglot boarding-house."[95] For Roosevelt, American values, identity, and citizenship were of the greatest value. Washington, Lincoln, "and the men of Valley Forge and the men of Gettysburg" were exemplary citizens who epitomized the greatness of the nation and provide an example for all to follow. "They were Americans. That is why we are proud to be their fellow countryman. That is why they have been an inspiration to the best men of all other nations," Roosevelt wrote. "There is no limit to the greatness of the future before America. But we can realize it only if we are Americans with all of the fervor of our hearts and all of the wisdom of our brains. We can serve the world at all only if we serve America first and best. We must feel in the very marrow of our being that our loyalty is due only to America, and that it not diluted by loyalty for any other nation or all other nations on the face of the earth." [96]

In modern times, Samuel Huntington believes American nationality and the American creed, as he terms it, face a survival challenge due to mass migration, multiculturalism, and a general weakening of American values. "The United States' national identity, like that of other nation-states, is challenged by the forces of globalization as well as the needs that global-ization produces among people for smaller and more meaningful 'blood and belief' identities," he wrote. "The United States ignores this challenge at its peril." [97]

Sherrill takes a more optimistic view: American civil religion, rather than being a static creed that is the sole dominion of white Protestant Americans, is an ever-evolving phenomenon that adapts and incorporates diversity—and in fact is the very force that enables pluralism in the United States. "American civil religion provides background, ideas and vocabulary for a national discussion. It is accessible to Americans if they've been here since 1620 or if they arrived from Vietnam six weeks ago. There are certain ways the country talks about itself as 'the land of opportunity,' an open soci-ety, democratic way of life, etc.—all of which have a pull on the imagination of people who are fleeing horrible circumstances elsewhere," he said.

Sherrill noted that different versions of civil religion exist and often compete in different regions of the country and among different ethnic groups: "Civil religion works at a national level and filters down into local communities; and it is very different on the East Coast, the West Coast and the Southwest. Every group in America that is religious and is serious about its national character incorporates civil religion in its own terms. Civil re-ligion in Los Angeles is a huge contest among so many different groups, each of which has its own version of the religious meaning of the coun-try. They would disagree on almost every issue except for the belief that America sanctions the smaller version that they enact in their particular neighborhood."

Separation of Church and State

> Precedents caution us to measure the idea of a civic religion against the
> central meaning of the Religion Clauses of the First Amendment, which
> is that all creeds must be tolerated and none favored. The suggestion that
> government may establish an official or civic religion as a means of avoid-
> ing the establishment of a religion with more specific creeds strikes us as a
> contradiction that cannot be accepted.
>
> — Supreme Court Justice Anthony Kennedy, *Lee vs. Weisman,* (1992)

Civil religion gets sticky and confusing in the church-state debate. Until
recently, the courts have not acknowledged the existence of civil religion.
Only recently has the Supreme Court used the term, but it still has no legal
standing.

"The existence of an American civil religion and its affinities and simi-
larities to traditional, sacral religion have clearly been the source of much
of the Supreme Court's confusion in its interpretation of the Establishment
Clause," wrote Yehudah Mirsky in the *Yale Law Journal.* "The problem
has been that given the absence of civil religion from the judicial lexicon,
courts have been deprived of a valuable analytic tool and source of historical understanding. They have not had at their disposal an adequate set of
paradigms and metaphors with which they could capture the contours of
public religion."[98]

In the 1992 case *Lee v. Weisman,* which banned benedictions at public
school graduation ceremonies, the Supreme Court acknowledged "civic
religion" for the first time, although without recognizing it as a matter of
law. "There may be some support, as an empirical observation . . . that
there has emerged in this country a civic religion, one which is tolerated
when sectarian exercises are not," Justice Anthony Kennedy wrote for the
Court majority. "If common ground can be defined which permits once
conflicting faiths to express the shared conviction that there is an ethic and
a morality which transcend human invention, the sense of community and
purpose sought by all decent societies might be advanced."[99]

But if civil religion takes the form of a school-sponsored prayer, even
a non-sectarian prayer, Kennedy said it constitutes an unacceptable contradiction with the Establishment Clause. "Though the First Amendment
does not allow the government to stifle prayers which aspire to these ends,
neither does it permit the government to undertake that task for itself," he
wrote. "A state-created orthodoxy puts at grave risk that freedom of belief
and conscience which are the sole assurance that religious faith is real, not
imposed."

In dissent, Justice Antonin Scalia, while not mentioning civil religion directly, invoked the Declaration of Independence—and its appeal to "divine Providence"—as the cornerstone of the nation's longstanding tradition of nonsectarian public prayer, which Scalia contends the Establishment Clause does not forbid.[100]

In other high court cases, former Justice Sandra Day O'Connor has assigned civil religion to a lesser god, "ceremonial deism"—formal language reserved for public ceremonies, but devoid of deeper religious meaning. "For centuries, we have marked important occasions or pronouncements with references to God and invocations of divine assistance. Such references can serve to solemnize an occasion instead of to invoke divine provenance," O'Connor wrote in *Elk Grove Unified School District v. Newdow*, a case challenging the Pledge of Allegiance—with the words "under God."[101] "Our continued repetition of the reference to 'one Nation under God' in an exclusively patriotic context has shaped the cultural significance of that phrase to conform to that context. Any religious freight the words may have been meant to carry originally has long since been lost."

Despite the outcomes of these cases, the mere fact that civil religion gets mention on the High Court advances it for further discussion. And on a divided court that considers challenges to the Establishment Clause on a case-by-case basis, the issue will inevitably come up again. In the meantime, church-state issues in the ongoing "culture wars" are fought out in lower courts.

Civil Religion and the Culture Wars

> The majority of Americans—certain of their belief in the existence of a God—are completely blind to the offensiveness of the words 'under God' in the nation's Pledge of Allegiance. This is precisely what one would expect to see as a result of religious bias, and the Framers' recognition of this sort of ecclesiastically based myopia is largely why the Religion Clauses were created.
>
> —Michael Newdow, *Newdow v. U.S. Congress* (2005)

The Ten Commandments, the Pledge of Allegiance, and other cultural-religious symbols have become touchstones in the so-called culture wars in America. Even public celebration of Christmas has become disputed, with a steady stream of lawsuits over holiday displays on public property. Every December ushers in new yuletide ballyhoo over the "correct" holiday greeting—"Merry Christmas" or "Happy Holidays"? (See chapter 7 for a detailed discussion of court challenges to holiday displays.) Squaring off in the trenches of the *Kulturkampf,* the secular partisans claim that religious America is trying to impose religion on them; and the other side claims secular America is trying to "kick God out" of every aspect of society—civil religious or otherwise. "Separationists object to the slightest scintilla of Christianity in the public sector," wrote author David Limbaugh. "When the smoke from the often cacophonous debate that surrounds these assaults on culture dissipates, what remains is the bald conclusion that the object of the separationists' desire is not to preserve religious liberty by limiting government's involvement in 'religion.' Rather, it is to remove, piece by piece, every vestige of Christianity in our culture and replace it with values they deem preferable." [102]

Ongoing challenges to the Pledge of Allegiance—"under God"—have become a flashpoint in the culture wars. California atheist Michael Newdow has filed a series of lawsuits demanding removal of the phrase, claiming its insertion in 1954 was blatantly sectarian and had nothing to do with promoting patriotism or national unity, as the Pledge is intended. Newdow rejects any argument that the phrase "under God" is passable in the context of civil religion or O'Connor's ceremonial deism. "In an effort to obscure the obvious, some have attempted to apply the rubric of 'ceremonial deism' to phrases such as 'under God.' Even momentarily accepting this as a constitutionally valid construct, history shows that this was definitely not the case for the Act of 1954," Newdow wrote. "The legislative history demonstrates that the Act of 1954 was passed for the purposes of endorsing Christian monotheism. The text—'under God'—intruded into the Pledge of Allegiance is patently, facially, unquestionably and clearly religious text." [103]

Newdow quotes exhaustively from the *Congressional Record* of 1954 to make his point. During the debates to amend the Pledge, many congressmen expressed their desire to thumb America's nose at the Soviet Union and its "atheistic communism"; [104] some congressmen directly expressed the need for Americans to affirm belief in God; while others echo the old themes of civil religion, as spelled out in the Declaration of Independence. Many congressmen mixed all of these sentiments together. "We see the pledge as a formal declaration of our duty to serve God, and our firm reliance, now as in 1776, on the protection of Divine Providence," said Senator Thomas A. Burke, a Democrat from Ohio, in casting his vote for the amendment inserting "under God" in the Pledge. [105] Rep. Louis C. Rabaut, a Democrat from Michigan and author of the bill to amend the Pledge, added, "The fundamental basis of our government is the recognition that all lawful authority stems from Almighty God." [106] Newdow retorts that these sentiments "are used to perpetuate the notion that 'real Americans' believe in God, and those who do not believe in God are second-class citizens, to be 'tolerated' by society."[107]

Newdow twice convinced lower federal courts that the Pledge was unconstitutional. The U.S. Supreme Court threw out one of his suits on a technicality, and another was on appeal at the time of this publication. The Becket Fund for Religious Liberty filed a brief on behalf of parents wishing to keep the Pledge as is, with the phrase "under God." The Becket brief, while not using the term "civil religion" specifically, traces the history of civil religious political philosophy in America: "Even before the Declaration of Independence, it has been an important part of our national ethos that we have inalienable rights that the state cannot take away, because the source of those inalienable rights is an authority higher than the state. In this way, the Pledge, like the Declaration and the Gettysburg Address, is a statement of political philosophy, not of theology. Anathematizing the phrase, 'one nation under God' would deprive government of perhaps the most potent rationale it has for declaring human rights to be inalienable."[108] Inclusion of the phrase "under God" in the Pledge, therefore, is not a religious or sectarian statement, but a reaffirmation of the nation's longstanding political philosophy, Becket concludes.

While a the battle over the Pledge is being waged, many lesser skirmishes are also being fought in the multi-front *Kulturkampf* which spans the broad disputed territory of religion and public life. In Cupertino, California, elementary school teacher Stephen Williams sued the school district in late 2004, accusing school officials of forbidding him to instruct students about the religious context of America's founding and prohibiting him from citing excerpts of the Declaration of Independence in his fifth-grade class. A group of parents, backed by the school principal and superintendent, contended that Williams was using the words of the Founders out of context in order to proselytize students for his Christian faith rather than to instruct them in history. The story made it to the television talk shows, sparking a minor national uproar. Williams, who was represented by the Alliance Defense Fund—a religious advocacy group—dropped his case in 2005.[109]

In 2003, Roy S. Moore lost his job as Chief Justice of the Alabama Supreme Court for refusing to remove a monument displaying the text of the Ten Commandments that he had placed the foyer of the state courthouse. The monument also included quotes invoking God from Thomas Jefferson, James Madison, and George Washington. Was Moore trying to establish his religion, or was he acting within the purview of civil religion, or both? (See more on Roy Moore in chapter 4.)

Such controversies illustrate the confusion and lack of understanding of civil religion: civil religion is not the religion of church and worship; civil religion is not Christianity, and it should not be confused or appropriated as such. The Supreme Court now recognizes the difference, but has not figured out a standard by which to judge it. For this reason, Mirsky suggests the usefulness of a formal recognition of civil religion: "While recognizing the idea and reality of civil religion cannot make the ambiguities simply go away, it can help courts ground their decisions in a coherent understanding of the social and cultural realities before them. The idea of a civil religion can serve as a supply tool with which courts can adequately comprehend the origins and function of public religion and do justice to enduring values while maintaining the integrity of the Establishment Clause." [110]

On the other hand, legal recognition of civil religion might also require a legal definition of civil religion, which would be an impossible task—similar, perhaps, to the Court's pornography paradigm: "We can't define it, but we know it when we see it." [111]

Curses on Civil Religion

Civil religion is a religion built from parts of others; and like Franken-stein's monster, it too now takes on a sinister being of its own, capable of destroying its creators. . . . One can only hope that the Supreme Court will one day come to its senses and use this pile [of spare parts] as the funeral pyre for American Civil Religion.

—Ryan J. Dowd, *Northern Illinois University Law Review* (2002)

The language of civil religion can be used to inform, motivate, and inspire, but it can also be used to pander, manipulate, control, and deceive. It can represent the best of the national character, but it can also degenerate into egoism, chauvinism, and hubris. In the mid-1800s, Alexis de Tocqueville observed Americans' sometimes annoying attitude of "chosenness."

"Not only are the Anglo-Americans united by their common opinions, but they are separated from all other nations by a feeling of pride," he wrote. "For the last 50 years, no pains have been spared to convince the inhabitants of the United States that they are the only religious, enlightened, and free people. They perceive that, for the present, their own democratic institutions prosper, while those of other countries fail; hence they conceive a high opinion of their superiority and are not very remote from believing themselves to be a distinct species of mankind." [112]

Civil religion has its many detractors and critics. Even Robert Bellah, considered the authority on civil religion in America, has developed an ambivalent attitude toward it because the term has so many conflicting definitions, and it is too often misconstrued to mean nationalism or the "idolatrous worship of the state."[113] Some observers criticized Reagan's "city on a hill" talk as vapid, shallow, and jingoistic, especially when so many Americans were abandoning their cities and retreating to suburbs and gated communities.[114]

Law and religion scholar Yehudah Mirsky said a primary weakness of civil religion is that it is based on myth, and myths can deceive. "The tone of American civil religion is more than often too celebratory. . . . America's moral failings, as democracy and as a nation ostensibly under God, are glossed over," Mirsky wrote. "To the extent that civil religion allows us to forget or perpetrate past injustices, it corrupts the polity and its governments' ability to function wisely."[115]

Roger Williams, founder of Rhode Island and an early spokesman for freedom of conscience, argued against state-established and state-mandated religion. In Williams' view, government corrupts religion, and religion corrupts government. Similarly, some argue that civil religion both competes with and corrupts *real* religion. "In hijacking God for its own purposes, governmentally sanctioned civil religion dilutes the potency and distorts the conception of various religious ideas," wrote legal commentator Ryan Dowd. "Perhaps the weight of its familiarity prevents members of mainstream Christianity and Judaism from seeing the offensiveness of American Civil Religion."[116]

C. Welton Gaddy, a pastor and president of the Interfaith Alliance, argues that in current political discourse, civil religion has degenerated into nothing more than "God talk," in which politicians, particularly President Bush, litter their speeches with religious references in order to pander to political and religious constituencies—particularly conservative Christians. "Nothing is inherently wrong with the presence of religious rhetoric in the public life of the nation," Gaddy wrote. "But not all God talk is the same; nor is it even religious in substance or motivation. Even while some God talk has about it the ring of authenticity—an honest reference to personal faith locked in a struggle to understand and comment on social-political issues—other God talk has about it the clang of deception or manipulation, the language of faith used to promote a particular politically partisan or narrow sectarian agenda."[117] In Gaddy's analysis, the current level of God-talk has the following deleterious effects: it stokes sectarian sentiments and thus creates divisiveness; it is employed as a tool of electoral politics and a studied strategy for advancing public policy; it cheapens the value of the language of faith by turning it into a utilitarian tool for advancing an agenda; and it threatens the vitality of democracy by shutting down debate and silencing opposing voices.

"Political operatives who depend on God talk to gain authority and to evoke popularity desacralize religion and turn God into a mascot for people advancing a particular brand of politics," Gaddy wrote. "To suggest that a person's failure to agree with them politically is a sign of the opponent's religious immaturity or, worse still, infidelity, redefines the substance and inclusive nature of religion in a most destructive manner." [118]

Because of these dangers, more than ever the public needs to understand the nature of civil religion and what buttons politicians are trying to push when they resort to God-talk. Gaddy and Sherrill agree that it is critical for journalists and the public to question politicians on their use of God-talk, ask for specific meaning and definition, and be ready to cross-examine. "It would lift the level of political and religious discourse if journalists would stop and ask, 'Wait just one fine minute, what do you mean by that?'" Sherrill said. "So much of it [civil religious language] out there goes unacknowledged and unstudied that can be more dangerous than useful; it can be used to create fraudulent sentiments." On the other hand, he noted, "civil religion involves some of the best resources we have as a nation. The power to compel and to elicit a sense of bonded-ness to one's fellow countryperson is the best part of civil religion when it works. I believe civil religion, if done with integrity and honesty, does represent the source of common aspirations if you don't push it too hard and make it too specific."

George W. Bush and "God-Talk"

> We Americans have faith in ourselves, but not in ourselves alone. We do not know, we do not claim to know all the ways of Providence, yet we can trust in them, placing our confidence in the loving God behind all of life and all of history.
>
> —George W. Bush, State of the Union Address (2003)

President Bush has been both praised and condemned for his public displays of religiosity and his religious rhetoric. Some mock Bush for his "faith-based presidency." Indeed, Bush's key word is "faith." He says the word often, and he says it with conviction, especially when discussing his Faith-Based and Community Initiative. So much does Bush focus on faith that critics say he crosses the murky line between what is civil religion and cynical "God talk." [119]

When Bush uttered the words "axis of evil," in his 2002 State of the Union

Address, many criticized him for crossing the line.[120] Bush elicited harsh criticism from the Muslim world when he likened the war on terrorism to a "crusade" to defend freedom.[121] In the same speech, Bush called the war on terror a "war against evil" itself, for which he was roundly derided. He often mixes the language of his faith with civil religion, and sometimes it's hard to distinguish the two. "Faith gives the assurance that our lives and our history have a moral design," he said at the 2002 National Prayer Breakfast.[122] While the first clause is a statement of faith, the second clause is a basic definition of civil religion: American democracy has a higher purpose.

Another key word in Bush's rhetoric is "liberty," which he often ties in with faith. "Liberty is both the plan of Heaven for humanity, and the best hope for progress here on Earth," Bush told the National Endowment for Democracy in 2003. "America has put our power at the service of principle. We believe that liberty is the design of nature; we believe that liberty is the direction of history. We believe that human fulfillment and excellence come in the responsible exercise of liberty. And we believe that freedom—the freedom we prize—is not for us alone; it is the right and the capacity of all mankind."[123]

Bush touches on the standard themes in American political rhetoric— liberty, freedom, and democracy—and transforms them into articles of faith. Liberty and democracy are the gifts of God's Providence; and by extension, it is America's duty to spread these gifts to all mankind. Critics argue that is this kind of misguided thinking that got the United States into the war in Iraq. The messianic notion that America is God's general in the war to spread divine liberty throughout the world brings the notion of "God on our side" to new levels of hubris. C. Welton Gaddy contends that Bush's "God talk," and the relentless infusion of religion into politics has corrupted both.

"The president's merger of political and religious language clearly suggested that the speaker's way was the right way, indeed, God's way, and that all who disagreed with him had chosen another path," Gaddy wrote in his chapter "God Talk in the Public Square" in *Quoting God*. "The public's present infatuation with 'God bless America'—whether as a genuine prayer for a righteous nation, as a patriot boast of divine blessing, or as strategic rhetoric employed to build support for a politician's candidacy for public office or for a national policy—epitomizes the reality, confusion and danger of God talk in the public square. So pervasive is the God talk phenomenon that it has contributed significantly to the politicization of religion and the 'religiofication' of politics in the national public square."

Much of Bush's political rhetoric came from Michael Gerson, who served as a key Bush aide and speechwriter until 2006. Gerson defends his choice of words and contends that civil religion is an essential element of a healthy society. "Every society, it seems to me, needs a standard of values that stands above the political order, or the political order becomes absolute," Gerson said at a 2004 conference on religion and public life. "Christianity is not identical to any political ideology. It has had great influence precisely because it judges all ideologies." [124]

Gerson explained there are five basic components to Bush's political-religious rhetoric: comfort in grief and mourning, the historic influence of faith on America, faith-based welfare reform, literary allusions to hymns and scripture, and reference to Divine Providence. Gerson said critics sometimes accuse him of "planting" code words in speeches in order to pander to particular religious and political constituencies—religious conservatives in particular. Gerson counters that a careful reading of his rhetoric places it well within the traditional framework of American civil religion as it has been enunciated throughout the centuries.

"I've actually had, in the past, reporters call me up on a variety of speeches and ask me where are the code words. I try to explain that they're not code words; they're literary references understood by millions of Americans," Gerson said. "They're not code words; they're our culture. It's not a strategy. It comes from my own background and my own reading of the history of American rhetoric. I think that American public discourse would be impoverished without it."

The Future of American Civil Religion

> From the point of view of republicanism, civil religion is indispensable. A republic as an active political community of participating citizens must have a purpose and a set of values. . . . A republic must attempt to be ethical in a positive sense and to elicit the ethical commitment of its citizens. For this reason, it inevitably pushes toward the symbolization of an ultimate order of existence in which republican values and virtues make sense.
>
> —Robert Bellah, *The Broken Covenant*

Civil religion and its conjoined philosophy, republican virtue, are crucial to America's continued existence as a democratic republic, Bellah argues. Civic virtue and civic faith are the bases of public morality that enable the American republic to function. It is not enough to have a well-designed constitution; the fulfillment of a nation's laws depends upon an ethical citizenry. "The republican state therefore has an ethical, educational, even spiritual role, and it will survive only as long as it reproduces republican customs and republican citizens," Bellah maintains. It is civic virtue that prevents a republic from degenerating into corruption and despotism. "Corruption is, in the language of the founders of the republic, the opposite of republican virtue. It is what destroys republics." Bellah fears the loss of civic virtue in America could lead to the loss of democratic rights and descent into authoritarianism, "remembering that republican and liberal regimes have been in the history of the planet few and brief." [125]

Civic virtue was a central theme in Edward Gibbon's monumental *History of the Decline and Fall of the Roman Empire* (1776). Gibbon assigns the loss of Roman civic virtue as a primary cause of the decline of the Empire and its eventual submission to barbarian tribes in the West. "That public virtue which among the ancients was denominated patriotism, is derived from a strong sense of our own interest in the preservation and prosperity of the free government of which we are members," Gibbon wrote. [126]

Anxiety about America's decline—in its morality, civic life, and military prowess—is deeply rooted in biblical and Roman archetypes. Parallels between ancient Rome and America are not just popular among modern pundits but were pervasive at the time of the nation's founding. "At a deeper level, the Roman attribute that preoccupied the imagination of the founders of the new nation was republican virtue," Bellah writes. "The history of Roman liberty served as both archetype and warning." [127] Rome's trajectory from glory to ruin still echoes like John Winthrop's warning to his Massachusetts colonists, "If we shall deal falsely with our God in this work . . . we shall . . . be consumed out of the good land whither we are going." [128]

American civil religion, as it began with Winthrop almost four centuries ago, has endured and evolved throughout the centuries, but it faces challenges on many fronts: Partisans in the culture wars challenge the legal basis of an America "under God"; politicians manipulate and debase the language; while intellectuals in the ideological wars strike at the heritage of American civil religion and its corrupt "Anglo-Saxon" roots.

In the face of its many modern challenges, Bellah says civil religion is in danger of fragmenting. "Instead of one American civil religion, it is argued, there are many civil religions; instead of one covenant, many. A few critics feel that the American experiment has been so badly botched that it is even questionable that we can survive as a single society. Others look to the emergence of new collective ideals quite different from those of the past in which pluralism and community will have a prominent place." [129]

Can one nation, "under God," continue to exist in such a state of plurality? Will civil religion be overtaken and replaced by reactionary ideologies and competitors like diversity and multiculturalism? Or will American civil religion incorporate the new ideals of diversity and multiculturalism within its tenets?

Sherrill takes an optimistic view: American civil religion is flexible and adaptable enough to survive and meet the needs of modern America, he says. "Civil religion has gone through permutation after permutation throughout the course of our history. Every significant historical event that the country passed through had to get folded into it somehow. There are signs and remnants of religion in places where you don't expect it. Civil religion is voracious and will gobble up anything it thinks useful."

In political-speak, civil religion gets gobbled up and mangled in the "spin" machine. Bellah and Sherrill warn against its abuse, which they say must be exposed in order to prevent its corruption. They argue what is needed is continual reform and renewal of America's civic spirit. If Winthrop's covenant is ever to be mended and realized, the ideals behind American civil religion must be reinvigorated.

"There is a need for a rebirth of imaginative vision," Bellah says. "As a first step, I would argue, we must reaffirm the outward or external covenant that includes the civil religion in its most classical form. The Declaration of Independence, the Bill of Rights, and the Fourteenth Amendment to the Constitution have never been fully implemented. . . . No one has changed a great nation without appealing to its soul, without stimulating a national idealism."[130]

The ideals and principles of republican virtue, as professed by Jefferson, Franklin, and Montesquieu, still ring modern today. Those basic habits, as identified in the Declaration of Independence, remain life, liberty, and the pursuit of happiness—unalienable rights, "endowed by their Creator," who takes great interest in what happens in America and its democratic experiment.

Finding the Common Threads of Religious Liberty

Déjà Vu

> It is by a mutual consent, through a special overvaluing providence and a more than ordinary approbation of the churches of Christ, to seek out a place of cohabitation and consortship under a due form of government both civil and ecclesiastical.
>
> —John Winthrop, "A Model of Christian Charity," 1630

> All civil states with their officers of justice in their respective constitutions and administrations are proved essentially civil, and therefore not judges, governors, or defenders of the spiritual or Christian state and worship.
>
> —Roger Williams, "The Bloody Tenant of Persecution," 1644

> In order to establish justice, we must invoke the favor and guidance of Almighty God.
>
> —Roy Moore, former Chief Justice, Alabama Supreme Court, 2001

During the 2004 presidential election campaign, a common refrain was heard across the media: America is polarized—more than anyone can remember. Controversy over critical moral and religious issues such as abortion, same-sex marriage, and the Pledge of Allegiance has pitted Americans against each other to an unprecedented degree, or so it might seem. Based on the tenor of talk shows, Web logs, and political strategists, it would appear America's national discussion is moving into dangerous uncharted territory.

But these debates are nothing new. Four centuries ago, the early Americans were arguing over the same basic issues: What is the place of religion in society? To what degree do we separate church from state? How does society tolerate people of different faiths—or no faith at all?

"It all boils down to the basic question, 'What kind of nation are we, and what kind of nation are we going to be?'" said First Amendment scholar Charles C. Haynes.[1] "In the 1600s, the argument was even less friendly than today."

The debate between John Winthrop, first governor of Massachusetts, and Roger Williams, founder of Rhode Island, embodies the early clash of philosophy between church and the embryonic American state. Winthrop and Williams were both Puritans. But while Winthrop sought to keep his Puritan colony tightly knit together and free of dissent, Williams advocated freedom of conscience and complete free exercise of religion.[2]

Winthrop and Williams emerge as archetypes in the ongoing debate regarding religion in American public life. In the seventeenth century, the terms of the debate and the posturing of opposing camps were much the same as they are today. In modern terminology, Winthrop would represent the conservative side, and Williams the liberal or radical view. Both men were deeply committed to their Christian faith, but their interpretations of the Bible led them to very different conclusions. "These were two very different visions of what kind of society could be built in this place," Haynes said. "If you go back in history, you can see how the same debate has echoed throughout the centuries. In Alabama today, you hear echoes of both." (Alabama Supreme Court Justice Roy Moore lost his job in 2003 after defying a court order to remove the Ten Commandments monument from the courthouse rotunda.)

Winthrop and Williams, despite their philosophical differences and occasional exasperation with one another, maintained friendship and civility—in contrast to some of today's modern shout-casts. "It was an argument between friends, and Winthrop and Williams remained friends throughout their entire lives. But their visions were very different," Haynes said.

City on a Hill

In the spring of 1630, John Winthrop, with a royal charter in hand, led a fleet of 11 vessels and 700 passengers from England to the Massachusetts Bay Colony.[3] On board the *Arbella*, Winthrop delivered his landmark sermon, "A Model of Christian Charity," in which he spelled out the mission he and his followers were about to embark upon: "Thus stands the cause between God and us: We are entered into a covenant with Him for this work; we have taken out a commission. . . . For we must consider that we shall be as a city upon a hill, the eyes of all people upon us. We have professed to enterprise on these actions upon these ends."[4]

Winthrop's language echoed the Old and New Testaments—especially Deuteronomy and Jesus' Sermon on the Mount. Many of Winthrop's followers saw him as a modern-day Moses leading his people into the new Promised Land, the "new Israel."[5] "John Winthrop was giving his fellow Puritans a vision of their mission: 'We are a special nation; we are an example to the world,'" Haynes said. "They thought of themselves as chosen agents of God, modeling themselves on the Hebrews, and entering into a covenant with God. It's a partnership with God, and God is investing in the community."

Winthrop's sermon continues, "If the Lord shall please to hear us and bring us in peace to the place we desire, then He hath ratified this covenant and sealed our commission, and will expect a strict performance of the articles contained it. But if we shall neglect the observation of these articles which are the ends we have propounded . . . the Lord will surely break out in wrath against us." Winthrop's language reflects the Puritans' particular interpretation of Christian theology and Calvinism—that God has chosen an "elect" group of people to receive His grace.[6] God's selection is determined by God alone and not earned by one's deeds, petitions, or by performing particular rituals. In the Puritan colony, one's deeds were taken as evidence of whether or not one was a "visible saint"—a member of the chosen elect.[7] But one could never know with complete certainty whether or not one was "chosen," which led to a certain anxiety.

"This is the heart of the Puritan paradox: If you are a Calvinist and believe the elect have already been determined, then why should you be worried? Calvinist liberation is the idea that there is nothing you can do for your salvation. That is solely in the hands of God. But Calvinist anxiety is, if you don't appear to be saved, then you probably aren't," Haynes said. "Winthrop's words tap into the Puritan anxiety: If you live up to what God requires, you will be blessed. If you fail to live up to it, you will be cursed. If you are chosen for this special mission, then you have an obligation to live up to what God requires."

Winthrop's sermon goes on to define his vision of community and men's obligation to one another: "Every man might have need of others, and from hence they might be all knit more nearly together in the bond of brotherly affection . . . always having before our eyes our commission and community in the work, our community as members of the same body." Here, the covenant is a collective one. For a good Puritan to live up to his covenant, he must be concerned with the welfare of the community and how others are living up to the covenant. "What one person does affects what others in the community doing; otherwise stated, 'You will be punished for what I am doing,'" Haynes said. "This philosophy translates into the moral underpinnings in the nation's laws; it has shaped our concern for education and our sense of purpose; it has shaped our priorities and what we do in the world and how we are connected to one another. Much of theology has gone out of it, but not the ideas and the philosophy."[8]

City on a Hill in Dissent

Dissent came to the Massachusetts Bay Colony, and it didn't take long to arrive. In 1631, Roger Williams sailed from England to Massachusetts in search of new spiritual soil. He took his first job as "teacher" at the First Church in Boston. "He astonished them almost at once by calling them a false church," wrote historian Martin E. Marty. "True Puritans, he insisted, must separate from the whorish Church of England; yet Bostonians clung to it, hoping to reform it from a distance."[9]

Although the Protestant Reformation had freed England and northern Europe from the Catholic Church, it did not break the bond between church and state. Established state churches—whether Protestant or Catholic—were still the order of the day. Williams was a radical separatist; he believed the true church must separate from what he regarded as the irreformably corrupt Church of England. Winthrop, on the other hand, hoped to purify the Anglican Church, but he did not want to create a confrontation with the crown. But for Williams, the Reformation was incomplete and Christianity was tainted so long as the state was involved.[10] "Williams believed any society founded on a state religion is corrupt: The state corrupts religion, and then religion corrupts the state. And a state that denies freedom of conscience is corrupt," Haynes explained. "Williams believed you cannot be a true Christian unless it is an act of conscience."[11]

Williams was searching for the true church he believed was lost all the way back in the year 313, when the Roman Emperor Constantine bestowed imperial favor on Christianity, creating a "Christian Empire" and setting the blueprint for 1,000 years of medieval Christian Europe. Church and state were "inseparate."[12] "For Williams, the worst word in the English language was 'Christendom.' When Christianity becomes Christendom, it is no longer Christianity; it is a corruption," Haynes said. "When people are Christian because the state is Christian—and it is to one's advantage to be a Christian—then they are hypocrites. Or, when people refuse to become Christians, the result is 'rivers of blood.'"[13]

Williams made his case for the cause of conscience dramatically in his 1643 publication "Queries of Highest Consideration," in which he wrote: "Oh! since the commonweal cannot without a *spiritual rape* force the consciences of all to one worship; oh, that it may never commit that rape in forcing the consciences of all men to one worship which a stronger arm and sword may soon (as formerly) arise to alter." [14] Williams developed these ideas further in his landmark 1644 treatise "The Bloody Tenant of Persecution." [15] In it, he makes the following proclamations:

- "First, that the blood of so many hundred thousand souls of Protestants and Papists, spilt in the wars of present and former ages, for their respective consciences, is not required nor accepted by Jesus Christ the Prince of Peace.
- "The doctrine of persecution for cause of conscience is proved guilty of all the blood of the souls crying for vengeance under the altar.
- "All civil states with their officers of justice in their respective constitutions and administrations are proved essentially civil, and therefore not judges, governors, or defenders of the spiritual or Christian state and worship.
- "God requireth not a uniformity of religion to be enacted and enforced in any civil state; which enforced uniformity (sooner or later) is the greatest occasion of civil war, ravishing of conscience, persecution of Christ Jesus in his servants, and of the hypocrisy and destruction of millions of souls.
- "It is the will and command of God (since the coming of his Son, the Lord Jesus), that permission of the most paganish, Jewish, Turkish or anti-Christian consciences and worships, be granted to all men."

Williams' detractors, particularly the Rev. John Cotton, pastor of the Boston church, argued that the state must protect the common good by correcting heretics, blasphemers, and idolaters. Cotton wrote an answer to the "Bloody Tenant" called "The Bloody Tenent, Washed, And Made White in the Blood of the Lambe"—to which Williams responded with yet another treatise with an even longer title, "The Bloody Tenant Yet More Bloody by Mr. Cotton's endeavor to wash it white in the Blood of the Lambe; of whose precious Blood, spilt in the Blood of his Servants; and of the Blood of Millions spilt in former and later Wars for Conscience sake, that Most Bloody Tenant of persecution for the cause of Conscience, upon a second Tryal, is found now more apparently and more notoriously guilty." [16]

Williams' radical ideas got him banished from the Massachusetts Bay Colony. His friends and foes alike could not fathom the level of religious freedom he advocated. "People thought Williams had to be out of his mind," Haynes said. "The form of liberty he advocated was dangerous. Surely the state has the right to defend itself against evil."

Williams believed the community, as a matter or priority, had to protect the individual conscience. His argument for freedom of conscience was grounded in a theological proposition. "Williams believed God created every human being with liberty of conscience," Haynes said. "God created human beings with the capacity to turn toward God or turn away. Society or government may not interfere with what God has done. People in any society have the right to be wrong. If they chose to turn away from God, that is between them and God. Williams had a supreme confidence that 'God can take care of God.'"

This opinion stood in sharp contrast with the general view of the day, which was more concerned with uniformity, according to Winthrop's vision of a community "knit together." Williams, on the other hand, argued for complete free exercise of religion, even for Quakers, Catholics, and Jews—a revolutionary idea at the time.[17] "Free exercise means the state does not have control of religion, and no one else had imagined a state could exist with that," Haynes said. "People thought free exercise meant chaos."

Free exercise is to be distinguished from its lesser cousin, toleration, which could always be withdrawn at the whim of a particular regime. "Williams believed that in the hands of government, toleration is a 'weasel word,'" Haynes said. "Toleration means that government can allow something one day and then disallow it the next. Toleration means the state still has control over what is Christian and what is not, and it can stamp out what is not in its purview. In terms of personal virtue, Williams might say toleration is good; but in the hands of government, it is dangerous."

Williams was also a man of his time. He called the Catholic Church the "Anti-Christ" and the "Whore of Babylon"; he accused the Church of England of "popery"; and he thought the Quakers were completely out of bounds. He quarreled with the Quakers verbally throughout his life.[18] "He thought everyone should understand the Gospel the way he understood it. He was not the founder of ACLU, and he had no love for all different groups. He debated the Quakers to the end and tried to convince them that they were wrong and he was right. The fact that Williams urged tolerance of groups he opposed made his argument for religious liberty even sharper," Haynes pointed out.[19]

Embryo of the First Amendment

In tracing the birth of the First Amendment, the most logical place to start is with Thomas Jefferson, James Madison, and the other Founders.[20] But the basis of religious liberty in America goes back much further, and it begins in these early debates.

The core idea behind the First Amendment's Establishment Clause—that the government should never interfere with an individual's freedom of conscience—comes from Roger Williams. "He was the first to use the term, 'separation of church and state.' The First Amendment—specifically the first 16 words—takes us all the way back to Williams," Haynes said. "Williams wanted people to go to church on their own free will, and not be coerced. This is where we get 'free exercise thereof.' Williams argued that you can't have free exercise if you have an established church. He believed we must build a 'hedge of separation between the garden of the Church and the wilderness of the world.' Otherwise there would be no chance of having the garden if the state is involved."

Martin Marty calls Williams "a premiere apostle of liberty"; and First Amendment historian William Lee Miller says Williams represents "the root of the matter" in the genealogy of religious liberty in America.[21] "Roger Williams represents the elusive possibility, the rare instance in which the Christian religion, perhaps even in its Puritan version . . . can find within itself the grace to overcome its own deficiencies and give over any effort at the subduing of all nations," Miller wrote.[22]

Williams spent most of his life searching for pure Christianity and the "true church." He became a Baptist, but later withdrew from the ministry and congregations, and became a kind of sect unto himself, or a "seeker" of his day.[23]

By the time the first Congress convened to pass the Bill of Rights in 1791, Roger Williams was a faded memory from colonial history, and he did not emerge as a popular figure for name-dropping among the Founders. Williams' role in shaping what was to become the First Amendment was important but indirect—primarily through his influence on political philosopher John Locke, who was influential among the Founders, and on Isaac Backus, an important spokesman for religious freedom during the Revolutionary era and the founding period. Backus, a Baptist minister from Massachusetts, argued for separation of church and state and against taxation for the support of the established church of Massachusetts, the Congregational Church (handed down from the Puritans).

"God alone is Lord of the conscience, and hath left it free from the doctrines and commandments of men," Backus wrote in "An Appeal to the Public for Religious Liberty Against the Oppression of the Present Day" (1773). "The requiring of an implicit faith, and an absolute blind obedience, is to destroy liberty of conscience—and reason also."[24]

Like Williams more than a century earlier, Backus used a basic theological argument: Interference with the human conscience is an offense against God, and attempts at such interference represent the worst kind of oppression. A similar argument cropped up later in the landmark Virginia Statute of Religious Freedom (1786), which begins as follows: "Whereas Almighty God hath created the mind free; that all attempts to influence it by temporal punishments or burdens, or by civil incapacitations, tend only to beget habits of hypocrisy and meanness, and are a departure from the plan of the Holy Author of our religion, who being Lord both of body and mind, yet chose not to propagate it by coercions on either." [25]

The author of the statute was Thomas Jefferson—not one for making theological arguments, but he found common cause with his dissenting religious counterparts for the cause of conscience. James Madison, who steered Jefferson's bill to passage in the Virginia Assembly, took the ball and ran with it when the time came to draft the U.S. Constitution and the First Amendment. [26]

The genealogy of the ideas Jefferson and Madison permanently imprinted on the United States goes back to early Colonial America, the radical wing of the Protestant Reformation, and the dissenting Puritans, of whom Williams is the primary—and perhaps still the most radical—spokesman. [27] "Roger Williams believed the same Reformed Protestant doctrines his principal opponents believed. But he applied them with a boldness and moral imagination quite beyond the point to which his fellow Puritans were willing to go, and with practical results for political life," Miller wrote.

The Legacy of Winthrop's Covenant

Williams' stubborn dissents and pointed arguments carried the essential elements of what would develop into the First Amendment a century and a half later. But it is Winthrop's vision of a "city on a hill," as expressed in his "Model of Christian Charity," that remains the dominant ideal in America. "You see these ideas throughout American history and still today," Haynes said. "If there is any one document that echoes out throughout our history to present time, it is this one."

Winthrop is a favorite for politicians to quote. Ronald Reagan built his presidential career around the image of the "city on a hill." Presidents who don't give a "city on a hill" speech are said to be lacking "the vision thing." George H. W. Bush wasn't able to capture Reagan's aura. Bill Clinton talked about a "new covenant," but didn't get far with it. George W. Bush has dusted off "Providence," which he often invokes in his formal speeches, including his 2005 State of the Union Address.[28] "You could take any election cycle, and things from Winthrop's sermon will be there," Haynes said. "I don't think you can be elected president of the United States without some kind of 'city on a hill' speech. It resonates with Americans."

Each political party claims Winthrop, but each party emphasizes different aspects of his philosophy. Republicans emphasize the "city on a hill," while Democrats emphasize the notion of community "knit together."

Missing from Winthrop's speech are the words "diversity" and "pluralism"—so dominant in today's political dialogue, but not part of the seventeenth-century Puritan reality.[29] "They [the Puritans] were after religious freedom for themselves, but not for other people," Haynes said. "Conformity was built into their society because much of what they envisioned depended on people having a shared understanding of what their society was going to be about." Politicians who invoke Winthrop today conveniently omit the lines immediately following his city on a hill reference: "If we shall deal falsely with our God . . . We shall shame the faces of many of God's worthy servants, and cause their prayers to be turned into curses upon us till we be consumed out of the good land whither we are going."

Only the "shining city" side of divine Providence is revealed on the political stump. But without a complete understanding of Winthrop's meaning, and without Williams' view to balance, the "shining" vision can easily degenerate into national chauvinism, triumphalism, and American exceptionalism. This misplaced mindset has been blamed for many of America's foreign policy failures and excesses—from the colonial war in the Philippines to the Vietnam War and second Iraq War. If "God is on our side," how can we possibly lose?[30]

According to Williams, neither Massachusetts nor any other American colony could ever be God's approximation of a "New Israel." Nor could the people of any country claim to be a special nation of "God's chosen people." Williams based this view on his "typological" interpretation of the Bible—that the Israel of the Old Testament was a one-time arrangement, and no subsequent nation could claim to be "God's chosen people."[31] But since being special and "chosen" are far more politically attractive than the alternative, the selectively appropriated Winthrop vision has won out.[32]

"Massachusetts Bay picked up and carried on the disposition . . . as chosen and favored by God, selected and cared for by a special providence; and that view entered into the bloodstream of America . . . and continues to add an element of self-righteousness to American self-interpretation to this day," Miller writes.[33]

Witch Trials, Civil Liberties, and the Puritan Legacy

The Puritans are generally not looked upon favorably in history books, popular culture, and the media. The Puritans are most commonly known not for Winthrop or Williams, but for the infamous Salem witch trials, in which about twenty-five people, including seven men, were executed by hanging, tortured to death, or died in prison.[34]

But despite the excesses of the witch trials, it was the Puritans themselves who put a stop to them. Increase Mather, a Puritan clergyman and president of Harvard College, played a prominent role in exorcising the witch hysteria. In his published sermon "Cases of Conscience Concerning Evil Spirits," Mather argued against the use of "spectral evidence" in the courtroom. Evidence had to be tangible. "It is better that ten suspected witches should escape than that one innocent person should be condemned," Mather wrote.[35] Revulsion and reaction against the witch trials led to important legal reforms and expansion of the rights of the accused, contributing to the development of political and religious rights in America. Puritan theology, although harsh and rigid in many respects, contained within it progressive elements that would point the way to more liberal paths. "The Protestant Reformers, and particularly the English and colonial Puritans, for all their sometimes zealous narrowness and for all their participation in intolerant episodes, still promulgated principles that sometimes led by implication beyond their own behavior: Every man his own priest. 'Justification' by God's free grace received by the individual believer's faith, instead of through the sacramental system of the Church . . . The Bible as the sole authority; the congregational, nonhierarchical, internally democratic church. These religious ideas had unintended social and political consequences—unintended and unwelcome to some; welcomed and explicitly affirmed by others," Miller wrote.[36]

The most important lasting legacy of the Puritans, according to Haynes, is government by constitution, which comes from the Puritans' idea of covenant—forming a compact or a charter. "We are a chartered people; we are not a tribe," he said. "The idea of covenant in the 1600s was to become the idea of constitution in 1700s. It is a religious idea that became secular. In many ways we have the Puritans to thank for our Constitution. Unfortunately this history—and the legacy of Winthrop and Williams—is lost to most people."

Morbid fascination with the Puritans' excesses tends to obscure their important contributions and ongoing influence on American society,

Haynes contends. "Most textbooks treat the Puritans as cartoon figures and stereotypes. The history books usually tell us how narrow-minded they were and just how 'puritan' they were; or, one of my favorite definitions of Puritanism—'the haunting fear that someone somewhere might be happy.' But the Puritans were not as dour as they are often depicted in textbooks. There was rum in the bottom of those ships; and they had sex, and they enjoyed it."[37]

Haynes believes that in order for Americans to truly understand themselves, it is important to reach a balanced understanding of the Puritans. "It is wrong to read through the lens of our stereotypes. It does us no good to demonize the Puritans, because it hurts our self-understanding as a people," he said. "The Puritans deeply shaped our culture. We are all heirs to their legacy, and we are all deeply influenced by the Puritans in many ways we don't know. I think all Americans are Puritans in some ways. If we distort them, we will have trouble understanding ourselves today."

After the seventeenth century, the Puritans evolved and faded into America's increasingly diverse tapestry. Like the rest of Americans in the "melting pot," they assimilated. But their strands remain deeply woven into American society.[38] The downside of the Puritans' legacy also remains deep within the nation's fabric, and is often expressed in certain forms of intolerance and fear of the "other," which began with the hatred of Catholics.[39] "Every time the nation faces a serious crisis, you see this anxiety come to the surface," Haynes said. "A lot of the rhetoric that used to be directed against Catholics you can now hear about American Muslims—that they can never be good Americans because of what they believe."

After the September 11 terrorist attacks, the Rev. Jerry Falwell, along with the televangelist Pat Robertson, blamed the devastation on atheists, abortionists, feminists, homosexuals, the American Civil Liberties Union, and the People for the American Way.[40] "Jerry Falwell's choice of words was so unfortunate; but if you go back to Winthrop's language, you can see an old theme: 'If we live up to what we are to be and what God requires, we will prosper. If we fail to obey God, we will be destroyed,'" Haynes said. "Since Sept. 11, many people are afraid we've fallen away and should return. They believe we are losing ground because we have fallen away from the source of our liberty and who we are as a people."

After the Civil War, many people similarly believed the devastation was caused by disobedience to God and a breach in the covenant.[41] "The Civil War was seen by many Americans as God's judgment on America, and many people believed the appropriate response was to amend the Constitution to include God and Jesus Christ. This came very close to passing. They felt the judgment of God on our nation had to be corrected, because of the great defect in the Constitution omitting God," Haynes said.

During the Cold War, fear of atheistic communism prompted Congress to insert the phrase "under God" in the Pledge of Allegiance. Now with a pending lawsuit aimed at expunging the phrase from the Pledge, many fear the consequences if it is removed.[42]

"Why should we care about prayer and the pledge? A strong segment of the population sees the United States as a God-blessed nation; that our liberties are inseparably linked to God's gift and his involvement in the American experiment. You don't have freedom unless you acknowledge the God who gave it to you. And if you deal falsely with God, you will be destroyed," Haynes says. "Many Americans feel the Puritan anxiety of the removal of God's blessing on America. This is a culture war issue in the deepest sense, because all could be lost. We need to have a perspective on these themes and realize how long we've been struggling with them and why they are so important to so many people."

The Ten Commandments

> While truth and law were founded on the God of all Creation,
> Man now, through law, denies the truth and calls it "separation."
> No longer does man see a need for God when he's in full control,
> For the only truth self-evident is in the latest poll.
>
> —Roy Moore, "Our American Birthright"

The Winthrop-Williams debate could easily carry right up to the Alabama Supreme Court rotunda, the epicenter of a battle over the Ten Commandments. Former Alabama Chief Justice Roy Moore stirred controversy in 2001 when he placed a monument to the Ten Commandments in the state Supreme Court building. Two years later, he was removed from office for refusing to remove it. In commenting on the issue, Moore often invokes Winthrop-like speech and reasoning. The Ten Commandments, he said, are a reminder of God's sovereignty over America's laws and freedoms.

"It is axiomatic that to restore morality, we must first recognize the source of that morality," Moore said at the dedication of the monument in 2001. "Many judges and other government officials across our land deny that there's a higher law. . . . Not only have they turned away from those absolute standards which form the basis of our morality and the moral foundation of our law, but they have divorced the Constitution and the Bill of Rights from these principles. As they have sown the wind, so we have reaped the whirlwind, in our homes, in our schools and in our workplaces."[43]

Was Moore attempting to establish his religion by placing the Ten Commandments monument in the courthouse?

"He advocates a theological and a civic vision of society that echoes back to this early vision [of Winthrop]. He is not arguing for a Biblical commonwealth, but close. He seems to be saying all law must be subordinate to God's law for it to be valid," Haynes said. "Roy Moore is reminding people not to forget God. And he's telling judges to look to a higher law; because when they don't, the country becomes a 'moral slum.' This is a view deeply felt by many Americans today."

Moore's monument also includes quotes from various Founding Fathers invoking God, including George Washington's Farewell Address, in which Washington states, "Let it simply be asked: Where is the security for property, for reputation, for life, if the sense of *religious obligation* deserts the oaths which are the instruments of investigation in courts of justice?"[44] Quotes from Thomas Jefferson, James Madison, and other founders invoking God, "nature's God" and the "Creator" are also inscribed on the monument.[45] The choice of Jefferson and Madison is ironic, given that the two were avowed secularists who fought not to "get God back into government" but to keep religion out of government. Such invocation of the Founders is often heard in the case for a "Christian nation." Miller warns against what he calls "selective appropriation of the Founding Fathers."[46]

"The most important of these Founders, intellectually speaking, was Thomas Jefferson, who shaped the phrases and formed the ideas that gave the nation its soul. Jefferson looked upon the old religions of mysteries, creeds, and emotion-charged symbols as 'shackles' on the human mind—impediments to the truths on which rested his new nation," Miller writes.[47]

In the context of the Winthrop-Williams dichotomy, Moore would find a philosophical ally in Winthrop—reaching back to the "Model of Christian Charity"—but a strong opponent in Williams. "Winthrop would agree with Roy Moore: God commands that the Ten Commandments remain; while Williams would say God commands them to come down," Haynes said.

"Rogues' Island"

In 1635, the General Court of Massachusetts found Roger Williams guilty of contempt and banished him from the colony. Williams went next door to Rhode Island and founded Providence in 1636. He governed the colony under the mandate of religious liberty—"a haven for the cause of conscience." [48] "Rhode Island was the first spot in human history where one's standing in civic order was completely disconnected from one's standing in religious community," Haynes says. "At the time, people thought you couldn't set up a society without an established religion. Williams opened up the proverbial Pandora's box."

Rhode Island became popularly known as "Rogue's Island," because it attracted so many misfits, according to Martin Marty. [49] The colony also became a haven for Quakers and Catholics, the most controversial and hated religious groups in the colonies at the time. Williams was not fond of either, but he insisted they must be allowed—and not merely tolerated, but given complete free exercise. "Among the people who came [to Rhode Island], the Quakers pushed even Williams to the limits of tolerance," Marty wrote. "Always the Quakers kept nettling Williams, but he defended their right to propagate their views."

Williams believed free exercise was God's mandate, and he advocated free exercise on theological grounds. "Williams argued that God required it," Haynes said. "Even if you didn't want Catholics and Quakers in your mix, you had to do it. Williams proclaimed, 'Here is a haven for the cause of conscience, not the sewer of New England.'"

In 1654, the first group of Jews to come to North America arrived in New Amsterdam (later to become New York). The governor, Peter Stuyvesant, was hostile toward the émigrés and forced them into ghettoes. Four years later, another group of Jews arrived in Rhode Island. Williams granted them free exercise and spared them persecution. [50] "The treatment of Jews is a test in particular for a person who held intensely to the truth of the Christian revelation, as Williams did, at the time, and among the folk with whom he lived, when religious beliefs were taken as seriously as some economic, political and scientific beliefs are taken now," Miller writes. [51]

In an age when Jews were subject to mass expulsions and various other forms of persecution, most synagogues were designed with trap doors for quick escape. But the Jews of Rhode Island were never forced into such a precarious situation—a fact Haynes said is important to remember in the current political atmosphere in the world: "Yes, we have a long way to go in the U.S.; but despite all of our faults and problems, here is something to think about: The Jews have never had to use that trap door. . . . That is who we are at our best. That is why I think the First Amendment is America's greatest gift to world civilization; and that is the legacy of Roger Williams."

Muslims in America

When Roger Williams said, "It is the will and command of God that permission of the most paganish, Jewish, Turkish or anti-Christian consciences and worships, be granted to all men," he meant religious liberty for *all*, including Muslims.[52]

This idea was as extraordinary in 1644 as it has been in America since the September 11, 2001, terrorist attacks—perpetrated in the name of Allah. During Williams' lifetime, the Muslim Ottoman Empire was pounding at Europe's back door, placing Vienna under siege for the second time in 1683, and potentially threatening the whole continent. The Ottomans had first attempted to take Vienna in 1529, following the momentum of their conquering of Constantinople and all of the former Byzantine lands in the Balkans. The second Battle of Vienna began, coincidentally, on September 11, 1683. The city was saved only when a Polish-allied army led by King Jan III Sobieski came to the rescue.[53]

Muslims elicited fear and loathing in the West then as they do now. The seventeenth-century English political philosopher John Locke, influential among America's Founding Fathers, discussed what he viewed as the problems of a Muslim living in a Christian society. "It is ridiculous for any one to profess himself to be a Mahometan only in his religion, but in everything else a faithful subject to a Christian magistrate, whilst at the same time he acknowledges himself bound to yield blind obedience to the Mufti of Constantinople [Istanbul], who himself is entirely obedient to the Ottoman Emperor and frames the feigned oracles of that religion according to his pleasure," Locke wrote in his 1689 treatise, "A Letter Concerning Toleration." Yet when the issue comes down to the matter of conscience, Locke joins with Williams: "Neither Pagan nor Mahometan, nor Jew, ought to be excluded from the civil rights of the commonwealth because of his religion."[54] Freedom of conscience, even a Muslim conscience, is paramount.

In the post-September 11 world, Muslims may prove the ultimate test of American tolerance and commitment to free exercise of religion. Many were shocked when U.S. Rep. Keith Ellison (D–Minn.), the first Muslim elected to Congress, swore his oath of office on a Koran—ironically, Thomas Jefferson's Koran. "I fear that in the next century we will have many more Muslims in the United States if we do not adopt the strict immigration policies that I believe are necessary to preserve the values and beliefs traditional to the United States of America and to prevent our resources from being swamped," wrote Virginia Congressman Virgil Goode (notwithstanding the fact that Ellison is not an immigrant).[55] Goode was widely condemned for his comments, but his sentiments were reinforced when Congress effectively killed a deal by Dubai Ports World—a United Arab Emirates-owned firm—to buy management rights to terminals at major U.S. ports.[56] The standoff pitted President Bush, who supported the deal, against both Democrats and his usual stalwart Republican supporters in Congress. Congressmen opposing the deal justified their posture on security grounds, while some on the other side of the argument said the real issue was religious and ethnic bias. "I think the near-hysteria about this is not warranted," said Senator John McCain of Arizona.[57]

The national conflicts filter down to the local level. In late 2006, a brouhaha broke out in Katy, Texas, between local community members and the Katy Islamic Association, which wanted to build a Mosque and community center on eleven acres of open land. Neighboring property owner Craig Baker threatened to race pigs on the edge of his land on Fridays, the Muslim day of *Jumu'ah*, or congregational prayer. Muslims consider pigs unclean and do not eat pork. Baker maintained that members of the Katy Islamic Association attempted to run him off his property, and he was merely holding his ground in defense, while the KIA claimed "a small minority of bigoted and close minded people" was opposing them.[58]

Despite these conflicts, Muslims are generally considered far more integrated into American society than in Europe, where conflict between Muslims and native Europeans is fierce and seemingly intractable. The intermittent *intifada* (uprising) in France's poor immigrant *banlieues* is a stark example of the clash of cultures and failure to integrate. The 2005 subway bombings in Great Britain and the ongoing series of thwarted bomb plots there have made "Londonistan" an epicenter of jihad. In the United States, optimists maintain that the nation's commitment to free exercise of religion, pluralism, and integration prevents the dismal scenario that Europe presents.

"What one hopes about these reciprocating persuasions [Christian, Jewish, Muslim] in the atmosphere of freedom is that each of the great religions can find within itself the moral resources to endorse on its own ground democracy and human rights and to overcome the inclination of all religions to become tribal," Miller wrote.[59]

"Dead White Males" and Diversity

The role of religion in public life and the notion of pluralism—and just how much of it we can tolerate—were critical issues 400 years ago just as they are today. An explanation of the origins of religious liberty in America could begin at many places, most obviously with the Founders—Jefferson and Madison in particular. Benjamin Franklin also had much to say about religion and public life, and his own life offers a case study of an exemplary citizen who set the blueprint for what it is to be an American.[60] "Benjamin Franklin was such an archetypical American, and he was the father of the country in so many ways," Haynes said. "His way of thinking about his life, his transformation, and his melding of the Puritan way of thinking with the Enlightenment really set the stage."

But the origins of religious liberty go even further back to the two conflicting visions of the "city on a hill" as embodied by Winthrop and Williams. They are enduring archetypes to this day. "These two visions of America continue to shape and frame the debate," Haynes says. "In our society, we are deeply struggling about how to deal with religion in public life in the most religiously diverse nation in the world. We really have to deal with these conflicts honestly and find out where they come from."

Since the 1960s, a growing chorus of intellectuals and academics has promulgated revisionist theories assailing the traditional canon of American history and literature as inherently racist and the tool of institutional oppression.[61] Some universities have gutted their American history and institutions requirements and replaced them with ethnic studies.[62] But viewing American history through reactionary ideologies only further distorts the present. Of all the "dead white males"[63] to walk across American history, Roger Williams must not be forgotten.

"If you think religious liberty is difficult and complicated, blame Williams, because it starts with Williams in Rhode Island," Haynes said. "That is the genius of the American experience—never use the engine of government to deny people the freedom to choose in matters of faith—Williams thought this was the way. Our public square ought to be just like this."

5

Religious Liberty in Public Schools

Finding Common Ground on the Battleground

> The public school is at once the symbol of our democracy and the most pervasive means for promoting our common destiny. In no activity of the State is it more vital to keep out divisive forces than in its schools, to avoid confusing, not to say fusing, what the Constitution sought to keep strictly apart.
>
> —Supreme Court Justice Felix Frankfurter,
> *McCollum v. Board of Education* (1948)

Nowhere is the battle for freedom of religion—and freedom *from* religion—more heated than in public schools, where the hearts and minds of children are involved. The issue of religion in public schools has left a long trail of court cases, and it continues to be a prime source of conflict, litigation, and precedent-setting Supreme Court decisions. Since 1987, the High Court has upheld school vouchers,[1] campus Christian clubs, and after-hours Bible study on school property;[2] but the Court has struck down prayers before football games,[3] prayers at graduation ceremonies,[4] and the teaching of creationism.[5] These matters are far from settled. The Court's decisions are frequently split 5 to 4, and it could easily reverse itself as new justices replace those retiring.

Religion is a nuclear hot potato for public schools. It is therefore no surprise that school boards and administrators have chosen to banish it. It is more expedient to omit religion from the curriculum and ban it from the campus than to risk a costly lawsuit.[6] But this solution is clearly not what former Supreme Court Justice Tom Clark had in mind when he wrote for the majority of the Court in striking down school-led Bible recitations in the landmark case of *Abington School District v. Schempp* (1963): "It might well be said that one's education is not complete without a study of comparative religion or the history of religion and its relationship to the advancement of civilization. It certainly may be said that the Bible is worthy of study for its literary and historic qualities. Nothing we have said here indicated that such study of the Bible or of religion, when presented objectively as part of a secular program of education, may not be effected consistently with the First Amendment."[7]

Surveys consistently show that Americans place a high value on religion. According to a 2004 Gallup poll, 82 percent of Americans said religion plays a "very important" or "fairly important" role in their lives. But Americans are divided on the pros and cons of religion's influence in public life. According to the Gallup poll, 33 percent of Americans would like to see less influence of organized religion; 26 percent would like to see more influence; and 39 percent believe the level of religion's influence is good at its present level. Working through these conflicting opinions in public schools is complicated indeed.

Charles C. Haynes, senior scholar at the First Amendment Center, argues that teaching *about* religion and religions is crucial in preparing young people to function in an increasingly diverse society. "The confusion and ignorance surrounding religious liberty and the Constitution leave Americans in a weak position to meet the challenges of exploding religious pluralism in the United States," he says. "We've got to rethink how we are preparing people to engage one another in the public square across their differences. Teaching about religion is only part of that."[8]

The Challenge of Neutrality

> The First Amendment requires the state to be a neutral in its relations with groups of religious believers and non-believers; it does not require the state to be their adversary. State power is no more to be used so as to handicap religions than it is to favor them.
>
> —Justice Hugo Black, *Everson v. Board of Education* (1947)

The concept of neutrality is the guiding principle for the government's relationship to religion. Neutrality means not favoring one religion over another, not favoring religion over non-religion, and vice-versa. The U.S. Supreme Court has become the final arbiter of what is and what isn't neutral with regards to religion in public schools. The Court applies the Establishment Clause more stringently to public schools because young people are more impressionable than adults, and students are a "captive audience" in a compulsory school system.

"Students in their early teens have not yet developed the critical acumen they will rely on only a few years later," historian Martin E. Marty wrote in

Education, Religion, and the Common Good. "While college students can tell the difference between imparting information and proselytizing, individuals at earlier education levels may not be able to do so. In elementary schools especially, where students often have a single teacher for most subjects, children may be more gullible, more easily influenced and manipulated, more exploitable."[9]

Since the 1940s, the Supreme Court has devised various tests to determine whether a state action violates neutrality and constitutes an establishment of religion. No one test is currently favored by the majority of the court, but two of the most referenced tests regarding religion in public schools include the "Lemon test" and the "compelling interest" test.

The Lemon test is derived from the 1971 Supreme Court case *Lemon v. Kurtzman,* in which the court struck down state programs in Rhode Island and Pennsylvania that subsidized the salaries of parochial school teachers. To pass the Lemon test, a governmental or school policy must meet the following criteria:

1. Reflect a clearly secular purpose;
2. Have the primary effect of neither advancing nor inhibiting religion; and
3. Avoid excessive government entanglement with religion.

If the public school or government policy fails to meet any of these three standards, the Court may deem it unconstitutional. In the *Lemon* case, the state policies in question met the first two standards, but failed number three, thus breaching the First Amendment's prohibition against a government establishment of religion.

"A law 'respecting' the establishment of religion is not always easily identifiable as one violative of the Establishment Clause. A given law might not establish a state religion but nevertheless be one 'respecting' that end in the sense of being a step that could lead to such establishment and hence offend the First Amendment," former Chief Justice Warren Burger wrote for the Court majority in *Lemon.*[10]

Oliver Thomas, an attorney and a consultant with the First Amendment Center, said another way to look at the Lemon test is *primary effect:* "What is the effect of what you're doing? Is the effect to accommodate religion or to promote religion?" Thomas asked. "In the arena of public schools, if you can't identify a primary educational purpose under the Lemon test, the law will usually fail."[11]

The Lemon test is not the final word for determining neutrality. Former

Supreme Court Justice Sandra Day O'Connor developed another test, called the "endorsement test," which asks if the law in question could be perceived by a "reasonable observer" as an endorsement of religion or disapproval of it.[12]

Justice Anthony Kennedy has developed still another test, known as the "coercion test," which some view as less stringent than other tests. Under Kennedy's criteria, the government does not violate the Establishment Clause unless it (1) provides direct aid to religion in a way that would tend to establish a state church, or (2) coerces people to support or participate in religion against their will.[13] Kennedy applied this test in the 1992 case *Lee v. Weisman*, in which the court declared school graduation prayers—even non-sectarian prayers—to be unconstitutional. The petitioner, Robert E. Lee, principal of Nathan Bishop Middle School in Rhode Island, argued that attending the graduation ceremony was a voluntary activity, not a requirement to receive a diploma; thus the students were not being forced to listen to the graduation prayer. Kennedy rejected this argument. "Everyone knows that in our society and in our culture high school graduation is one of life's most significant occasions. A school rule which excuses attendance is beside the point. Attendance may not be required by official decree, yet it is apparent that a student is not free to absent herself from the graduation exercise in any real sense of the term *voluntary*," Kennedy wrote. Thus the school policy was unconstitutional by virtue of its "coerciveness," according to Kennedy. "The Constitution forbids the State to exact religious conformity from a student as the price of attending her own high school graduation. This is the calculus the Constitution commands. A state-created orthodoxy puts at grave risk that freedom of belief and conscience which are the sole assurance that religious faith is real, not imposed," Kennedy wrote.

The Court applies different tests in different circumstances, and it is likely those tests will continue to expand and evolve as the Court moves through its ongoing docket of First Amendment cases. "Although the Court's interpretation of the Establishment Clause is in flux, it is likely that for the foreseeable future, a majority of the justices will continue to view government neutrality toward religion as the guiding principle," Haynes and Thomas wrote in *Finding Common Ground: A Guide to Religious Liberty in Public Schools*.

The Challenge of Diversity

> I agree with the Court that the religious scruples of the Amish are op-
> posed to the education of their children beyond the grade schools,
> yet . . . if a parent keeps his child out of school beyond the grade school,
> then the child will be forever barred from entry into the new and amazing
> world of diversity that we have today.
>
> —Justice William O. Douglas, *Wisconsin v. Yoder* (1972)

Many people blame the Supreme Court for "kicking God out of the schools" during the 1960s, when it ruled against state-sponsored school prayer and Bible readings.[14] But religious-oriented instruction had been largely removed from public schools much earlier. The process began around the turn of the last century when Catholics, Jews, and other non-Protestant immigrants arrived in sufficient numbers to challenge the monopoly of the old educational establishment.

"The presence of new peoples challenged everything that had previously been privileged, including once unquestioned educational assumptions," Marty writes.[15] Such assumptions included presentation of the King James Bible from a Protestant perspective. In response, ethnic groups established parochial schools in an effort to preserve their cultural and religious heritage. But as immigration continued, pressure from the increasingly diverse population mounted on public schools, and administrators voluntarily began eliminating Bible study. At the time, most Protestants were adamant that school curriculum not include Christianity from a Catholic viewpoint or make any mention of the pope.[16]

The Supreme Court did not get involved until the 1940s. In the landmark 1948 case *McCollum v. Board of Education,* the Court ruled against the Champaign (Ill.) County school district's policy of allowing outside religious teachers to provide religious instruction for grades four through nine. The program was set up, theoretically, to allow Protestant, Catholic, and Jewish teachers provide the religious instruction, and students who did not wish to participate could be excused. Nevertheless, the Court rejected the Champaign school's "entanglement" with religion.[17] "Here not only are the state's tax-supported public school buildings used for the dissemination of religious doctrines, the State also affords sectarian groups an invaluable aid in that it helps to provide pupils for their religious classes through use of the state's compulsory public school machinery. This is not separation of Church and State," Justice Hugo Black wrote.[18]

Five years before *McCollum,* during the height of World War II, Justice

Sidebar 5.1. | Evolving Models of Public Schools

Historically, public schools have followed the following models with respect to religion:

- *The sacred public school:* During the nineteenth century, public schools in the United States were de facto Protestant schools. Christianity was presented from a Protestant viewpoint. By the turn of the century, pressure from increasing diversity resulted in an informal "disestablishment" of the Protestant model. "The sacred public school model began to fall apart early in the 20th century in what some people call the 'second disestablishment.' The Protestant consensus about public education broke down," according to Charles Haynes.
- *The secular public school:* In response to a series of Supreme Court cases beginning in the 1940s, which challenged the remaining religious elements in public schools, many public schools eliminated all mention of religion in any context. Many school administrators misinterpreted the Supreme Court opinions to mean that the First Amendment prohibits schools from making any mention of religion in any context. Reaction to this situation has led many parents to give up on public education and turn to parochial schools or home schooling for their children.
- *The civil public school:* Public schools may teach *about* religion when it's in the appropriate context and does not involve proselytizing, according to Supreme Court decisions. The civil public school model also accommodates the First Amendment rights of students to express their religious views on campus so long as they are not disruptive. The First Amendment Center advocates this model through the First Amendment Schools project.

Source: Haynes and Thomas, *Finding Common Ground*, 5–6; 31–34. Also see Marty, *Education, Religion, and the Common Good*, 37–39.

Robert Jackson made an equally poignant statement on the meaning of the First Amendment when the Court struck down compulsory flag salutes and recitations of the Pledge of Allegiance. "Probably no deeper division of our people could proceed from any provocation than from finding it necessary to choose what doctrine and whose program public educational officials shall compel youth to unite in embracing. Ultimate futility of such attempts to compel coherence is the lesson of every such effort from the Roman drive to stamp out Christianity as a disturber of its pagan unity, the Inquisition, as a means to religious and dynastic unity, the Siberian exiles as a means to Russian unity, down to the fast failing efforts of our present totalitarian enemies. Those who begin coercive elimination of dissent soon find themselves exterminating dissenters. Compulsory unification of opinion achieves only the unanimity of the graveyard," Jackson wrote in *West Virginia State Board of Education v. Barnette* (1943).[19]

Today, with some 3,000 religious groups in the United States, the challenge is how to maintain national unity and basic civility amidst this state of plurality. Haynes believes the solution lies in the values espoused by the nation's founders when they constructed the Bill of Rights.[20] "Since there is not, and cannot be, a religious consensus, what are the civic values that Americans of all faiths (or none) hold in common? American citizens must return to the democratic principles articulated in the Religious Liberty clauses of the First Amendment. Religious liberty, or freedom of conscience, is at the heart of what it means to be an American citizen," Haynes and Thomas emphasize.[21]

Free Exercise

> Students have the right to express religious views in class discussion or in assigned work, provided that their expression falls within the scope of the discussion or the assignment. . . . School authorities are not permitted to discriminate against student expression simply because of its religious character.
>
> — Federal Judge Samuel Alito, *C.H. v. Oliva* (2000)

Public school students and teachers retain their First Amendment rights to the free exercise of religion and free speech during the school day, within certain parameters. Or, in the words of former Supreme Court Justice Abe Fortas, "it can hardly be argued that either students or teachers shed their constitutional rights to freedom of speech or expression at the schoolhouse gate."[22]

So, although the school principal cannot lead an official school prayer over the loudspeaker, students or teachers may pray privately; or students may meet in designated rooms to pray, so long as the meetings are not led by teachers or administrators. Similarly, students may wear religious clothing so long as it is not disruptive, and teachers may wear nonobtrusive jewelry, such as a cross or a Star of David, but may not wear clothing that is fashioned as an advertisement for their religion. Like most other issues regarding the First Amendment and schools, the broad guidelines for the free exercise of religion—and its limitations—have been set out by the Supreme Court and federal courts.[23]

The Establishment Clause, the Free Exercise Clause, and the Free Speech Clause all came into play in the in the 1990 case *Board of Education of Westside Community Schools v. Mergens,* in which a student at Westside High School in Omaha, Nebraska, requested—and was denied—permission to form a Christian club at the school. The school argued that since organized student activities are an integral part of its educational mission, approval of the proposed Christian club would effectively incorporate religious activities into the school's official program, thus endorsing participation in the religious club and providing the club with an official platform to proselytize other students. The student, Bridget Mergens, sued the school, claiming that it had violated her constitutional freedom of speech, freedom of association, and free exercise of religion. In addition, she said the school violated the 1984 federal Equal Access Act, which prohibits public secondary schools from discriminating against students who wish to meet to discuss religious, political, or philosophical issues. The Equal Access Act applies to schools that provide a "limited open forum," which takes place when schools allow "noncurriculum related student groups to meet on school premises during noninstructional time," according to the law.[24]

The Supreme Court ruled in Mergens' favor on the basis that the school violated the Equal Access Act. The school attempted to argue that the act was unconstitutional under the Establishment Clause, but the Court disagreed. "There is a crucial difference between government speech endorsing religion, which the Establishment Clause forbids, and private speech endorsing religion, which the Free Speech and Free Exercise Clauses protect. We think that secondary school students are mature enough and are likely to understand that a school does not endorse or support student speech that it merely permits on a nondiscriminatory basis," Justice Sandra Day O'Connor wrote for the Court. "Although a school may not itself lead or direct a religious club, a school that permits a student-initiated and student-led religious club to meet after school, just as it permits any other student group to do, does not convey a message of state approval or endorsement of the particular religion."

Justice Thurgood Marshall concurred with the Court, but he noted the "intersection" of the Establishment Clause and the Free Speech Clause: "The introduction of religious speech into the public schools reveals the tension between these two constitutional commitments, because the failure of a school to stand apart from religious speech can convey a message that the school endorses, rather than merely tolerates, that speech. Recognizing the potential dangers of school-endorsed religious practice, we have shown particular vigilance in monitoring compliance with the Establishment Clause in elementary and secondary schools."

The newest member of the Supreme Court, Justice Samuel Alito, invoked *Mergens* while ruling in a school-related free exercise case while he was a federal judge on the U.S. Court of Appeals. The case, *C.H. v. Oliva*, involved a kindergarten student named Zachary who drew a picture of Jesus for a class assignment on the Thanksgiving holiday. The poster was initially placed in the school hallway. The school removed the poster, then put it back up in a less conspicuous place.

"Zachary's teacher told the students to make posters depicting what they were 'thankful for.' Zachary drew a picture of Jesus. . . . The subject matter of the poster was specified by Zachary's teacher: something for which he was thankful as the Thanksgiving holiday approached. His poster fell within the specified subject matter," Alito wrote. "The poster was given discriminatory treatment because of the viewpoint that it expressed, because it expressed thanks for Jesus, rather than for some secular thing. This was quintessential viewpoint discrimination. . . . Viewpoint discrimination strikes at the heart of the freedom of expression."[25]

Alito said that even in a "closed forum," such as a classroom, public schools may not engage in viewpoint discrimination unless the school's action can pass "strict scrutiny," the most rigorous form of judicial review.[26] Although in this case Alito was dissenting from his colleagues on the Third Circuit Court of Appeals, in his new job on the Supreme Court he might very well be in the majority. (See chapter 7 for further analysis of Alito's judicial record.)

Free exercise in public schools has numerous other parameters, as defined by the Supreme Court and federal courts:

• Prayer meetings: Students are free to pray before meals, read their Bibles, gather for prayer in designated areas, or meet at the flagpole for prayer before school begins. "In fact, a school might be guilty of violating the student's free-speech and free-exercise rights if it tried to prohibit such non-disruptive religious activities," according to Haynes and Thomas.

Teachers and administrators, however, may not join students in such activities, because their presence could be construed as an endorsement of religion. School employees are permitted to meet and discuss religious issues with other adults.[27]

• Proselytizing: Students are allowed to express their religious viewpoints on campus and even invite others to join their religious group so long as they are not disruptive or disrespectful of the rights of other students. "A student should not be allowed to pressure or coerce others in a public school setting, but within these broad parameters a student has wide latitude to exercise his faith," Haynes says.[28]

• Classroom assignments: Students may express their beliefs about religion in a class assignment so long as the expression is relevant to the assignment. But teachers retain a great deal of control over assignments and other matters related to teaching the curriculum. "Public school teachers may also enforce viewpoint-neutral rules concerning such matters as the length of an oral presentation or written assignment," Alito wrote.[29]

• Oral reports and proselytizing: Students are not permitted to sermonize or proselytize before the classroom in the name of freedom of speech. This would violate the rights of the other students in the classroom, who are a "captive audience."[30]

• Student clubs: If school policy permits extracurricular student groups, religious groups must be given equal treatment, pursuant to the 1984 federal Equal Access Act. Teachers or other adults may attend student club gatherings, but they are not allowed to lead the meetings.[31]

Vouchers

> In a society as religiously diverse as ours, the Court has recognized that we must rely on the Religion Clauses of the First Amendment to protect against religious strife, particularly when what is at issue is an area as central to religious belief as the shaping, through primary education, of the next generation's minds and spirits.
>
> —Justice Stephen Breyer, *Zelman v. Simmons-Harris* (2002)

One of the hottest debates in recent years has involved school vouchers—credits given by the state to parents to send their children to private schools. In the case of *Zelman v. Simmons-Harris* (2002), the Supreme Court decided that a school voucher program in Ohio did not violate the First Amendment. But the Court split 5–4, leaving the issue far from settled.

Voucher proponents say vouchers rescue children from failing schools and challenge public schools to do a better job. Critics say vouchers siphon needed funding from public schools and create the potential for sectarian strife—a primary concern Justices David Souter and Stephen Breyer cited in their dissents. Souter noted that the vast majority of the voucher money went to parochial schools—thus, according to Breyer, creating an excessive government "entanglement" with religion. "Religious teaching at taxpayer expense simply cannot be cordoned from taxpayer politics," Souter wrote. "And every major religion currently espouses social positions that provoke intense opposition. Not all taxpaying Protestant citizens, for example, will be content to underwrite the teaching of the Roman Catholic Church condemning the death penalty. Nor will all of America's Muslims acquiesce in paying for the endorsement of the religious Zionism taught in many religious Jewish schools, which combines a nationalistic sentiment in support of Israel with a deeply religious element. Nor will every secular taxpayer be content to support Muslim views on differential treatment of the sexes, or, for that matter, to fund the espousal of a wife's obligation of obedience to her husband, presumably taught in any schools adopting the articles of faith of the Southern Baptist Convention."

But the majority of the Court did not express such concerns. Writing for the majority, Chief Justice William Rehnquist upheld the Cleveland program on the following bases:

- The program serves a secular purpose—to educate disadvantaged children in a "demonstrably failing public school system."
- The program is "neutral in all respects towards religion"—it neither advances nor inhibits religion.
- Ohio does not coerce voucher recipients into attending religious schools, and provides parents with a range of valid alternatives, including staying in public school, tutoring, charter schools, and secular private schools.

The *Zelman* outcome follows the reasoning of the 1947 landmark case *Everson v. Board of Education*, which involved a New Jersey state program that covered the transportation costs of sending children to Catholic schools. The Supreme Court held that the program was constitutional, because the primary purpose of sending the children to Catholic schools was for education and not religious indoctrination.[32]

The Court's ruling in the *Zelman* case gave immediate encouragement to proponents of voucher systems throughout the United States. But given the close division on the Court, the controversy will likely continue. "The Zelman case is an interesting example of where we break down in our society as to how we understand the relationship between church and government, and those who would build a higher wall [between church and state] versus those who want a lower wall with some holes in it," Haynes said.[33]

Thomas said the voucher debate will likely continue in the following arenas:

- Congress: Legislation in Congress would be the most sweeping way to promote vouchers nationwide.
- State legislatures: Efforts to launch voucher programs would be complicated in the 37 states that have stringent establishment clauses in their own constitutions.
- State supreme courts: Another venue likely for voucher battles, which would produce a variety of results.
- Statewide referenda: Voucher proponents have attempted to take the issue directly to voters eight times in seven states (twice in Michigan). All proposals were defeated.

Public policy debate also focuses on the question of whether diverting public money to private schools undermines the public school system. As time passes, data from the Cleveland program as well as Milwaukee's voucher program may shed some light on this issue.[34]

Haynes believes the *Zelman* decision may have the broader effect of encouraging public schools to address issues of religion and to gain a better understanding of the First Amendment. "My sense is it will motivate public schools to do better on religion and religious liberty in general if they realize the reason why many people are supporting vouchers is linked to their concern about religion and values in public schools, and how their faith is treated and how their values are treated," he says.[35]

Monkey Trials

To be sure, Darwin's theory of evolution is imperfect. However, the fact that a scientific theory cannot yet render an explanation on every point should not be used as a pretext to thrust an untestable alternative hypothesis grounded in religion into the science classroom or to misrepresent well-established scientific propositions.

—Judge John E. Jones III, *Kitzmiller v. Dover Area School District* (2005)

The issue of evolution vs. creationism remains a highly continuous dispute, dating back to the infamous 1925 "Scopes Monkey trial," in which a high school biology teacher was put on trial for teaching evolution.[36] Eighty years later, the dispute is still alive and well and has recently been all over the U.S. map: in 2005, a federal judge in Pennsylvania struck down the teaching of "intelligent design" as an alternative to the teaching of evolution;[37] also in 2005, a federal judge struck down a Georgia school district policy that declared evolution "a theory, not a fact";[38] and the issue has been hotly contested for several years on the Kansas Board of Education.[39]

In Dover, Pennsylvania, proponents of intelligent design received a stinging rebuke from Judge John E. Jones, who called intelligent design "creationism re-labeled." The judge devoted a substantial portion of his 139-page opinion to showing how "ID" proponents on the Dover Area School Board testified falsely, "or lied outright under oath on several occasions" to advance their agenda. "An objective observer would know that ID and teaching about 'gaps' and 'problems' in evolutionary theory are creationist, religious strategies that evolved from earlier forms of creationism. Next, and as stated, religious opponents of evolution began cloaking religious beliefs in scientific-sounding language and then mandating that schools teach the resulting 'creation science' or 'scientific creationism' as an alternative to evolution," Judge Jones wrote. "Although Defendants attempt to persuade this Court that each Board member who voted for the biology curriculum change did so for the secular purposed of improving science education and to exercise critical thinking skills, their contentions are simply irreconcilable with the record evidence. Their asserted purposes are a sham."[40]

The evolution vs. creationism skeleton continues to rattle in various locales, particularly in Kansas. In 2005, the Kansas Board of Education revised the Kansas Scientific Education Standards "to incorporate scientific criticisms into the science curriculum that describes the scientific case for the theory of evolution."[41] Board member John Bacon said the new standards would help eliminate "scientific dogma."[42] But in early 2007, with several new members, the reconvened board rejected the 2005 revisions and defined science as "a human activity of systematically seeking natural explanations for what we observe in the world around us," adding that "science currently has no tools to test explanations using non-natural (such as supernatural) causes."[43] But the new board adopted the standards by a 6 to 4 vote, making the controversy far from settled.[44]

Numerous other issues related to religious liberty and public schools remain unsettled and the source of potential conflict. Among them:

- Moments of silence: Moments of silence led by public schools may be permitted so long as the practice is "neutral" and does not encourage prayer. In the 1985 Supreme Court case *Wallace v. Jaffree,* the court struck down an Alabama "moment of silence" policy because its explicit purpose was to promote prayer.[45]
- Distribution of religious literature: Some court decisions have prohibited the distribution of any publication that is not sponsored by the school. Other cases, particularly *Tinker v. Des Moines Independent Community School District,* uphold the rights of students to express their views in a variety of ways, including print—"subject to the school's right to suppress such publications if they create substantial disruption, harm the rights of other students or infringe upon other compelling interests of the school," Haynes and Thomas wrote.[46]
- Dress codes: This is a hotly contested issue on which the Supreme Court has not yet weighed in. Many schools have adopted uniform policies or dress codes that ban hats and other articles of clothing linked to gang affiliation. The lower courts have usually upheld student uniforms. But schools must still accommodate students' free exercise rights to wear religious headwear, crosses, or other symbols. Some courts apply the *Tinker* standard to student dress. "Under the Tinker standard, school officials cannot regulate student expression unless they can reasonably forecast that the expression will cause a material interference or substantial disruption of the school environment," Haynes wrote.[47]

First Amendment battles often arise when advocates of religion have tried to retain or reinstate expressions of faith in schools, or when religious groups challenge the secular establishment. These are the "culture wars."[48] A few examples:

- Opposition to "secular humanism": Religious parents have accused schools of deliberately attempting to undermine religion by promoting a world view that a belief in a deity is not important.
- Opposition to the "new age" movement: In the 1980s, some advocates accused schools of trying to introduce out-of-the-mainstream religion, paganism, and other mystical practices into curriculum.
- Opposition to fantasy literature: Recently, some parents have objected to discussion of the *Harry Potter* children's books on the grounds that magical elements in their plots undermine Christianity and promote Satanism.

Haynes said that while claims of widespread secular humanist conspiracies were exaggerated, many people missed the crucial point: If schools avoid any mention of religion, then children learn that religion is unimportant and are unable to discern the importance of different forms of thought and belief.[49]

Defining the Common Good

> The First Amendment is the epitome of public justice and serves as the Golden Rule for civic life. Rights are best guarded and responsibilities best exercised when each person and group guards for all others those rights they wish guarded for themselves. . . . All who uphold the American Constitution are defenders of the rights of all faiths. From this axiom, that rights are universal and responsibilities mutual, derives guidelines for conducting public debates involving religion in a manner that is democratic and civil.
>
> —The Williamsburg Charter, 1988

More than sixty years after the Supreme Court began enforcing separation of church and state in public schools, the myriad details in the practical arrangements have yet to be worked out, and it is likely the Court will be considering school-related First Amendment cases for many years to come. Given the amount of resources that have gone into defending such lawsuits over the years, it is no wonder that many school administrators would rather eliminate any mention of religion in curriculum than risk having to use their limited financial resources on attorneys' fees.

"Nor is there much surprise that some people in this pluralist society have thought the best way to deal with the religious issue is to rule it out of bounds, to exclude questions of faith from education and other public spheres," Martin Marty notes in *Education, Religion, and the Common Good.* "Church-state separation traditions give good reasons for citizens to be careful about introducing or expanding subjects like religion in tax-supported public institutions. . . . Introducing religion on curricular terms, some say, only opens the way for proselytizing and witnessing groups to get a foot in the door."[50]

But exclusion is neither legally nor morally nor practically supported, Marty argues. In *Abington v. Schempp,* Justice Clark clearly left open the door to the importance of teaching *about* religion as opposed to religious advocacy and indoctrination. Marty argues that teaching about religion, done in the context of a liberal, secular education, is critical to advancing the common good in America. Given the importance Americans place on religion, as is shown in the Gallup Poll year after year, the issue cannot be ignored indefinitely. Young Americans, however sheltered in early life, will eventually be cast out into a world where they will have to converse with people of competing faiths and deal with complex controversies like abortion, stem-cell research, and their own children's education. "In the midst of global, national and local change affecting worldviews and public action, religion is too widespread and too deep a phenomenon not to be reckoned with in primary or at least secondary schools and thereafter. To say this is to do no public relations favor to religion, because the disturbing sides of religion will be up for examination as much as the positive sides," Marty writes.[51]

On the other hand, many people will argue, with strong validity, that religion is a private affair—something that belongs in the home and the sanctuary. Breaching the "wall of separation" that Thomas Jefferson envisioned only opens the door to the kind of civil and sectarian strife that the First Amendment is intended to prevent. But, Marty argues, one inevitably brings his or her worldviews—shaped by faith or otherwise—to the public square. The "wall" can never be absolutely realized, he says: "One's personal beliefs have an unavoidably public dimension. As people bring different core personalities and worldviews into the public [square] where people interact, they also bring along various understandings of education's purpose. How should education contribute to the common good? What kind of society are we trying to construct? On the surface, the intersections of religion and education may not be obvious. . . . But if you think for a moment, you may realize that a better question is, where does religion not come into all of this? You will not get very far into any educational issues without somehow bumping into religious themes."[52]

How *about* Religion?

> The secular public school did not imply indifference to the basic role of religion in the life of the people, nor rejection of religious education as a means of fostering it. . . . The non-sectarian or secular public school was the means of reconciling freedom in general with religious freedom.
> — Justice Felix Frankfurter, *McCollum v. Board of Education* (1948)

How can public schools teach about religion without falling down the slippery slope of proselytizing and violation of the First Amendment? The proposition has many challenges and pitfalls.[53]

In 2004, a controversy arose in Cupertino, California, involving a fifth-grade teacher who handed out teaching materials with references to God in the writings of John Adams, Thomas Jefferson, George Washington, and other Founders. The teacher, Stephen Williams, maintained he was merely illustrating Christianity's influence on America's founding. A group of parents complained that Williams was appropriating this material to proselytize for his faith. The school principal placed Williams under scrutiny, and Williams responded with a federal lawsuit against the school district, alleging that the principal prohibited him from teaching the Declaration of

---

Sidebar 5.2. | Teaching about Religion

First Amendment scholars Charles Haynes and Oliver Thomas say that public schools can teach *about* religion using the following approaches:

- *An academic approach*: Public schools should make students aware of religion and its impact on American society and world history. The academic approach contrasts with devotional worship.
- *Neutrality and fairness*: Public schools may study religion as long as they don't practice it, promote it, or denigrate it. "Classroom discussions concerning religion must be conducted in an environment that is free of advocacy on the part of the teacher," Haynes and Thomas write.
- *Diversity*: Schools may inform students about various religious beliefs and expose students to a diversity of religious views. But public schools may not promote any particular belief.
- *Separating religion from values*: Schools may teach ethical viewpoints or standards of behavior, but they may not invoke religious authority in doing so.
- *Religious displays*: Using religious symbols and texts, such as the Ten Commandments, is permissible so long as they are tied to a specific lesson in an academic context. Permanent displays of the Ten Commandments are not permitted.

Source: Haynes et al., *The First Amendment in Schools*, 52–55. See the First Amendment Center faqs page: http://www.firstamendmentschools.org/freedoms/faq.aspx ?id=12956.
Also see Marty, *Education, Religion, and the Common Good*, 45–46.

Independence. The story made it to the television talk shows, sparking a minor national uproar. Williams has since dropped the case.[54]

In a different kind of scenario, teaching *about* religion in a public school setting might pose a challenge for a teacher who is indifferent or hostile toward religion. "When teachers teach 'about' religion, faith may either get reduced to something so bland that it leads to a misreading of religion or become something so volatile that it will disrupt school and community life," Marty warns. "How to teach 'about' religion without implying judgments of truth and error?"[55]

The key to successfully teaching about religion and keeping within the spirit of the First Amendment is always to distinguish the academic study of religion from religious indoctrination and faith formation, according to Haynes and Thomas: "Study about religion is important if students are to value religious liberty, the first freedom guaranteed in the Bill of Rights. Moreover, knowledge of the roles of religion in the past and present promotes cross-cultural understanding essential to democracy and world peace."[56]

6

Transforming Lives and Transforming Government

Faith-Based Initiatives

A New Course

> Our faith-based institutions display [the] spirit of prayer and service
> in their work every day. People of faith have no corner on compassion.
> But people of faith need compassion if they are to be true to their most
> cherished beliefs. For prayer means more than presenting God with our
> plans and desires; prayer also means opening ourselves to God's priorities,
> especially by hearing the cry of the poor and the less fortunate.
>
> —President George W. Bush, Annual National Prayer Breakfast, 2005

President George W. Bush's Faith-Based and Community Initiative marks a
significant new course in national policy toward social welfare that is rivaled
in recent history only by Lyndon B. Johnson's "Great Society" program and
the "War on Poverty" in the 1960s. The initiative also marks a major shift in
the federal government's relationship with religious organizations, raising
questions regarding the separation of church and state and the meaning of
the First Amendment.

The scope of the initiative is expansive: In 2004, the White House reported that seven agencies awarded $2 billion in competitive grants to
faith-based organizations, representing more than 10 percent of the grants
awarded by the agencies. From 2003 to 2004, five of the seven agencies—the
departments of Health and Human Services, Housing and Urban Development, Justice, Labor, and Education—increased the dollar amounts of
grants to faith-based organizations by 14 percent, bringing the total for the
five agencies to $1.3 billion.[1]

The story of the Faith-Based Initiative exemplifies the mantra that "all
news is local": the president's grand national policy filters down to the
multitude of faith-based agencies that provide social services in local communities. Housing for the poor, soup kitchens, substance abuse treatment,
child care, employment services, teen pregnancy counseling, health care

services—these are just some of the social services faith-based groups are providing with financial assistance from the federal government. "The country has embarked on a new welfare experiment that utilizes faith-based providers as equal partners," said Ram A. Cnaan, a professor at the University of Pennsylvania's School of Social Work.[2]

In partnering with faith-based organizations, President Bush says his aim is to tap into America's "armies of compassion" to better serve those in need. "I believe one of the most effective ways our government can help those in need is to help the charities and community groups that are doing God's work every day. That's what I believe government ought to do. I believe government needs to stand on the side of faith-based groups, not

---

Sidebar 6.1. | Different Shapes of Faith-based Organizations

• *Local congregations*: Groups of people who gather for worship. As part of their missions, congregations may carry out social outreach or contribute money to specified social causes. Examples of the kinds of social action carried out by congregations include food pantries, clothing donation, in-home assistance and visitation to the elderly, transportation, and providing space for Alcoholics Anonymous meetings.

• *Interfaith coalitions or faith-based coalitions:* These are groups of different congregations, denominations, or religions that join together for a common cause or to provide large-scale services that are beyond the scope of a single congregation. These nonprofit organizations are often referred to as 501(c)(3) organizations, according to their Internal Revenue Service classification. "The difference between congregations and faith-based organizations: A congregation is a place where people go to pray; faith-based 501(c)(3)s are not places of worship, but organizations guided by religious principles," says Richard Nathan of the Nelson A. Rockefeller Institute of Government.[1]

---

1. Richard P. Nathan, "Gaining Perspective on Faith-Based Issues" (lecture presented at the FACS/Pew Journalism, Religion & Public Life seminar, entitled "Church & State: The Future of Faith-Based Initiatives," Feb. 3, 2003, at the *Orlando Sentinel* in Orlando, Fla.), http://facsnet.org/issues/faith/nathan.php

(*continued on page 114*)

(continued from page 113)

- *Citywide and region-wide sectarian agencies:* Catholic Charities, the Salvation Army, Lutheran Children and Family Service, and Jewish Family and Children's Services are examples of such agencies. These groups are religious-based organizations that maintain affiliation with the originating religious body while developing services and programs that are provided primarily by professional staff and significantly funded by government revenue.
- *National projects and organizations under religious auspices:* Examples of this sort of arrangement are the Habitat for Humanity, the YMCA, and the YWCA. "In this model, a central headquarters coordinates and monitors the activities of the local branches and dictates the parameters within which they can function. While the services are provided locally, often at the neighborhood level, the national headquarters represents all chapters," according to Cnaan.
- *Para-denominational advocacy and relief organizations:* These groups are not formally affiliated with any religion, but they are influenced by or based on religious principles. "Often a group of concerned citizens who are members of a particular denomination or religion may form an organization for the purpose of helping others. Although not formally affiliated with any congregation, denomination or other form of organized religion, these organizations freely acknowledge that their activities are influenced by denominational or religious doctrines," Cnaan writes.
- *Religiously affiliated international organizations:* Examples include the Catholic Relief Committee, the International Friends Service Committee, and the American-Jewish Joint Distribution Committee. "In many countries in which these organizations are active, they are defined as and operated as nongovernmental organizations (NGOs); in other countries they take the form of missionary agencies," says Cnaan.

Source: Cnaan, *The Newer Deal*, 25–26, 295.

against faith-based groups, when they come to saving lives," Bush said in a 2004 speech.[3]

As benevolent as it sounds, Bush's Faith-Based Initiative raises serious issues regarding the separation of church and state. The Supreme Court interprets the First Amendment as requiring government *neutrality* in matters of religion and prohibiting *excessive entanglement* between government and religious institutions. "The Bush Administration has sought to remove barriers to participation by faith-based organizations; but in so doing, may also have weakened long-standing walls preventing religious groups from inserting spiritual activities into secular services," according to a report for the Roundtable on Religion and Social Welfare Policy at the Rockefeller Institute of Government, State University of New York. "The administration's test of the constitutional limits of religious neutrality on the part of government has inspired both strong support and fierce opposition, manifest in a series of lawsuits brought by opponents. This litigation has brought, and will continue to bring, various aspects of the Faith-Based Initiative under judicial scrutiny."[4]

Regardless of whether one agrees with the president's policy or philosophy, America's "armies of compassion" are a real phenomenon. According to a 2002 Gallup Poll, 41 percent of the respondents said they had donated time to a religious group during the past 12 months, and 44 percent reported having donated time to other charitable causes. The combined results from the two questions: 60 percent of Americans said they have volunteered for one or both of those types of organizations over the past 12 months. "The United States has the highest rate of volunteerism in the world, and the U.S. has the largest amount of people spending the largest amount of hours [committed] to causes of their heart," Cnaan said.

Faith and Philanthropy

> Although the Americans have in a manner reduced selfishness to a
> social and philosophical theory, they are nevertheless extremely open to
> compassion.
>
> —Alexis de Tocqueville, *Democracy in America* (1835)

Alexis de Tocqueville, the great observer of America in the nineteenth century, noted that Americans tended to be both strongly religious and equally zealous in their quest for wealth and prosperity. The solution to these seemingly contradictory impulses was to fuse the two into the notion of "enlightened self-interest"—the benefit of one meant the benefit of all. "The Americans are fond of explaining almost all the actions of their lives by the principle of self-interest rightly understood; they show with complacency how an enlightened regard for themselves constantly prompts them to assist one another and inclines them willingly to sacrifice a portion of their time and property to the welfare of the state," Tocqueville wrote in *Democracy in America*.[5]

How does philanthropy fit into this equation? The general wealth generated by the nation produces the resources with which to give; and individual values and convictions compel people to give. In America, there is an abundant and quantified "supply side" of social capital, which is expressed in philanthropy and giving to causes. Religious congregations are a primary point of giving. "The high correlation between giving to charities and involvement in religious organizations is not coincidental. For many people, giving to others is central to their religious beliefs. Given this historical chain of charity, it is evident that giving is rooted in religious belief," Cnaan writes in his book *The Newer Deal*.[6]

The financial impact of religious congregations in the United States is substantial: In 2005, the country had more than 350,000 congregations, with total revenue of about $93 billion.[7] Congregations contribute significant chunks of their budgets to charitable causes, estimates ranging from 15 to 20 percent,[8] which translates to $14–$19 billion. Members of congregations contribute billions more in volunteer time.[9] "The sheer size of the religious sector in America suggests its potential as a player in community development programs. . . . Congregations are repositories and stewards of significant resources—time, talent, and treasure," note Southern Methodist University professors Robert V. Kemper and Julie Adkins.[10]

A study by the Independent Sector shows that people who give their time and money to religious organizations are more likely than others to contribute to larger civic causes as well. Of all American households that give to charitable causes, 59 percent give to both their congregation and outside charitable organizations, compared to 31 percent who give only to secular organizations and 10 percent who give only to their congregations. In dollar terms, households that donate to both their congregation and outside charitable causes contribute an average of $2,247 per year to both—with $958 of the total going to secular organizations; while households that donate only to secular organizations contribute an average of $623 per year.[11] "Faith-based generosity, whether measured in terms of dollars or time, is real, measurable and carries considerable impact," the study concludes. "The finding that those who give to religious organizations are both more likely to give to secular organizations and to give more generously of both time and money should and will have important consequences for many aspects of our society . . . [especially] in a moment in which Faith-Based Initiatives are being debated as one means to provide services to needy populations."

But there is a limit to what religious congregations can accomplish in terms of providing for the nation's social service needs, according to Mark Chaves, a professor of sociology at the University of Arizona. Chaves says that congregations most commonly meet short-term needs or engage in short-term projects, such as preparing Thanksgiving meals or volunteering for Habitat for Humanity. Individuals or small groups within the congregation often undertake these projects rather than the congregation at large.[12] Most congregations are not equipped to handle more complex social services, such as job training or combating domestic abuse, even with government funding. When one examines the percentages of congregations that participate in such programs, "the numbers get very small very fast," Chaves says.

It is the larger faith-based coalitions and sectarian agencies such as Catholic Charities and the Salvation Army, which have done business with the government for decades, that are best positioned to perform the level of social services the government requires.[13] (For a historical synopsis of social services and faith-government collaborations, see the Appendix, "From the Poor House to Charitable Choice.")

Sidebar 6.2. | Congregations and Social Services

Congregations perform a variety of basic social services, such as food and clothing collections, but the more complex social services they provide at low levels, according to Mark Chaves of the University of Arizona. For example, congregations engage in the following programs at these rates:

• Domestic violence programs—4 percent.
• Prison-related programs—2 percent.
• Substance abuse programs—2 percent.
• Tutoring and mentoring—1 percent.
• Job training—less than 1 percent.

When congregations conduct social services, they do so most often in collaboration with the government or other nonprofits. According to Chaves' research, about 59 percent of congregations with service programs collaborate with secular organizations; 21 percent collaborate with government agencies.

Source: Chaves, Congregations in America, chap. 3.

Executive Decision

> The Executive power shall be vested in a President of the United States of America. . . . The Congress may by law vest the appointment of such inferior officers, as they think proper, in the President alone, in the courts of law, or in the heads of departments.
>
> —United States Constitution, Article 2

Just nine days after he took office in 2001, President George W. Bush issued two executive orders creating the White House Office of Faith-Based Community Initiatives, and also creating sub-offices of Faith-Based Community Initiatives within five Cabinet agencies: the Department of Health and Human Services, the Department of Housing and Urban Development, the Department of Labor, the Department of Justice, and the Department of Education.[14]

The president's orders were the beginning of the end of what Bush called a "legacy of discrimination against faith-based charities." The president ordered an audit of each of the five Cabinet agencies to identify barriers to the participation of faith-based organizations in the delivery of social services. In August 2001, the White House released "Unlevel Playing Field," which summarized the findings of the audits. The document reported a "widespread bias" against faith-based organizations and favoritism toward "large and entrenched" social service providers.[15] "Both faith-based and community organizations should have an equal opportunity to obtain federal funding, if they choose to seek it," the report states. "Too much is done that discourages or actually excludes good organizations that simply appear 'too religious'; too little is done to include groups that meet local needs with vigor and creativity but are not as large, established or bureaucratic as the traditional partners with the federal government. This is not the best way for government to fulfill its responsibilities to come to the aid of needy families, individuals and communities."

Sidebar 6.3. | Unlevel Playing Field

The White House report "Unlevel Playing Field" cited 15 barriers to federal funding of faith-based organizations, among them:

• *Pervasive suspicion about faith-based organizations:* "An overriding perception by federal officials that close collaboration with religious organizations is legally suspect," the report states.

(continued on page 119)

(*continued from page 118*)

- *Restrictions on religious elements of organizations*: For example, according to the report, government officials have pressured churches that host Head Start programs to remove or cover up religious art, symbols, and other items. Similarly, faith-based organizations applying for Community Development Block Grants that are located in houses of worship have been told that they would qualify for support only if they first removed references to "God" from their mission statements.

- *Denial of faith-based organizations' right to hire or exclude staff based on religious preference*: Title VII of the Civil Rights Act of 1964 prohibits employment discrimination on the basis of religion, but churches and religious organizations are exempt from the provision. In other words, religious organizations are allowed to hire on the basis of religious creed. "Nevertheless, federal agencies sometimes require faith-based social service charities interested in partnering with government to surrender their long-held freedom to define their religious mission by hiring like-minded, like-hearted staff," the report states.

- *Non-implementation of Charitable Choice provisions*: Charitable Choice legislation, the precursor to Bush's Faith-Based Initiative, was enacted in 1996 to loosen restrictions on faith-based groups in the federal grant-making process. "Charitable Choice has been essentially ignored by federal administrators," the report states.

- *Barriers to smaller community-based organizations and newcomers*: Some grant applications are so lengthy and complicated that it is not feasible for smaller groups to complete the process. Well-established grantees are sometimes rubber-stamped year-to-year, thus crowding out the newcomers, according to the report. "The nonprofit organizations that administer social services funded by Washington are typically large and entrenched—in an almost monopolistic fashion," the report states.

The president's Faith-Based Initiative seeks to tear down the barriers and inequities detailed in "Unlevel Playing Field." Core elements of the initiative include the following:

- Faith-based organizations are placed on equal footing with secular organizations in competing for federal grants for social service programs. In other words, the government must assert the principle of neutrality between religious and non-religious social service providers.

• Faith-based organizations that enter contracts with the government are allowed to retain their religious character and may not be required to "secularize" their offices or mission statements in order to participate.[16]

• Faith-based organizations retain their right to hire staff on the basis of religious affiliation. But organizations may not discriminate in any way against those whom they serve. In other words, beneficiaries of social services may not be forced to participate in religious activities as a condition of receiving services that are funded by the government.

• Faith-based organizations may not use government funds for religious purposes; but when funding is provided indirectly—as through vouchers—providers have permission to intertwine religious and secular activities.

During his first term, Bush issued additional executive orders creating Faith-Based Community Initiatives offices within five more agencies: the Department of Agriculture, the Department of Commerce, the Department of Veterans Affairs, the Agency for International Development, and the Small Business Administration.[17] Each sub-office has a director and staff, who monitor, oversee, and encourage partnership with faith-based groups.

Sidebar 6.4. | Where the Dollars Go

The White House Office of Faith-Based and Community Initiatives grant catalog lists 150 federal grant programs representing more than $50 billion that are available for faith-based organizations. To further facilitate the process, the president created a "Compassion Capital Fund"—which spent about $100 million from 2002 to 2004—to support the training of small faith-based groups in grant writing, staff development, and management. Below is a list of programs and expenditures by participating government agencies:

• *Department of Health and Human Services:* The biggest funder of faith-based groups among all of the participating federal agencies, HHS also manages the Compassion Capital Fund. In 2004, HHS grants to faith-based organizations totaled $681 million, representing a 20 percent increase from the previous year, the White House

(*continued on page 121*)

(continued from page 120)

reported. HHS funds a variety of programs, including abstinence programs to reduce teen pregnancy, promoting marriage as a means of reducing poverty, assisting children of incarcerated parents, substance abuse treatment, and child care for low-income families.

- *Department of Housing and Urban Development:* The second largest player in the Faith-Based Initiative. In 2004, HUD grants to faith-based organizations totaled $545 million, representing 23.3 percent of its total grant funding. HUD-funded programs include affordable housing for the elderly and people with disabilities, emergency shelter, housing for people suffering from AIDS, promotion of home ownership, rural housing, and economic development.

- *U.S. Department of Agriculture:* In 2004, USDA grants to faith-based organizations totaled $149 million, representing 7 percent of the total amount funded by the USDA. Grant and loan programs open to faith-based providers include rural rental housing programs, farm labor housing, community food projects, and rural broadband connection. New USDA rules are the first to allow funding for construction of buildings that can be used for both religious worship and the delivery of government-funded social services.

- *Department of Justice:* In 2004, DOJ grants to faith-based organizations totaled more than $59 million, constituting a 15 percent increase from the previous year. Through the Faith-Based Initiative, DOJ has expanded funding of programs dealing with juvenile delinquency, crime victims, domestic violence, and the reentry of felons into society.

- *Department of Labor:* In 2004, DOL grants to faith-based organizations totaled $34.4 million, representing a 203 percent increase from the previous year. DOL grants available to faith-based organizations include the Prisoner Re-entry Initiative, Workforce Investment Boards, and the DOL's Employment and Training Administration. New DOL rules allow it to provide job-training vouchers for faith-based professions, including employment at churches, synagogues, temples, and other faith groups.

- *Department of Education:* In 2004, Department of Education grants to faith-based organizations totaled $15 million, representing a 115 percent increase from the previous year. ED grants available to

(continued on page 122)

(*continued from page 121*)

faith-based providers include the Safe and Drug Free Schools program, mentoring programs, physical education, and adult education. Old ED rules prohibited funding for "pervasively sectarian" organizations; new rules clarify that the department does not consider religious character or affiliation in deciding who may qualify for grants.

• *U.S. Agency for International Development:* Operating under the State Department, USAID responds to disasters, provides food and health care, and promotes economic development in developing countries. The 2004 rule changes allow faith-based organizations to participate in USAID programs. Through this program, the Bush administration has been particularly interested in promoting abstinence and behavioral changes as a means of combating the spread of AIDS. In 2004, USAID grants to faith-based organizations totaled $522 million, representing more than 14 percent of the total amount awarded. Through USAID, the Faith-Based Initiative has truly gone global.

Source: Information on Faith-Based and Community Initiatives grant programs is available on the White House website and the websites of the various Cabinet agencies as follows:
http://www.whitehouse.gov/government/fbci/grants-catalog-index.html
http://www.usda.gov/fbci/index.html
http://www.usda.gov/fbci/funding_fbci.html
http://www.hud.gov/offices/fbci/
http://www.dol.gov/cfbci/funding.htm
http://www.ed.gov/about/inits/list/fbci/grants.html
http://www.usaid.gov/our_work/global_partnerships/fbci/

Also see "Getting a Piece of the Pie: Federal Grants to Faith-Based Social Service Organizations," The Roundtable on Religion and Social Welfare Policy, 2006: http://www.religionandsocialpolicy.org/publications/publication.cfm?id=70.

The president's executive orders not only require equal treatment for faith-based groups, but the federal agencies involved are required to devise outreach programs to encourage faith-based groups to apply—a kind of affirmative action for faith-based groups that have suffered past discrimination, in the president's view.

The president's program is controversial because, among other reasons, it was advanced entirely at the president's discretion, without legislation from Congress. In 2001, the House passed a bill that followed closely the administration's proposal, but the Senate balked. Subsequent attempts to get legislation passed failed. Undaunted, President Bush proceeded with his Faith-Based Initiative using his executive powers.[18] "I got a little frustrated in Washington because I couldn't get the bill passed out of the Congress. They were arguing process. I kept saying, wait a minute, there are entrepreneurs all over our country who are making a huge difference in somebody's life; they're helping us meet a social objective. Congress wouldn't act, so I signed an executive order—that means I did it on my own," Bush said to a round of applause at the 2004 conference in Los Angeles.[19]

Many observers in Congress and elsewhere aren't so sure this is a good way for government to do its business, but the president has proceeded throughout his administration with little in the way of "checks or balances" to stop his program. Although many faith-based programs have been challenged in the courts, the lawsuits have done little to slow down the march forward. "The Bush Administration has made concerted use of its executive powers and has moved aggressively through new regulation, funding, political appointees and active public outreach efforts to expand the federal government's partnerships with faith-based social service providers in ways that don't require Congressional approval," according to a Roundtable report.[20]

The president is not entirely out on his own in promulgating faith-based partnerships. The basis of Bush's Faith-Based Initiative was legislated by Congress in the 1996 Charitable Choice legislation, which sought to break down barriers to the participation of faith-based organizations in government partnerships to provide social services.[21]

Transforming Lives

> The best way to help heal those who hurt is to bring all the resources of our country to bear. And the most powerful resource of all is the ability to transform lives through faith.
>
> —George W. Bush, addressing the 10th Anniversary
> Celebration of the Power Center, Houston, 2003

When President Bush speaks about his personal faith, even his political opponents believe that he speaks from the heart, particularly when he recounts his own story of giving up alcohol through faith and being born again. "I can't think of anything more vital in America than to have a program aimed at changing drug addiction in America, and a program that will allow faith-based programs to be an integral part of helping somebody kick alcohol and drugs. I say that because I know firsthand what it takes to quit drinking, and it takes something other than a textbook or a manual. To change a person's heart, you can change their life," Bush said in a 2003 speech.[22]

The president has a sizable chorus to join him: Testimonials to the successes of faith-based substance-abuse recovery programs are abundant.[23] Similarly, faith-based prisoner rehabilitation programs claim to dramatically reduce recidivism rates by transforming lives through faith.[24] Former Indiana Senator Dan Coates often told the story of the Gospel Mission, a drug-treatment center for homeless men in Washington, D.C., which boasts a 66 percent success rate while, just blocks away, a government-operated shelter spends 20 times more per person with only a 10 percent success rate.[25] "What's most essential to successful rehabilitation is a whole-person approach which treats the physical, mental, educational and spiritual needs of each person," reads an Association of Gospel Rescue Missions report. "The spiritual component of rescue mission rehabilitation helps restore self-esteem, teach forgiveness and provide a renewed sense of purpose. Without the spiritual, the individual is left to deal with recovery only through their own limited emotional resources."[26]

Another side to the argument for faith-based initiatives is the idea that government social services are bureaucratic, cold, and uncaring and the perception that the government's attitude toward the people it serves ranges from indifferent to inhumane. The image of the gray civil servant, mechanically upholding the rules of a rigid bureaucracy, is the stuff of lore.[27] "It is a time when most Americans, not only Republicans and conservatives, assume that the state has failed to provide adequate welfare," Cnaan says. "The trendsetters in our society—journalists, politicians, foundations and social leaders—are sending the same message. That message is that the public views the government's handling of welfare as inept, ineffective, and demeaning; and that there is a groundswell of support for social services provided in an efficient, effective and humane manner. In other words, there is a growing support for the type of social services provision that is construed to be the hallmark of the religious community."[28]

Another important corollary of the Faith-Based Initiative is a long-fermenting idea that government welfare programs are counterproductive and actually encourage dependency by making it easy. Marvin Olasky, in his book *The Tragedy of American Compassion*, chronicles the "tough love" approach to welfare in early America, in comparison to the "entitlement" philosophy that requires nothing of the welfare recipient and asks no questions. Olasky quotes Gospel Mission Superintendent Lincoln Brooks as saying: "For a program to be effective, it must be redemptive."[29] Although testimonials to this truism are abundant, detailed studies testing it are not. "While more elaborate, scientific studies are under way, the White House has relied largely on anecdotal evidence to support the view that faith-based approaches produce better long-term results," according to a Roundtable report.[30]

Subsequent comparative studies have shown that "secular" social service programs and faith-based approaches are each effective in their own ways, but the proposition that one approach is better than the other is inconclusive.[31] "There is no data to say faith-based organizations are more effective or efficient, but there is no data to say they are less effective," Cnaan notes. "In principle, when you allow more groups to compete—when you open the door for more groups to participate—you increase the chances of quality. But without testing it, we don't know."[32]

No "Inherently Religious Activities"

> And so the faith-based initiative that I've launched recognizes the need there be separation of church and state—the state should never be the church, and the church certainly should never be the state. But the state should never fear the good works of the church. And the truth of the matter is, there's a culture inside government which resents and fears religious charities, and has discriminated against them. We're changing that.
>
> —George W. Bush, speaking at the 122nd
> Knights of Columbus Convention, 2004

President Bush's executive orders prohibit any direct government funding for "inherently religious activities such as worship, religious instruction or proselytization." This rule is central to the administration's claim that the Faith-Based Initiative is in keeping with the First Amendment and the separation of church and state.[33]

At first glance, the rule against inherently religious activities would seem sensible and appropriate. But Ira C. Lupu and Robert W. Tuttle at George Washington University Law School say the rule is an insufficient guide for maintaining constitutionality. For one thing, the First Amendment, as affirmed by the Supreme Court, already prohibits direct government funding of religious activity. More important, activity that is not necessarily "inherently religious" can be carried out in a religious way.[34] "Training, education, counseling and other service activities are not 'inherently religious,' but they may be conducted in highly religious ways," Lupu and Tuttle wrote in a legal analysis of Faith-Based Initiatives. "For example, a faith-intensive substance abuse treatment program would not be considered inherently religious—substance abuse treatment can be provided by religious or non-religious providers—but the courts have held that direct government funding of a program with significant religious content would nonetheless violate the Establishment Clause."

In order to remain constitutional, Faith-Based Initiatives will have to limit "specific religious activity" in whatever context, Lupu and Tuttle conclude. "The Supreme Court's most recent decisions regarding the Establishment Clause emphasize the secularity of the government's purpose at issue, neutrality between religion and nonreligion, and the concern that government not be responsible for religious indoctrination," they write. "Although the Supreme Court's Establishment Clause jurisprudence once required the exclusion of 'pervasively sectarian organizations' from participation in any government-financed service program, that law has changed dramatically over the past 15 years. The law on the Establishment Clause now focuses attention on the religious content of the service financed by the government, not on the religious character of the organization providing that service."

Another key word in Bush's rule is no "direct" government financing for religious activities. This may also seem reasonable and sensible at first, but it leaves the door open to indirect government financing of such activities. Many of the faith-based programs are provided indirectly through vouchers, which people can exchange for service with the provider of their choice, including faith-intensive providers. The U.S. Court of Appeals upheld this type of arrangement in *American Jewish Congress v. Corporation for National and Community Service.*[35] The Supreme Court rejected an appeal.[36]

Another administrative rule President Bush issued in 2004 prohibits the use of government funds to acquire, construct, or rehabilitate buildings—"to the extent that those structures are used for inherently religious activities." But the government may fund buildings used for both religious and nonreligious activities, so long as the funding covers only "the portion attributable to eligible activities," according to the rule.[37]

The problem here is determining just what percentage of a particular use goes to what, raising the issue of "excessive entanglement" between government and religion, as defined by the Supreme Court in the landmark case *Lemon v. Kurtzman.* "Because compliance with this rule depends on grantee's ability to distinguish between proper and improper uses of government-financed facilities, the incomplete information given by the 'inherently religious' standard in this context places grantees at a heightened risk," write Lupu and Tuttle. "Second, even if the rules were correct in identifying the set of constitutionally prohibited direct expenditures, the rule fails to satisfy an additional requirement under the Supreme Court's Establishment Clause jurisprudence—it provides no adequate safeguards to protect against improper diversion of government funds for religious uses. None of the newly promulgated rules includes provisions for monitoring appropriate uses of shared facilities."

All of the potential conflicts arising from inherently religious activity, specific religious activity, and entanglement point to the nature of faith-based organizations: quite logically, faith-based organizations are inherently religious. But the call to social service, as commanded by one's faith, confers other important benefits on society, as President Bush recognizes.

"It is important for any discussion of religious-based social services to distinguish between social ministry (a way of serving the community) and social mission/gospel mission (a proselytizing vehicle)," Cnaan writes. "At times, the two may overlap, as when a congregation helps others as a means of spreading the Gospel and saving souls. It is also the case when members heed a call to practice their faith by helping others in need."[38]

From the perspective of many professional social service workers, faith-based providers will always possess an ulterior motive and a hidden agenda—which is not necessarily solving someone's worldly problems but saving someone's soul. Secular social service professionals argue that they provide services in an impartial way, free from proselytizing and inappropriate impositions on their clients. The different approaches of faith-based and secular social service providers have resulted in a rift between the two groups, according to Cnaan. "Religious institutions may and do conflict and clash with social work values and principles on issues ranging from abortion and birth control to the status of women and gays and lesbians in society," he writes. "We also acknowledge that some religious groups and organizations were, are and will be among the leading conservative forces in society. Nevertheless, there is no unified religious front regarding social issues. There were and continue to be numerous religious groups and organizations at the forefront of social care."

Redefining Separation of Church and State

Since the founding of our country, there have been popular uprisings against procuring taxpayer funds to support church leaders, which was

> one of the hallmarks of an established religion. . . . That early state con-
> stitutions saw no problem in explicitly excluding *only* the ministry from
> receiving state dollars reinforces our conclusion that religious instruction
> is of a different ilk.
>
> — Chief Justice William Rehnquist, *Locke v. Davey* (2004)

With his Faith-Based Initiative, President Bush has redrawn the line in the sand that separates church and state. Some say he has crossed the line. The standoff has spurred an avalanche of lawsuits so numerous that Faith-Based Initiative litigation is approaching its own sub-field of First Amendment law. Every year, the Roundtable on Religion and Social Welfare Policy releases an annual Faith-Based Initiative "State of the Law" report—always in excess of 100 pages.[39] In 2006, Judge Robert W. Pratt, chief judge of the U.S. District Court in Iowa, released a whopping 140-page opinion in *Americans United for Separation of Church and State v. Prison Fellowship Ministries*, which involved a religious-based prisoner rehabilitation program.[40]

"Establishment Clause analysis, especially in the consideration of direct aid programs, is essentially an exercise in line-drawing," Lupu and Tuttle wrote in *State of the Law 2006.* "One side of the line represents the set of activities permitted within a government-funded program; the other side of the line represents the set of activities that the government may not directly finance."[41]

Litigation has been complicated by the fact that the Faith-Based and Community Initiative has been pursued entirely at the executive level, without legislation from Congress. The administration asserts that it is immune from legal challenges to the initiative brought by taxpayers, and the Supreme Court has buttressed this claim. In *Hein v. Freedom from Religion Foundation (2007)*, the Court ruled that taxpayers do not have constitutional "standing" to challenge executive spending that incurs into Establishment Clause territory.[42] Writing for the Court in a 5–4 decision, Justice Samuel Alito said taxpayers only have standing to challenge congressional spending. Justices Clarence Thomas and Antonin Scalia would have gone further—preventing challenges to either executive or congressional spending. "Is a taxpayer's purely psychological displeasure that his funds are being spent in an allegedly unlawful manner ever sufficiently concrete and particularized to support Article III standing?" Scalia asked, referring to the section of the Constitution that defines the judiciary and the parties who may appeal to it. "The answer is plainly no."[43] In dissent, Justice David H. Souter wrote, "If the executive could accomplish through the exercise of discretion exactly what Congress cannot do through legislation, Establishment Clause protection would melt away."[44]

The current state of litigation echoes Bush's war parlance—"We're not winning, but we're not losing." He has won a number of legal victories, but suffered several losses in advancing his Faith-Based Initiative.[45] The administration's policy received legal boosts recently with favorable decisions in *American Jewish Congress v. Corporation for National and Community Service,* in which a federal appeals court rejected a challenge to a faith-based teacher training program;[46] and in *Lown v. the Salvation Army,* in which a federal district court dismissed challenges to the selective employment practices of a faith-based organization.[47] But in *Americans United for Separation of Church and State v. Prison Fellowship Ministries,* a federal district judge struck down a Christian rehabilitation program for prisoners. "The state, through its direct funding of InnerChange, hopes to cure recidivism through state-sponsored prayer and devotion," Judge Robert W. Pratt wrote in his lengthy opinion. "While such spiritual and emotional 'rewiring' may be possible in the life of an individual and lower the risk of committing other crimes, it cannot be permissible to force taxpayers to fund such an enterprise under the Establishment Clause."[48]

While the "taxpayer standing" technicality has complicated several recent challenges to the Faith-Based Initiative, other court challenges sound familiar themes in Establishment Clause jurisprudence. The 2004 case *Locke v. Davey* centered around government "vouchers" used for educational purposes—similar to the 2002 case *Zelman v. Simmons-Harris* discussed in chapter 5, in which the Supreme Court ruled that vouchers used to send children to parochial schools are constitutional.

But in *Locke v. Davey,* the Supreme Court ruled that Washington State could deny state scholarship funding for college students majoring in divinity. The initial plaintiff, Joshua Davey, invoked the *Zelman* case, arguing that if students in the Cleveland City School District could use vouchers to attend parochial schools, he should be permitted to apply his scholarship toward a divinity degree at a Christian college. The state of Washington justified its exclusion of divinity majors based on Article I, section 11 of the state constitution, which states that "no public money or property shall be appropriated for or applied to any religious worship, exercise or instruction, or the support of any religious establishment."[49]

The Supreme Court, in a 7–2 decision, upheld Washington's "state's right" to maintain more stringent separation between church and state than what is required in the First Amendment. Washington is one of many states that have so-called Blaine amendments in their state constitutions. Blaine Amendments, which were passed during the nineteenth century in reaction to the growth in Catholic education, prohibit any state funding of religious education. Although the outcome of the *Davey* case did not hang on Washington's Blaine Amendment, ongoing court cases, including a challenge to Florida's school voucher program, could have a broader impact on Faith-Based Initiatives in "Blaine" states.[50]

The outcome of *Locke* could also have an important impact on the Bush administration's claim that religion and religious providers of social services are always entitled to a "level playing field" to share government financing. The *Locke* case is also significant because numerous Faith-Based Initiative programs employ vouchers for training purposes.[51]

"The substance and tenor of the court's opinion in *Locke v. Davey* is likely to provide substantial ammunition to states that wish to exclude programs with explicitly religious content from state-financed service, whether voucher-financed or directly financed," Lupu and Tuttle write. "We expect that the courts will uphold state discretion to exclude educational or social service programs that involve worship or religious teaching."[52]

Politics, Pandering, and Influence-Peddling

George W. Bush has placed the faith agenda on the table in ways it never has been before. In promoting his faith-based agenda, he has targeted African-American churches in a big way. This has been a very targeted effort—a black church strategy that the Bush Administration has advanced in an effort to gain support and win a larger black vote. The Republican White House has made a concerted effort to explain the Faith-Based Initiative, and explain to the clergy and faith leaders how they can position themselves to receive federal money for their organizations.

— R. Drew Smith, Scholar-in-Residence at Morehouse College,
at a 2004 seminar on religion and public life

President Bush's Faith-Based Initiative has drawn controversy for its political overtones in election years, particularly when the political campaigns swing through minority communities.

During the 2004 presidential campaign, Jim Towey, then-director of the White House Office of Faith-Based and Community Initiatives, spent the majority of his travel time in a dozen battleground states where he often met with community leaders to promote the Initiative. In January 2005, the *Los Angeles Times* published an investigative piece documenting Faith-

Based Initiative grants to black churches and community organizations, which often correlated with church ministers' endorsement of the GOP.[53]

During the 2002 congressional race, representatives from the White House Office of Faith-Based and Community Initiatives traveled to at least six states to appear at Republican-sponsored events and alongside Republican candidates, as chronicled by the Roundtable on Religion and Social Welfare Policy. "The events often targeted black audiences, including one South Carolina event sponsored by the state Republican Party and attended by 300 black ministers, who later received letters on GOP stationary containing instructions on how to apply for grant money," according to the Roundtable.[54]

Many black ministers and members of the Congressional Black Caucus are highly suspicious. Congressman Elijah E. Cummings of Maryland, an outspoken critic of the Faith-Based Initiative, believes the program not only violates the constitutional separation of church and state but also threatens to undermine the credibility of black churches and faith-based organizations that accept money from the government. "Since the movement to abolish slavery, the most important political contribution of American religion has been to challenge the immorality or amorality of the state—not to support our secular power centers," Cummings says. "If social justice ministries become financially dependent upon continued political support, who will remain to challenge this society's failure to live up to our shared religious and philosophical values? . . . Our churches must carefully guard their historic mission of caring for those who cannot care for themselves."[55]

Black ministers and Democrats aren't the only ones wary of President Bush's Faith-Based Initiative. An unlikely source of criticism was the Christian televangelist and one-time presidential contender Pat Robertson, who, although approving of portions of Bush's faith-based concept, objected to the possibility of government money going to non-Christian or non-Jewish groups. As he put it, "the same government grants given to Catholics, Protestants and Jews must also be given to the Hare Krishnas, the Church of Scientology, or Sun Myung Moon's Unification Church—no matter that some may use brainwashing techniques, or that the founder of one claims to be the messiah and another that he was Buddha reincarnated."[56]

Robertson's objections and Cummings' concerns raise two important issues of contention that the framers of the First Amendment intended to prevent: sectarian conflict and corruption of both the church and the state when the two are empowered by one another. Roger Williams argued in the seventeenth century that the state, when it attempts to enforce an official religion, corrupts religion because its body of "believers" have been coerced by the state rather than drawn by their own consciences.[57] Likewise, a church empowered by the state corrupts the state. Thomas Jefferson and James Madison emphasized this point. Madison wrote extensively of "the danger of silent accumulations and encroachments by ecclesiastical bodies" upon government.[58] In the span of early American thinking, the equation was developed: separation of church and state was required to prevent the church from corrupting the government and to prevent the government from corrupting the church. This is the logic behind the Religious Liberty Clauses of the First Amendment.

The Supreme Court has repeatedly emphasized the necessity of the First Amendment to prevent sectarian conflict. "In a society as religiously diverse as ours, the Court has recognized that we must rely on the Religion Clauses of the First Amendment to protect against religious strife," wrote Justice Stephen Breyer in the *Zelman* case.[59]

As the issue of strife applies to Pat Robertson's criticism of Faith-Based Initiatives, if one's tax money is allocated to a religious organization one disagrees with or opposes, the potential for religious conflict increases accordingly. Justice David Souter envisioned various such scenarios in his *Zelman* opinion: "Every major religion currently espouses social positions that provoke intense opposition. Not all taxpaying Protestant citizens, for example, will be content to underwrite the teaching of the Roman Catholic Church condemning the death penalty. . . . Nor will every secular taxpayer be content to support Muslim views on differential treatment of the sexes, or, for that matter, to fund the espousal of a wife's obligation of obedience to her husband."

The *Zelman* case, like many before the current Supreme Court, was decided by a narrow 5 to 4 vote, meaning the issue is far from settled, and a change of one vote could reverse policy. It is no surprise, then, that the nomination of new members to the High Court causes such political storms.

A "Notable Innovation"

> At its heart, a religion-based service provider aims to transform lives.
> —Amy Sherman, "Cross Purposes: Will Conservative Welfare
> Reform Corrupt Religious Charities?" *Policy Review*, 1995

President Bush speaks passionately about the power of faith, volunteerism, and the strength of America's religious congregations. He frequently speaks of the power of faith to "transform lives," giving testimony from his own personal experience. Faith-based organizations are good at what they do because they change hearts, Bush says.

Therein lies the central dilemma of Faith-Based Initiatives: Can and should government rely on faith-based organizations, which at their core aim to transform lives through the power of God, to provide the nation's social service needs? And can this be done without trampling the long-held tradition of "no establishment" of religion?

For President Bush, the answer is clear: "Our government must not fear the application of faith into solving social problems. We must not worry about people of faith receiving taxpayers' money to help people in need. In my judgment, that doesn't obscure the line of church and state; it enhances the capacity of state to save lives, by tapping into this fundamental powerful resource of ours, the heart and soul of the American people."[60]

The president's call for "neutrality" and a level playing field for faith-based organizations bumps up against the contrary philosophy—that faith-based organizations are fundamentally different and should be treated as such. "The principal constitutional arguments against the Initiative rest on the contrary premise that faith-based organizations are constitutionally unique, and that such organizations must therefore be disqualified in their competition for grants and contracts to perform government service," according to Lupu and Tuttle.[61]

And can the Bush administration really practice "neutrality" when the president is such an outspoken advocate of faith-based solutions to social problems?

Such questions will likely be on the court docket for years to come. Also, President Bush's use of executive power in lieu of legislation will have a lasting impact on American politics and government. "In the absence of new legislative authority, the president has aggressively advanced the Faith-Based Initiative through executive orders, rule changes, managerial realignment in federal agencies and other innovative uses of the prerogatives of his office. Whether or not one agrees with the policy objective, the character and scale of the Bush Faith-Based Initiative—because it has been carried out so methodically and across the whole federal establishment— must be regarded as a notable innovation in executive action," according to the Roundtable.[62]

Beyond the constitutional and policy controversies surrounding President Bush's Faith-Based Initiative, two important points must not be overlooked: Faith-based philanthropy is a significant part of American life, and religious organizations play a vital role in serving the nation's needy. If faith-based organizations suddenly disappeared from the scene, their absence would be painfully felt. Cnaan writes: "Were the religious community to withhold its social and communal involvement, no other force would step in to fill the void. Others in the profession may disagree and say that this is a non-issue and that only public nonsectarian services should be provided in a modern democracy. Such a stance, however, would be at the expense of the needy and disadvantaged members of our society."[63]

On the other hand, passing the nation's social service burden to the faith-based community through a policy of devolution is equally unworkable, Cnaan argues: "We should not believe for a minute that the religious community can handle our social ills outside a well-planned, well-executed and well-maintained public, private, nonprofit and civic partnership. While religious-based organizations have become central to the operation of local human service networks, the assumption that they could eventually take over the nation's huge social welfare apparatus is nothing short of fantasy."[64]

Richard Nathan, director of the Roundtable on Religion and Social Welfare Policy, believes faith-based organizations and government social services will always have distinct roles. There are some social services that faith-based organizations are well suited to deliver; others are better left to the government. "Some things the government is not very well-positioned to deal with, and yet they mean a lot in society. Family values is one. Politicians talk about family values all the time, but those things are very hard to transmit. For example, churches can provide marriage and family counseling, but it would be hard to imagine government taking on this role," Nathan says.[65] Government does try to promote good citizenship and civic responsibility through public education. Welfare reform speaks of strengthening family values, preventing out-of-wedlock births, discouraging teen pregnancy, encouraging two-parent families, and strengthening marriage. But there are limits to what government can achieve in these areas. "I think this is the most interesting area for which faith-based organizations seem to be so appropriately suited," Nathan says.

Appendix

From the Poor House to Charitable Choice

> The machinery of church and state must be kept separate, but the output of each must mingle with the other to make social life increasingly wholesome and normal. Church and state are alike but partial organizations of

humanity for special ends. Together they serve what is greater than either: humanity. Their common aim is to transform humanity into the kingdom of God.

—Walter Rauschenbusch, *A Theology for the Social Gospel*, 1917

Collaboration between government and faith-based groups in delivering social services did not begin with George W. Bush's Faith-Based Initiative. It is part of a long process that has evolved significantly since America's beginnings. In early Colonial times, churches in England and America were less involved in social welfare; they were more embroiled in squabbles over doctrine, conflict with the Catholic Church, and the ongoing Protestant Reformation.

In Elizabethan England, the Poor Laws were enacted to provide relief for the indigent. In 1601, the Poor Law Act established a national welfare system, which was funded with property taxes and administered at the local parish level. This was the basis for what would become a county-based social service system in America. In 1723, following lobbying efforts by the Society for the Promotion of Christian Knowledge, Parliament passed the Workhouse Test Act, which established parochial workhouses for the poor. This early faith-based initiative aimed to discourage pauperism by requiring work in exchange for only the most austere living and working environment.[66]

The Poor Laws also extended to Colonial America, and, as in England, "tough love" was the applied practice of the day. Cotton Mather (1663–1728), pastor of Boston's North Church, explained the philosophy in his influential pamphlet, *An Essay to Do Good*: "If there be any idle persons among them [your neighbors], I beseech you, cure them of their idleness; Don't nourish 'em and harden 'em in that; but find employment for them; find 'em work; set 'em to work; keep 'em to work. Then, as much of your other bounty to them, as you please."[67]

As in England, the Poor Law regime in America meant that the municipal authorities were responsible for the needy, not the churches. A notable exception was pre-Revolutionary Virginia, where Anglican clergymen often served concurrently as municipal Poor Law officials. But in the other colonies, the differentiation in the roles of church and government was reinforced by the fact that most colonies had established churches, such as the Anglican Church in the South and the Congregationalist Church in New England.

"In the establishment system, clergy are discouraged from developing social ministries, as such efforts are difficult to organize and unnecessary to establish the credibility and importance of the church in the community," writes Cnaan. "While clergy salaries are financially secured and legally preferred under the wings of the state, the clergy are not compelled to make special efforts to recruit new members, revive their preaching, or manifest a dynamic leadership style. This being the case, clergy are not accountable to their congregants, but are the local representatives of the state and its church."[68]

Following the Revolution and the disestablishment of state churches, independent religious organizations became increasingly involved in assisting the needy. In the late 1800s, in response to the growing social problems associated with industrialization, urbanization, and immigration, churches in cities across the country mobilized. The Social Gospel Movement, led by Walter Rauschenbusch and other progressive ministers, sought to transform society into the image of the "Kingdom of God" by focusing on both personal and social salvation.[69] "The idea was to introduce the Christian spirit and heritage into the social order," Cnaan says. "The Social Gospel Movement represented an attempt to respond to serious social problems of the time such as slums, labor unrest, urban blight, and exploitation of the poor. . . . The power of the Social Gospel was in its wide reach and the fact that a social theology managed to move so many people into being involved in social services provision and social change."[70]

The late 1880s also saw the advent of large "parachurch" organizations like the Salvation Army, which developed a significant social services network that included soup kitchens, rescue shelters, employment offices, thrift shops, and clinics. Catholic, Jewish, and Lutheran organizations responded to the needs of their growing immigrant communities. "In fact, social service was so central to Catholicism in America that many nineteenth-century Catholic orders were first founded in order to operate a particular school, orphanage, or hospital," writes Cnaan.[71]

During the Great Depression in the 1930s, Franklin Roosevelt's New Deal marked the advent of the modern welfare state and ascendancy of the government as the primary caretaker of the needy. Lyndon B. Johnson's "Great Society" program and the "War on Poverty" sought to revive the spirit of the New Deal. But Johnson's domestic initiatives were eclipsed and undermined by the war in Vietnam.

From the 1950s to the 1980s, the federal government expanded partnerships with the country's largest faith-based social service providers, such as the Salvation Army, Catholic Charities, Jewish Family and Children's Services, and Lutheran Social Services. The large bureaucratic structures of these organizations were well suited for government collaboration. But beyond these select partnerships, smaller faith-based groups were largely shut out of the government process until the 1990s and the advent of Charitable Choice.[72] "By law, regulation or simply bureaucratic habit, [federal] agencies excluded faith-based organizations from [participating in social service] programs or subjected them to burdens not imposed on analogous non-religious providers," according to Lupu and Tuttle.[73]

In the 1980s, Ronald Reagan ushered in the age of "devolution" in social services.[74] Devolution shifted the responsibility for administration of social services from the federal government to state and local governments and nonprofit organizations. Devolution also implied the end of "entitlements" to the poor. Reagan's view was that "big government" was the problem, and its well-intentioned social service programs were causing more problems than they were solving. Reagan famously summed up his sentiment in his take on the Parable of the Good Samaritan. "The story of the Good Samaritan has always illustrated to me what God's challenge really is. He crossed the road, knelt down, bound up the wounds of the beaten traveler, the pilgrim, and carried him to the nearest town. He didn't go running into town and look for a caseworker to tell him that there was a fellow out there that needed help. He took it upon himself," Reagan said in 1982.[75]

Bill Clinton carried the policy of devolution forward, in his own form, in his pledge to "end welfare as we know it."[76] In 1996, Clinton signed into law the Personal Responsibility and Work Opportunity Reconciliation Act, a sweeping welfare reform package. One of its provisions, known as "Charitable Choice," opened the door to greater participation of faith-based organizations in providing social services. Charitable Choice, which was sponsored by then-Senator John Ashcroft, prohibits the exclusion of faith-based organizations from the federal grant process on the basis of religious affiliation or character. In addition, the law allows faith-based organizations to retain their religious missions and symbols while providing social services funded by the government.[77]

Prior to Charitable Choice, faith-based groups were typically required to form separate nonprofit organizations, with a secularized mission, in order to contract with the government. Charitable Choice ended that requirement. The law also specified that faith-based organizations did not give up their Title VII right to hire staff based on religious affiliation as a condition of doing business for the government.

Charitable Choice laid the groundwork for George W. Bush's Faith-Based Initiative five years later. Much of Bush's initiative is an implementation of Charitable Choice, which the administration contends was resisted, thwarted, or ignored by federal agencies. "The Charitable Choice concept aims to challenge and eliminate perverse bureaucratic rules and regulations that have often hampered civic-minded, public-spirited partnerships between government and faith-based social service providers. Charitable Choice was written to respond point-by-point to various inappropriate restrictions by explicitly protecting religious charities from pressures to secularize their programs, abandon their religious character or sacrifice their autonomy," according to the White House report "Unlevel Playing Field."[78]

Not surprisingly, Charitable Choice raised many of the same concerns as Bush's Faith-Based Initiative regarding separation of church and state. "The issue of government using public money to support faith-based social services does not exist elsewhere in the world," Cnaan points out.[79] "In Europe, the central governments are the provider of social services, and church-state conflicts are not an issue. In the United States, we take it for granted that religious groups provide social services, but it wasn't always that way."

Beyond the "Wall of Separation"

The Supreme Court and the First Amendment

A Porous Wall

The "establishment of religion" clause of the First Amendment means at least this: Neither a state nor the federal government can set up a church. Neither can pass laws which aid one religion, aid all religions, or prefer one religion over another. Neither can force nor influence a person to go to or to remain away from church against his will or force him to profess a belief or disbelief in any religion. No person can be punished for entertaining or professing religious beliefs or disbeliefs, for church attendance or non-attendance. No tax in any amount, large or small, can be levied to support any religious activities or institutions, whatever they may be called, or whatever form they may adopt to teach or practice religion. Neither a state nor the federal government can, openly or secretly, participate in the affairs of any religious organizations or groups and vice versa. In the words of Jefferson, the clause against establishment of religion by law was intended to erect *"a wall of separation between Church and State."*

> —Justice Hugo Black, delivering the majority opinion of the Court
> in *Everson v. Board of Education of Ewing Township* (1947)

The concept of a "wall" of separation between church and state is a useful metaphor but is not an accurate description of the practical aspects of the relationship that in fact exists. The Constitution does not require complete separation of church and state; it affirmatively mandates accommodation, not merely tolerance, of all religions, and forbids hostility toward any. Anything less would require the "callous indifference" that was never intended by the Establishment Clause.

> —Chief Justice Warren Burger, delivering the majority opinion
> in *Lynch v. Donnelly* (1984)

Like most of the rights enumerated in the Bill of Rights, those granted in the Religious Liberty Clauses of the First Amendment are not clear-cut or absolute, nor are the interpretations of these sixteen monumental words set in stone or unchanging. School vouchers for parochial schools, religious displays on public property, and prayers before Congress and even the Supreme Court are examples of where total separation of church and state breaks down.

Accommodating certain aspects of religion in public life, while barring others, has been the tortuous task of the Supreme Court. The lines of separation and accommodation have changed significantly since the 1940s, when the Court began a wholesale re-evaluation of the Religious Liberty Clauses—and their application to the states and local governments.[1] Over the past sixty-plus years, the Court's philosophy has changed significantly, and it continues to evolve. Old metaphors for describing "separation of church and state" are being cast aside, while new ones are being introduced.

In the landmark 1947 case *Everson v. Board of Education*, the Court adopted the "wall of separation" metaphor, which many have lamented ever since. In *Everson*, which dealt with the use of public funds for the transportation of children to parochial schools, Justice Hugo Black cited Thomas Jefferson's 1802 letter to the Danbury Baptist Association, in which Jefferson explained his vision of separation of church and state: "I contemplate with sovereign reverence that act of the whole American People which declared that their legislature should make 'no law respecting an establishment of religion, or prohibiting the free exercise thereof,' thus building a wall of separation of church and state."[2]

For Black, the "wall" was the applicable metaphor for an absolute separation of church and state. "That wall must be kept high and impregnable. We could not approve the slightest breach," Black wrote.[3] Ironically, his ruling in *Everson* did permit public funds to be used for the transportation of children to parochial schools. Apparently, the wall did not extend to the moon. Nonetheless, the Court was stuck with the "wall" metaphor for years to come, and many subsequent justices have tried to shake off its shadow.

"Judicial caveats against entanglement must recognize that the line of separation, far from being a 'wall,' is a blurred, indistinct, and variable barrier depending on all the circumstances of a particular relationship," former Chief Justice Warren Burger wrote in the landmark case *Lemon v. Kurtzman* (1971). "Our prior holdings do not call for total separation between church and state; total separation is not possible in an absolute sense. Some relationship between government and religious organizations is inevitable."[4]

For former Chief Justice William Rehnquist, Burger's "blurred barrier" was no less problematic than the wall. "In the 38 years since *Everson,* our Establishment Clause cases have been neither principled nor unified. Our recent opinions, many of them hopelessly divided pluralities, have with embarrassing candor conceded that the 'wall of separation' is merely a 'blurred, indistinct, and variable barrier,'" Rehnquist wrote in his dissenting opinion in *Wallace v. Jaffree* (1985), in which the majority of the Court held that an Alabama law authorizing a one minute period of silence in public schools violated the Establishment Clause.

"The 'wall of separation' between church and state is a metaphor based on bad history, a metaphor which has proved useless as a guide to judging. It should be frankly and explicitly abandoned," Rehnquist continued. "The crucible of litigation has produced only consistent unpredictability, and today's effort is just a continuation of the sisyphean task of trying to patch together the 'blurred, indistinct, and variable barrier' described in *Lemon.* We have done much straining since 1947, but still we admit that we can only 'dimly perceive' the *Everson* wall. Our perception has been clouded not by the Constitution, but by the mists of an unnecessary metaphor." [5]

In lieu of the blurred barrier, how can the Court's current position be defined? Although the Court is so often divided, the results of its recent decisions are often called "accommodationist"; that is, the government may acknowledge and even support certain facets of religion without creating an "Establishment."

"Government policies of accommodation, acknowledgment, and support for religion are an accepted part of our political and cultural heritage," Justice Anthony Kennedy wrote in *Allegheny County v. ACLU* (1989). [6] "Rather than requiring government to avoid any action that acknowledges or aids religion, the Establishment Clause permits government some latitude in recognizing and accommodating the central role religion plays in our society. Any approach less sensitive to our heritage would border on latent hostility toward religion, as it would require government in all its multifaceted roles to acknowledge only the secular, to the exclusion and so to the detriment of the religious."

Diversity has become an important factor in the modern Court's decisions. Holiday displays that embody diversity get points, as in the *Allegheny* case, in which the Court approved a display that included a Christmas tree and a menorah. But as part of the same case, the Court struck down a nativity scene that lacked diversity in its presentation.

"This nation is heir to a history and tradition of religious diversity that dates from the settlement of the North American continent. Sectarian differences among various Christian denominations were central to the origins of our republic. Since then, adherents of religions too numerous to name have made the United States their home, as have those whose beliefs expressly exclude religion," wrote former Justice Harry Blackmun for the Court in *Allegheny*. "Precisely because of the religious diversity that is our national heritage, the Founders added to the Constitution a Bill of Rights, the very first words of which declare: 'Congress shall make no law respecting an establishment of religion, or prohibiting the free exercise thereof . . . ' Perhaps in the early days of the republic these words were understood to protect only the diversity within Christianity, but today they are recognized as guaranteeing religious liberty and equality to the infidel, the atheist, or the adherent of a non-Christian faith such as Islam or Judaism."

But within the broad scope of "accommodation," even with diversity factored in, there is always the possibility of accommodating too far—skirting over that blurry line into something beyond what the Framers intended in the Religious Liberty Clauses. Some would use the Free Exercise Clause as an instrument for establishing their own religion or asserting dominance of the majority. The Court has recognized this contradiction of logic and refuses to permit it. "In a pluralistic society there may be some would-be theocrats, who wish that their religion were an established creed, and some of them perhaps may be even audacious enough to claim that the lack of established religion discriminates against their preferences," Blackmun wrote in *Allegheny*. "But this claim gets no relief, for it contradicts the fundamental premise of the Establishment Clause itself. The anti-discrimination principle inherent in the Establishment Clause necessarily means that would-be discriminators on the basis of religion cannot prevail. To be sure, some Christians may wish to see the government proclaim its allegiance to Christianity in a religious celebration of Christmas, but the Constitution does not permit the gratification of that desire, which would contradict the logic of secular liberty it is the purpose of the Establishment Clause to protect."

Testing the Establishment Clause

> The language of the Religion Clauses of the First Amendment is, at best, opaque. . . . In the absence of precisely stated constitutional prohibitions, we must draw lines with reference to the three main evils against which the Establishment Clause was intended to afford protection: sponsorship, financial support, and active involvement of the sovereign in religious

activity. Every analysis in this area must begin with consideration of the cumulative criteria developed by the Court over many years. Three such tests may be gleaned from our cases. *First, the statute must have a secular legislative purpose; second, its principal or primary effect must be one that neither advances nor inhibits religion; finally, the statute must not foster an excessive government entanglement with religion.*

— Chief Justice Warren Burger, delivering the majority opinion in *Lemon v. Kurtzman* (1971)

No fixed, per se rule can be framed. . . . We have repeatedly emphasized our unwillingness to be confined to any single test or criterion.

— Chief Justice Warren Burger, delivering the majority opinion in *Lynch v. Donnelly* (1984)

Over the course of the past sixty years, the Supreme Court has laid down large volumes of case law and various criteria, or "tests," for judging cases involving the Establishment Clause. In the 1971 case *Lemon v. Kurtzman,* the Court established the so-called *Lemon* test to determine whether or not a law meets constitutional muster. The *Lemon* test asks three questions:

1. Does the law in question have a secular purpose?
2. Does it advance or inhibit religion?
3. Does it foster excessive government entanglement with religion?

If a law fails any of these three "prongs," the Court may deem it unconstitutional. In *Lemon,* the Court found that programs subsidizing the salaries of parochial school teachers in Rhode Island and Pennsylvania constituted "excessive entanglement" between government and religion, thus violating the Establishment Clause.

Chief Justice Burger, writing for the majority of the Court, explained the purpose of the test: "Political division along religious lines was one of the evils at which the First Amendment aimed, and in these programs, where successive and probably permanent annual appropriations that benefit relatively few religious groups are involved, political fragmentation and divisiveness on religious lines are likely to be intensified. As well as constituting an independent evil against which the Religion Clauses were intended to protect, involvement or entanglement between government and religion serves as a warning signal."

Although the Supreme Court frequently refers to the *Lemon* case, in recent years justices have more often criticized it than adhered to it. Justices Clarence Thomas and Antonin Scalia and Chief Justice Rehnquist have been outspoken opponents of the *Lemon* test. "The *Lemon* test has no more grounding in the history of the First Amendment than does the 'wall' theory upon which it rests," Rehnquist wrote in his dissenting opinion in *Wallace v. Jaffree.* "The three-part test represents a determined effort to craft a workable rule from a historically faulty doctrine; but the rule can only be as sound as the doctrine it attempts to service. The three-part test has simply not provided adequate standards for deciding Establishment Clause cases, as this Court has slowly come to realize. Even worse, the *Lemon* test has caused this Court to fracture into unworkable plurality opinions, depending upon how each of the three factors applies to a certain state action."

In lieu of *Lemon,* some justices have created their own tests. Retired Justice Sandra Day O'Connor, who was often the swing vote on the Court, developed what she called the "endorsement test." Under this test, cases should be observed from the standpoint of "a reasonable observer [as to] whether a challenged governmental practice conveys a message of endorsement of religion," she wrote in *Allegheny County v. ACLU* (1989). The heart of O'Connor's test is her belief that endorsement "sends a message to nonadherents that they are outsiders, not full members of the political community, and an accompanying message to adherents that they are insiders, favored members of the political community," as she wrote in *Allegheny.* "The endorsement test captures the essential command of the Establishment Clause, namely, that government must not make a person's religious beliefs relevant to his or her standing in the political community by conveying a message that religion or a particular religious belief is favored or preferred."

Justice Anthony Kennedy, who criticized O'Connor's endorsement test *in Allegheny,* devised his own test, called the "coercion test." This test asks two questions:

1. Does the law in question aid religion in a way that would tend to establish a state church?
2. Does the law coerce people to support or participate in religion against their will?

"Government may not coerce anyone to support or participate in any religion or its exercise; and it may not, in the guise of avoiding hostility or callous indifference, give direct benefits to religion in such a degree that it in fact establishes a state religion or religious faith, or tends to do so," Kennedy wrote in *Allegheny.*

The coercion test is designed for accommodation of longstanding traditions, such as legislative prayer and prayer before the opening of the Supreme Court, which a "faithful application" of O'Connor's endorsement test would preclude, Kennedy wrote. "Either the endorsement test must invalidate scores of traditional practices recognizing the place religion holds in our culture, or it must be twisted and stretched to avoid inconsistency with practices we know to have been permitted in the past, while condemning similar practices with no greater endorsement effect simply by reason of their lack of historical antecedent. Neither result is acceptable."

O'Connor was equally critical of Kennedy's test: "An Establishment Clause standard that prohibits only 'coercive' practices or overt efforts at government proselytization, but fails to take account of the numerous more subtle ways that government can show favoritism to particular beliefs or convey a message of disapproval to others, would not, in my view, adequately protect the religious liberty or respect the religious diversity of the members of our pluralistic political community," she wrote in *Allegheny*.

Debates over how to judge the Establishment Clause are not likely to end soon, and new members of the court are sure to introduce their own views. Justice Thomas takes a strikingly different interpretation of the Establishment Clause, analyzed below.

Testing Free Exercise Claims

The door of the Free Exercise Clause stands tightly closed against any governmental regulation of religious beliefs as such. Government may neither compel affirmation of a repugnant belief, nor penalize or discriminate against individuals or groups because they hold religious views abhorrent to the authorities.

—Justice William Brennan, writing for the Court
in *Sherbert v. Verner* (1963)

It may fairly be said that leaving accommodation to the political process will place at a relative disadvantage those religious practices that are not widely engaged in; but that unavoidable consequence of democratic government must be preferred to a system in which each conscience is a law unto itself or in which judges weigh the social importance of all laws against the centrality of all religious beliefs.

—Justice Antonin Scalia, delivering the majority opinion
in *Employment Division v. Smith* (1990)

The Court distinguishes between "belief" and "action based on belief" when considering free exercise claims.[7] The Court also closely examines the state's interest and necessity, especially when public safety is involved.

As with Establishment Clause cases, the Court applies particular tests developed from precedent.

In the 1963 case *Sherbert v. Verner*, the Court developed the now widely applied "compelling interest" test. The case involved a Seventh Day Adventist, Adeil Sherbert, who was fired from her job for refusing to work on Saturday, recognized as the Sabbath for Adventists, and then was denied unemployment compensation. The Court ruled that the state, in denying unemployment benefits, "substantially infringed" upon Sherbert's free exercise of religion.[8]

Justice William Brennan, writing for the majority of the Court, asked if a "compelling state interest" justified the infringement. He found none. Only a situation that would "endanger paramount interests" of the state or "pose some substantial threat to public safety, peace or order" would permit the government to place limitations on the free exercise of religion, Brennan concluded.

The South Carolina Supreme Court's ruling against Sherbert "forces her to choose between following the precepts of her religion and forfeiting benefits, on the one hand, and abandoning one of the precepts of her religion in order to accept work, on the other hand. Governmental imposition of such a choice puts the same kind of burden upon the free exercise of religion as would a fine imposed against appellant for her Saturday worship," Brennan wrote.

The Court departed from the *Sherbert* standard in the 1990 case *Employment Division v. Smith*. The case involved two drug and alcohol abuse rehabilitation counselors, Alfred Smith and Galen Black, who were fired from their jobs and denied unemployment benefits for using peyote during Native American religious ceremonies.[9] Smith and Black appealed the state's action, and the Oregon Supreme Court ruled in their favor, citing the *Sherbert* standard. The state's action in denying them unemployment compensation "significantly burdened [their] religious freedom in violation of the Free Exercise Clause," the Oregon court found.

But Supreme Court Justice John Paul Stevens said the state court erred by not considering the fact that peyote possession is a felony in Oregon. The *Sherbert* case and other similar free exercise cases involved actions that were "perfectly legal," Stevens wrote. "Their results might well have been different had the employees been discharged for criminal conduct, since the First Amendment protects legitimate claims to the free exercise of religion, not conduct that a State has validly proscribed."[10]

Scalia, writing for the Court, said because Oregon's controlled substance law was not aimed at regulating anyone's religious beliefs, but was an across-the-board criminal prohibition, Smith and Black could not unilaterally claim an exemption from the law. "We have never held that an individual's religious beliefs excuse him from compliance with an otherwise valid law prohibiting conduct that the state is free to regulate," Scalia wrote. "Respondents in the present case, however, seek to carry the meaning of 'prohibiting the free exercise [of religion]' one large step further. They contend that their religious motivation for using peyote places them beyond the reach of a criminal law. . . . To make an individual's obligation to obey such a law contingent upon the law's coincidence with his religious beliefs, except where the state's interest is 'compelling'—permitting him, by virtue of his beliefs, 'to become a law unto himself,' contradicts both constitutional tradition and common sense."

The Court declined to apply the *Sherbert* compelling interest standard because "what it would produce here—a private right to ignore generally applicable laws—is a constitutional anomaly," Scalia wrote. "Even if we were inclined to breathe into *Sherbert* some life beyond the unemployment compensation field, we would not apply it to require exemptions from a generally applicable criminal law."

Justice Harry Blackmun, in his dissent, said the Court should uphold the *Sherbert* standard, which he said would demonstrate that Oregon had no compelling interest in its prohibition of peyote without a religious exception. Nor did the state demonstrate that the religious use of peyote had actually harmed anyone, Blackmun wrote. "The carefully circumscribed ritual context in which respondents used peyote is far removed from the irresponsible and unrestricted recreational use of unlawful drugs. The Native American church's internal restrictions on, and supervision of, its members' use of peyote substantially obviate the state's health and safety concerns."

Blackmun warned that the rollback of free exercise liberties in *Smith* would cause "a wholesale overturning of settled law concerning the Religion Clauses of our Constitution." In fact, following the *Smith* decision, numerous lower court cases were decided against religious groups and individuals, prompting Congress to pass the Religious Freedom Restoration Act (RFRA) of 1993.[11] The act, signed into law by President Bill Clinton, sought to restore the *Sherbert* standard of compelling interest. Key elements of the law are as follows: "Government may substantially burden a person's exercise of religion only if it demonstrates that application of the burden to the person (1) is in furtherance of a compelling governmental interest; and (2) is the least restrictive means of furthering that compelling governmental interest."

But in 1997, the Supreme Court declared the Religious Freedom Restoration Act unconstitutional as it applied to state and local governments. The Court said application of law beyond the federal level exceeded Congress's powers as enumerated in the Fourteenth Amendment, thus "contradicting vital principles necessary to maintain separation of powers and the federal-state balance," as Justice Anthony Kennedy wrote in *City of Boerne v. Flores.*[12]

Also, by attempting to force states and local governments to prove their "compelling interest" in any law that might "substantially burden" free exercise of religion, the Court said Congress was actually changing the meaning of the First Amendment by adding additional conditions upon which "free exercise" is judged. In so doing, Congress stepped on the judiciary's toes by attempting to dictate the means by which the Free Exercise Clause is interpreted, something the Supreme Court guards for itself.[13] "Legislation which alters the meaning of the Free Exercise Clause cannot be said to be enforcing the Clause. Congress does not enforce a constitutional right by changing what the right is. It has been given the power to enforce, not the power to determine what constitutes a constitutional violation," Kennedy wrote.

Since *Boerne,* at least twelve states have passed their own religious freedom restoration acts in order to enforce "compelling interest" in their own jurisdictions. In some states, including Minnesota, Massachusetts, and Wisconsin, courts have held that the compelling interest test is applicable to free exercise claims by virtue of their own state constitutions.[14]

Congress, in response to the *Boerne* decision, enacted the Religious Land Use and Institutionalized Persons Act of 2000. Less sweeping than Religious Freedom Restoration Act, RLUIPA addresses land use regulation and the religious exercise of people institutionalized by the state, including prisoners. In 2005, the Supreme Court upheld the act in *Cutter v. Wilkinson.*[15]

Despite the *Boerne* decision, the Religious Freedom Restoration Act is still applicable at the federal level (the Court struck down RFRA only as it applied to the states and local governments). In *Gonzales v. O Centro Espirita Beneficente Uniao Do Vegetal* (2006), RFRA was used to uphold a Brazilian religious sect's use of *hoasca,* a tea brewed from plants unique to the Amazon rainforest that contain the hallucinogen dimethyltryptamine (DMT), a Schedule I controlled substance under federal law. "Application of the Controlled Substances Act would substantially burden a sincere religious exercise," Chief Justice John Roberts wrote for a unanimous court. "The government's argument [against the Brazilian sect] echoes the classic rejoinder of bureaucrats throughout history: 'If I make an exception for you, I'll have to make one for everybody, so no exceptions.' But RFRA operates by mandating consideration, under the compelling interest test, of exceptions to rules of general applicability." [16]

Happy Holidays

> It would be ironic if the inclusion of the crèche in the display, as part of a celebration of an event acknowledged in the Western World for 20 centuries, and in this country by the people, the executive branch, Congress, and the courts for two centuries, would so "taint" the exhibition as to render it violative of the Establishment Clause.
>
> —Chief Justice Warren Burger, delivering the majority opinion
> in *Lynch v. Donnelly* (1984)

> When viewed in its overall context, the crèche display violates the Establishment Clause.
>
> —Justice Harry Blackmun, delivering the majority opinion
> in *Allegheny County v. Greater Pittsburgh ACLU* (1989)

The Supreme Court has considered holiday symbols on public property several times in recent years and has arrived at differing and seemingly contradictory conclusions. In *Lynch v. Donnelly* (1984), the Court upheld, in a 5–4 decision, the constitutionality of a nativity scene in Pawtucket, R.I.[17] But in *Allegheny County v. ACLU* (1989), the Court struck down a nativity display in the Allegheny County Courthouse, although in the same case it gave its OK to a menorah and Christmas tree display next to the city-county building.

In deciding these cases, each particular holiday display was carefully scrutinized for its size, placement, and overall effect. The Court also delved into the history of public holiday displays in America, the legacy of sectarian conflict, and religious diversity. Justices reached sharply different conclusions.

In *Lynch v. Donnelly*, the issue centered around a holiday display erected by the city of Pawtucket, but located in a private park. The display included a Santa Claus house, a Christmas tree, a banner that read "Season's Greetings," and a crèche, or a nativity scene. The challenge focused on the crèche, which a slim minority of justices said violated the Establishment Clause.

"The 'primary effect' of including a nativity scene in the city's display is, as the district court found, to place the government's imprimatur of approval on the particular religious beliefs exemplified by the crèche," Justice William Brennan wrote in his dissenting opinion. "Those who believe in the message of the nativity receive the unique and exclusive benefit of public recognition and approval of their views." Tracing the history of the Christmas holiday and nativity scenes in America, Brennan noted that, contrary to common assumptions, Christmas was not widely observed in America until well into the nineteenth century, when Lutheran and Catholic immigrants introduced their celebration traditions into the popular mainstream. Early American Protestants objected to Christmas celebrations as part of "the sinister theology of 'Popery,'" Brennan wrote. "At the time of the adoption of the Constitution and the Bill of Rights, there was no settled pattern of celebrating Christmas, either as a purely religious holiday or as a public event. Second, the historical evidence, such as it is, offers no uniform pattern of widespread acceptance of the holiday and indeed suggests that the development of Christmas as a public holiday is a comparatively recent phenomenon. . . . In sum, there is no evidence whatsoever that the Framers would have expressly approved a federal celebration of the Christmas holiday including public displays of a nativity scene."

But the majority of the Court took a different reading of the history and determined that the holiday display was simply an acknowledgment of the nation's religious heritage that did not create an "excessive entanglement" between government and religion. In addition, the majority found that the display fulfilled both religious and secular purposes that did not advance religion in any discernable way. "Our history is pervaded by official acknowledgment of the role of religion in American life, and equally pervasive is evidence of accommodation of all faiths and all forms of religious expression and hostility toward none," Chief Justice Burger wrote for the majority. "This history may help explain why the Court consistently has declined to take a rigid, absolutist view of the Establishment Clause. We have refused to construe the religion clauses with a literalness that would undermine the ultimate constitutional objective as illuminated by history."

Burger said Brennan's focus on the sectarian implications of Christmas and holiday displays was misplaced. "There is an unbroken history of official acknowledgment by all three branches of government of the role of religion in American life from at least 1789," Burger wrote. "The Court has acknowledged that the fears and political problems that gave rise to the religion clauses in the 18th century are of far less concern today. We are unable to perceive the Archbishop of Canterbury, the Bishop of Rome, or other powerful religious leaders behind every public acknowledgment of the religious heritage long officially recognized by the three constitutional branches of government. Any notion that these symbols pose a real danger of establishment of a state church is farfetched indeed."

Five years later, the Court reached a differing conclusion, narrowly, in *Allegheny County v. ACLU*. As in *Lynch,* the Court closely considered the size, design, positioning, and "overall context" of the crèche in question.

"Here, unlike in *Lynch,* nothing in the context of the display detracts from the crèche's religious message," Justice Blackmun wrote for the majority. "The *Lynch* display comprised a series of figures and objects, each group of which had its own focal point. Santa's house and his reindeer were objects of attention separate from the crèche, and had their specific visual story to tell. . . . Here, in contrast, the crèche stands alone: It is the single element of the display on the grand staircase [in the Allegheny County Courthouse]." The overall effect of the display was to convey a religious message; thus, Allegheny County had "transgressed this line between church and state," Blackmun concluded.

Justice Anthony Kennedy disagreed, saying the Court's view "reflects an unjustified hostility toward religion, a hostility inconsistent with our history and our precedents." Kennedy said the Court majority distracted itself by focusing so closely on the details of the display and its presentation. The Court, he wrote, was in danger of falling into "a jurisprudence of minutiae. A reviewing court must consider whether the city has included Santas, talking wishing wells, reindeer, or other secular symbols as 'a center of attention separate from the crèche.' After determining whether these centers of attention are sufficiently 'separate' that each 'had their specific visual story to tell,' the Court must then measure their proximity to the crèche. . . . The majority also notes the presence of evergreens near the crèche that are identical to two small evergreens placed near official county signs. . . . After today's decision, municipal greenery must be used with care."

The *Allegheny* case also included a separate challenge to another holiday display outside the city-county building. The display included a menorah flanked by a 45-foot Christmas tree and a sign saluting liberty. Unlike the nativity scene in the courthouse, the more diverse outdoor display passed constitutional muster. The "combined effect" of the display was to recognize both Christmas and Hanukkah as part of the same winter holiday season, not an endorsement of either faith, Blackmun wrote. Again, he emphasized the physical attributes of the display, in addition to the particular meanings of the tree and the menorah, which both have secular and religious dimensions: "In the shadow of the tree, the menorah is readily understood as simply a recognition that Christmas is not the only traditional way of observing the winter-holiday season. In these circumstances, then, the combination of the tree and the menorah communicates, not a simultaneous endorsement of both the Christian and Jewish faiths, but instead, a secular celebration of Christmas coupled with an acknowledgment of Hanukkah as a contemporaneous alternative tradition."

Justice O'Connor agreed, saying the Christmas tree and the menorah, combined with the sign saluting liberty, conveyed a message of pluralism and freedom of belief during the holiday season, and therefore, "could not be interpreted by a reasonable observer as an endorsement of Judaism or Christianity or disapproval of alternative beliefs."

The split *Allegheny* outcome met with scalding criticism from dissenting justices. Kennedy called the decision "bizarre"; Clarence Thomas said the decision "can only be described as silly";[18] and Scalia said the Court was "conspicuously bereft" of an understanding of the nation's history. "I find it a sufficient embarrassment that our Establishment Clause jurisprudence regarding holiday displays has come to require scrutiny more commonly associated with interior decorators than with the judiciary," Scalia said of the *Allegheny* decision.[19]

Limited Diversity

> We live in a pluralistic society. Our citizens come from diverse religious traditions or adhere to no particular religious beliefs at all. If government is to be neutral in matters of religion, rather than showing either favoritism or disapproval towards citizens based on their personal religious choices, government cannot endorse the religious practices and beliefs of some citizens without sending a clear message to nonadherents that they are outsiders or less than full members of the political community.
>
> —Justice Sandra Day O'Connor, concurring opinion
> in *Allegheny County v. ACLU* (1989)

> If all actions thought to be religiously commanded [were subject to the Court's "compelling interest" standard] . . . any society adopting such a system would be courting anarchy. That danger increases in direct proportion to the society's diversity of religious beliefs, and its determination to coerce or suppress none of them. Precisely because we are a cosmopolitan nation made up of people of almost every conceivable religious preference,

and precisely because we value and protect that religious divergence, we cannot afford the luxury of deeming *presumptively invalid,* as applied to the religious objector, every regulation of conduct that does not protect an interest of the highest order.

—Justice Antonin Scalia, writing for the Court
in *Employment Division v. Smith* (1990)

Increasingly, the words "diversity" and "pluralism" show up in the modern Court's opinions. The Court often praises diversity and speaks of its historic importance in America. Diversity is most often invoked in Establishment cases, where it is cited as central to religious liberty in the American tradition. But the Court stops short of some forms of diversity, particularly when it comes to free exercise claims. In the 1990 case *Employment Division v. Smith,* the Court struck down the use of peyote in Native American religious ceremonies. Religious-based polygamy also crosses the line of what is constitutionally acceptable, the Court ruled in the landmark 1878 case *Reynolds v. United States.*

Diversity took center stage in *Allegheny County v. ACLU* (1989), in which the Court favored the diversity of a holiday display that included a Christmas tree and menorah. Writing for the majority, Justice Harry Blackmun spoke of diversity not only as a civic value, but also a constitutional mandate: The Christmas tree coupled with the menorah display, he wrote, embodied "a recognition of cultural diversity [and] . . . the respect for religious diversity that the Constitution requires."

Justice Sandra Day O'Connor, concurring, factored diversity into her "endorsement test" when weighing Pittsburgh's holiday display. Because it represented diverse religious traditions, the menorah–Christmas tree combo was fully permissible, unlike the religiously homogenous crèche: "A reasonable observer would, in my view, appreciate that the combined display is an effort to acknowledge the cultural diversity of our country and to convey tolerance of different choices in matters of religious belief or nonbelief by recognizing that the winter holiday season is celebrated in diverse ways by our citizens. The endorsement standard recognizes that the religious liberty so precious to the citizens who make up our diverse country is protected, not impeded, when government avoids endorsing religion or favoring particular beliefs over others."

Justice William Brennan, dissenting in *Allegheny,* scoffed at so much ado about diversity and said it had no basis in constitutional law. "Justices Blackmun and O'Connor appear to believe that, where seasonal displays are concerned, more is better. Whereas a display might be constitutionally problematic if it showcased the holiday of just one religion, those problems vaporize as soon as more than one religion is included," Brennan wrote. "I know of no principle under the Establishment Clause, however, that permits us to conclude that governmental promotion of religion is acceptable so long as one religion is not favored. We have, on the contrary, interpreted that clause to require neutrality, not just among religions, but between religion and nonreligion." Brennan said the "diversity" embraced by the majority of the Court was, in fact, a false diversity—which, in reality, was a Christian-centric view in disguise. "Contrary to the impression the city and Justices Blackmun and O'Connor seem to create, with their emphasis on 'the winter-holiday season,' December is not the holiday season for Judaism. Thus, the city's erection alongside the Christmas tree of the symbol of a relatively minor Jewish religious holiday, far from conveying 'the city's secular recognition of different traditions for celebrating the winter-holiday season (Blackmun),' or 'a message of pluralism and freedom of belief (O'Connor),' has the effect of promoting a Christianized version of Judaism. The holiday calendar they appear willing to accept revolves exclusively around a Christian holiday," he wrote.

But diversity carried the day. Justice Anthony Kennedy, concurring with the majority with respect to the menorah and Christmas tree, but not crèche, joined the chorus on diversity: "In my view, the principles of the Establishment Clause and our nation's historic traditions of diversity and pluralism allow communities to make reasonable judgments respecting the accommodation or acknowledgment of holidays with both cultural and religious aspects. No constitutional violation occurs when they do so by displaying a symbol of the holiday's religious origins," he wrote.

Diversity is on shakier ground when it comes to free exercise cases. In *Employment Division v. Smith* (1990), the Court ruled that Native American rituals may not include the ingestion of peyote when the state prohibits it. The respondents, Alfred Smith and Galen Black, argued that the sacramental use of small quantities of peyote in the Native American Church is comparable to the sacramental use of small quantities of alcohol in Catholic and Orthodox Christian masses. But Justice Antonin Scalia, writing for the Court majority, rejected the argument and instead warned of the dangers of too much diversity: "It is hard to see any reason in principle or practicality why the government should have to tailor its health and safety laws to conform to the diversity of religious belief. Any society adopting such a system would be courting anarchy, but that danger increases in direct proportion to the society's diversity of religious beliefs, and its determination to coerce or suppress none of them."

Scalia changed his tune substantially fifteen years later in *Gonzales v. O Centro Espirita,* which involved the sacramental use of psychedelic tea. "This demonstrates you can make an exception [to federal drug laws] without the sky falling," he said during oral arguments. "The Religious Freedom Restoration Act says there can be an exception to all federal statutes where there is a religious objection and a court makes a finding there can be an exception."[20]

Scalia did express concern that the general principle of religious exceptions to federal law might be stretched to polygamy. In the 1878 case *Reynolds v. United States,* the Court upheld federal law banning polygamy. The case remains precedent today. In *Reynolds,* the court distinguished between religious *belief*—which is protected by the First Amendment—and *action* based on belief, which is not.[21]

"Laws are made for the government of actions, and while they cannot interfere with mere religious belief and opinions, they may with practices," wrote Chief Justice Morrison R. Waite for the Court. "Suppose one believed that human sacrifices were a necessary part of religious worship, would it be seriously contended that the civil government under which he lived could not interfere to prevent a sacrifice? Or if a wife religiously believed it was her duty to burn herself upon the funeral pile of her dead husband, would it be beyond the power of the civil government to prevent her carrying her belief into practice?"[22]

Rather than calling for a "celebration of diversity," Waite invoked Western values as the appropriate standard to follow with respect to marriage. "Polygamy has always been odious among the northern and western nations of Europe, and, until the establishment of the Mormon Church, was almost exclusively a feature of the life of Asiatic and of African people. At common law, the second marriage was always void, and from the earliest history of England polygamy has been treated as an offense against society," he wrote.

When it comes to symbolism, such as that embodied in holiday displays, the Court places diversity on a pedestal; but when it comes to action based on religion, diversity is put under sharp constraints and must conform to the morality of the majority. Issues involving the right of conscience, however, are given greater leeway.

Issues of Conscience

> When one's belief collides with the power of the state, the latter is supreme within its sphere and submission or punishment follows. But, in the forum of conscience, duty to a moral power higher than the state has always been maintained. . . . Putting aside dogmas with their particular conceptions of deity, freedom of conscience itself implies respect for an innate conviction of paramount duty. The battle for religious liberty has been fought and won with respect to religious beliefs and practices, which are not in conflict with good order, upon the very ground of the supremacy of conscience within its proper field.
>
> —Chief Justice Charles Evans Hughes,
> dissenting in *United States v. MacIntosh* (1931)

> The rule respondents favor would open the prospect of constitutionally required religious exemptions from civic obligations of almost every conceivable kind, ranging from compulsory military service, the payment of taxes, to health and safety regulation such as manslaughter and child neglect laws, compulsory vaccination laws, drug laws, and traffic laws. . . . The government's ability to enforce generally applicable prohibitions of socially harmful conduct, like its ability to carry out other aspects of public policy, cannot depend on measuring the effects of a governmental action on a religious objector's spiritual development.
>
> —Justice Antonin Scalia, *Employment Division v. Smith* (1990)

Significantly missing from the Religious Liberty Clauses of the First Amendment is the word "conscience" or the phrase "freedom of conscience," but the issue of conscience is a critical part of the underlying philosophy of the First Amendment. James Madison's original proposal for the First Amendment addressed the right of conscience. "The civil rights of none shall be abridged on account of religious belief or worship, nor shall any national religion be established, nor shall the full and equal rights of conscience be in any manner, or on any pretext, infringed," Madison's draft read.[23]

The amendment underwent several compromise drafts and was ultimately massaged into its present form, absent the word, "conscience." Although not mentioned in the Bill of Rights, issues of conscience are still given weight by the Supreme Court and Congress. Conscientious objectors to war, Seventh Day Adventists who refuse to work on Saturdays, and those who wish to refrain from reciting the Pledge of Allegiance are all given deference.[24]

"Both morals and sound policy require that the state should not violate the conscience of the individual. All our history gives confirmation to the view that liberty of conscience has a moral and social value which makes it worthy of preservation at the hands of the state. So deep in its significance and vital, indeed, is it to the integrity of man's moral and spiritual nature that nothing short of the self-preservation of the state should warrant its violation; and it may well be questioned whether the state which preserves its life by a settled policy of violation of the conscience of the individual will not in fact ultimately lose it by the process," wrote former Chief Justice Harlan Fiske Stone.[25]

In the 1963 case *Abington v. Schempp*, in which the Court struck down compulsory Bible readings and prayer in public schools, Justice Tom C. Clark traced the right of conscience in America all the way back to Roger Williams, the great spokesman for religious liberty and the cause of conscience in early Colonial America: "Nothing but the most telling of personal experiences in religious persecution suffered by our forebears could have planted our belief in liberty of religious opinion any more deeply in our heritage. It is true that this liberty frequently was not realized by the colonists, but this is readily accountable by their close ties to the Mother Country. However, the views of Madison and Jefferson, preceded by Roger Williams, came to be incorporated not only in the Federal Constitution but likewise in those of most of our states. This freedom to worship was indispensable in a country whose people came from the four quarters of the earth and brought with them a diversity of religious opinion."[26]

The issue of conscience has no greater import than in matters of life and death, as in the case of conscientious objection to war. Deference to conscientious objectors has deep roots in America. Quakers (the Society of Friends), Mennonites, and the Brethren have long been recognized as "peace churches," which profess a doctrine of nonviolence, nonresistance, and pacifism. These groups were often persecuted for their beliefs and their refusal to take up arms. Rights and protection for conscientious objectors were granted not by the Constitution, nor by the Bill of Rights, but by long-standing tradition and "legislative grace."[27] "The conscientious objector is relieved from the obligation to bear arms in obedience to no constitutional provision, express or implied; but because, and only because, it has accorded with the policy of Congress thus to relieve him," wrote Chief Justice Charles Evans Hughes in *United States v. MacIntosh* (1931).[28]

The Supreme Court has upheld the rights of conscientious objectors numerous times. It has also placed limitations. In *MacIntosh,* the Court upheld the denial of a Canadian man's application for American citizenship because he would not swear the oath of citizenship in full—he would not swear to bear arms in defense of the United States "unless he believed the war to be morally justified." Justice George Sutherland, himself born in England, countered that "exemption from serving in the armed forces of the nation in time of war is dependent upon the will of Congress and not upon the scruples of the individual."

In the 1965 case *United States v. Seeger,* the Court upheld the right of conscientious objection to individuals who did belong to traditional churches. However, the Court did not extend the right to objection based on purely personal or political grounds. The case involved three men who professed personal religious beliefs against war, but claimed no affiliation with a peace church. The Court compared the men's statements to the provisions of the Universal Military Training and Service Act, which allowed conscientious objection based on "religious training and belief"—further defined as "an individual's belief in a relation to a Supreme Being involving duties superior to those arising from any human relation, but [not including] essentially political, sociological, or philosophical views or a merely personal moral code." The Court went through intricate intellectual gymnastics as to the definition of religion and the meaning of Supreme Being as defined in the law, and concluded, in the words of Justice Tom C. Clark, writing for the majority, "The test of belief 'in a relation to a Supreme Being' is whether a given belief that is sincere and meaningful occupies a place in the life of its possessor parallel to that filled by the orthodox belief in God of one who clearly qualifies for the exemption."[29]

Clark applied this test to the three individuals involved in the Seeger case, and all passed, thus establishing judicial precedent for broadened criteria for conscientious objectors. "The history of the Universal Military Training and Service Act belies the notion that it was to be restrictive in application and available only to those believing in a traditional God," Clark wrote. "Thus, while shifting the test from membership in such a church to one's individual belief, the Congress nevertheless continued its historic practice of excusing from armed service those who believed that they owed an obligation, superior to that due the state, of not participating in war in any form."

The Supreme Court has upheld the right of conscience in many other contexts. Seventh-Day Adventists and Jehovah's Witnesses have often become ensnared in state restrictions to free exercise, and the Court more often than not sides with them. In *Sherbert v. Verner* (1963), the Court ruled that individuals could not be forced to the choice between their dictates of faith and the requirements of the state. Specifically, the government may not burden a Sabbatarian with the choice of observing the Sabbath or complying with employment rules. Justice William Douglas, concurring with the majority, wrote: "an individual's scruples or conscience [are] an important area of privacy which the First Amendment fences off from government. The interference here is as plain as it is in Soviet Russia, where a churchgoer is given a second-class citizenship, resulting in harm though perhaps not in measurable damages."

As in the case of conscientious objectors, the Court has placed limitations on the right of conscience in free exercise cases. Free exercise does not mean *carte blanche* permission to do whatever one wants in the name of religion. Or, as Douglas put it in *Sherbert,* "the Free Exercise Clause is written in terms of what the government cannot do to the individual, not in terms of what the individual can exact from the government."

Back to the Future: Scalia, Thomas, and Rehnquist

The Establishment Clause prohibits Congress from enacting legislation respecting an *establishment* of religion; it does not prohibit Congress from enacting legislation "respecting religion" or "taking cognizance of religion." . . . In short, the view that the Establishment Clause precludes Congress from legislating respecting religion lacks historical provenance, at least based on the history of which I am aware. Even when enacting laws that bind the states pursuant to valid exercises of its enumerated powers, Congress need not observe strict separation between church and state, or steer clear of the subject of religion.

—Justice Clarence Thomas, concurring in *Cutter v. Wilkinson* (2005)

The First Amendment's authors did not simply prohibit the establishment of a state church or a state religion, an area history shows they regarded as very important and fraught with great dangers. Instead, they commanded that there should be no law respecting an establishment of religion. A law may be one respecting the forbidden objective while falling short of its total realization. A law "respecting" the proscribed result, that is, the establishment of religion, is not always easily identifiable as one violative of the clause. A given law might not establish a state religion, but nevertheless be one "respecting" that end in the sense of being a step that could lead to such establishment, and hence offend the First Amendment.

—Chief Justice Warren Burger, writing for the majority
in *Lemon v. Kurtzman* (1971)

In the past sixty years of jurisprudence, the Supreme Court has taken an expansive view of the Establishment Clause. Not only does it mean that Congress shall not establish a national religion, but it also prohibits laws' that "respect that end" or "tend to do so"—in the words of Justices Burger and Kennedy, respectively. In other words, although prayers at graduation ceremonies and nativity scenes in city hall don't go all the way in establishing a religion, they go part way, and therefore are unconstitutional.

A minority of the current Supreme Court interprets the Establishment Clause as much more limited in its scope. The most conservative members of the Court, Justices Scalia and Thomas, are sometimes described as "strict constructionist," "textualist," or "originalist" in their views of the Establishment Clause. Generally, they believe that the Establishment Clause prohibits Congress only from establishing a national religion, but nothing prohibits Congress from passing laws "respecting religion" in myriad ways that fall short of creating an establishment.[30]

In *Lee v. Weisman* (1992), in which the Court struck down nonsectarian benedictions at public school graduations, Scalia dissented, insisting that the Establishment Clause must be understood in a historical context, and not viewed as a continually malleable document: "The history and tradition of our nation are replete with public ceremonies featuring prayers of thanksgiving and petition. From our nation's origin, prayer has been a prominent part of governmental ceremonies and proclamations. But the Court is so oblivious to our history as to suggest that the Constitution restricts preservation and transmission of religious beliefs to the private sphere."

The meaning of establishment—and its prohibition in the First Amendment—can be found in Colonial Virginia, where the Anglican Church was the established church, and the general population was taxed to support the church whether they agreed with the church's doctrine or not, Scalia wrote. "The coercion that was a hallmark of historical establishments of religion was coercion of religious orthodoxy and of financial support by force of law and threat of penalty. Typically, attendance at the state church was required; only clergy of the official church could lawfully perform sacraments; and dissenters, if tolerated, faced an array of civil disabilities. The Establishment Clause was adopted to prohibit such an establishment of religion at the federal level, and to protect state establishments of religion from federal interference."

Nonsectarian benedictions at public school graduation ceremonies do not come close to this kind of coercion, Scalia argued; and the Court, in prohibiting such public prayers, had turned itself into a "bulldozer of its social engineering . . . [that] lays waste a tradition that is as old as public school graduation ceremonies themselves, and that is a component of an even more longstanding American tradition of nonsectarian prayer to God at public celebrations generally."

Chief Justice Rehnquist, who died in 2005, took a historical and "strict constructionist" view of the First Amendment. In his opinions, Rehnquist thoroughly traced the history of the First Amendment, arguing that recent interpretations of the Establishment Clause deviate from what the Founders intended.

"The true meaning of the Establishment Clause can only be seen in its history," Rehnquist wrote in his dissenting opinion in *Wallace v. Jaffree* (1985). "None of the members of Congress who spoke during the debate [in 1789] expressed the slightest indication that they thought the language before them from the Select Committee, or the evil to be aimed at, would require that the government be absolutely neutral as between religion and irreligion. The evil to be aimed at, so far as those who spoke were concerned, appears to have been the establishment of a national church, and perhaps the preference of one religious sect over another."

Justice Thomas takes his conservative peers' constructions a step further: Thomas has challenged the Establishment Clause's applicability to states via the Fourteenth Amendment. Before the Fourteenth Amendment, the Bill of Rights applied only to the federal government and not to the states— some of which retained their established churches into the early nineteenth century. Because the Establishment Clause is a "negative" freedom—it prevents Congress from doing something—it is distinguished from the Free Exercise Clause, which protects an individual right. Therefore, "it makes little sense to incorporate the Establishment Clause" into state jurisdiction, Thomas wrote in *Elk Grove Unified School District v. Newdow*. State laws respecting religion, therefore, are a matter of "states rights," over which the federal government should not have jurisdiction. "The text and history of the Establishment Clause strongly suggest that it is a federalism provision intended to prevent Congress from interfering with state establishments."

Under this view, states could theoretically re-establish official churches. Thomas points out that the Establishment Clause was specifically designed to protect and preserve the individual state establishments that existed at the time, such as the Congregationalist Church in Massachusetts and Connecticut. "Congress need only refrain from making laws respecting an establishment of religion; it must not interfere with a state establishment of religion. For example, Congress presumably could not require a state to establish a religion any more than it could preclude a state from establishing a religion," Thomas wrote in *Cutter v. Wilkinson.*

In the 2002 case *Zelman v. Simmons-Harris,* Thomas upheld Cleveland's school voucher program on similar grounds—that the Fourteenth Amendment has been misapplied to make the Establishment Clause applicable to the states. "The wisdom of allowing states greater latitude in dealing with matters of religion and education can be easily appreciated in this context. Respondents advocate using the Fourteenth Amendment to handcuff the state's ability to experiment with education," Thomas wrote. "By contrast, school choice programs that involve religious schools appear unconstitutional only to those who would twist the Fourteenth Amendment against itself by expansively incorporating the Establishment Clause. Converting the Fourteenth Amendment from a guarantee of opportunity to an obstacle against education reform distorts our constitutional values and disserves those in the greatest need."

Thomas's view of the Establishment Clause and the Fourteenth Amendment is at odds with the majority of the Court and longstanding precedent.

"The proposition that the several states have no greater power to restrain the individual freedoms protected by the First Amendment than does Congress is firmly embedded in constitutional jurisprudence," wrote Justice John Paul Stevens in *Wallace v. Jaffree.* "The First Amendment was adopted to curtail Congress' power to interfere with the individual's freedom to believe, to worship, and to express himself in accordance with the dictates of his own conscience, and the Fourteenth Amendment imposed the same substantive limitations on the states' power to legislate. The individual's freedom to choose his own creed is the counterpart of his right to refrain from accepting the creed established by the majority. Moreover, the individual freedom of conscience protected by the First Amendment embraces the right to select any religious faith or none at all."

The Catholic Court?

> The Constitution does not protect a right to an abortion.
>
> —Samuel Alito, on a job application to the Justice Department, 1985

> There is nothing in my personal views based on faith or other sources that would prevent me from applying the precedent of the Court faithfully under the principles of *stare decisis.*
>
> —John Roberts, during his confirmation hearings before the Senate, 2005

The newest members of the Supreme Court, Chief Justice John Roberts and Samuel Alito, both George W. Bush appointees, are considered conservative jurists. But neither is considered an ideological "originalist," and whether they will side with Scalia and Thomas on religious liberty issues remains to be seen.

Both Roberts and Alito are Catholics—joining Thomas, Scalia, and Kennedy—and thus giving the Court a Catholic majority of five in nine. The issue of the justices' religious affiliation has arisen primarily as it pertains to their views on *Roe v. Wade* (1973), whose precedent made abortion a constitutional right. Will the Catholic jurists' opinions be swayed by the Church's stance on abortion?

During Roberts' Senate confirmation hearings, Senator Arlen Specter (R-Pa.) backed into the issue directly: "When you talk about your personal views and, as they may relate to your own faith, would you say that your views are the same as those expressed by John Kennedy when he was a candidate, when he spoke to the Greater Houston Ministerial Association in September of 1960, quote, 'I do not speak for my church on public matters and the church does not speak for me,' close quote?"

"I agree with that, Senator. Yes," Roberts replied.[31]

During Alito's confirmation hearing, the Senate grilled him about his 1985 statement, "The Constitution does not protect a right to abortion." Alito told the Senate he made the statement "from my vantage point in 1985, and that was as a line attorney in the Department of Justice in the Reagan administration." Alito assured senators he would approach the abortion issue with "an open mind," and he emphasized the importance of *stare decisis,* or precedent.[32]

Many observers believe the strategy of the Court's conservative wing will be to slowly chip away at *Roe v. Wade,* rather than overturn it in one fell swoop. Roberts has ruled in favor of certain constraints pertaining to abortion. In *Ayotte v. Planned Parenthood* (2006), he led the court in a unanimous ruling—written by O'Connor—that states may require parental notification of abortions, provided that such laws include exceptions for medical emergencies. As a deputy solicitor general in the Department of Justice, Roberts argued in favor of Department of Health and Human Services policy that prohibits federally subsidized medical providers from discussing abortion with patients. The Supreme Court's ruling in that case, *Rust v. Sullivan* (1991), resulted in what is sometimes known as the abortion "gag rule." In 2007, the Court ruled 5–4 to uphold a federal law banning "partial-birth abortion" in *Gonzales v. Carhart.* The Catholic members of the Court—Alito, Roberts, Scalia, Kennedy and Thomas—formed the majority in the case.[33] Pro-life advocates are hoping the new composition of the Court will turn the tide further in their favor, while the pro-choice camp is increasingly nervous.

The issue of the death penalty is sometimes viewed as another "litmus test" of a justice's moral and religious views. The Catholic Church strongly opposes the death penalty, which Pope John Paul II called "cruel and unnecessary."[34] But Alito, during his fifteen years on the U.S. Third Circuit Court of Appeals, ruled consistently against murder defendants who received the death penalty—this, despite the fact that he is a Catholic. In a 2007 decision, Alito, Roberts, Scalia, Kennedy, and Thomas ruled in favor of reinstating a death sentence for a two-time Arizona murderer who told his trial judge, "if you want to give me the death penalty, just bring it right on." The 5–4 decision in *Schriro v. Landrigan* placed all five Catholic members of the Court in favor of the death penalty.[35]

In summary, one could characterize the Catholic jurists' records as conservative, but it would be difficult to characterize their records as "Catholic." Alito's and Roberts' personal opinions on abortion and the death penalty may—or may not—represent how one's religious teaching informs judicial thinking. If faith does happen to factor into any justice's decision regarding abortion, its influence could just as easily come from conservative Protestantism as from Catholicism, since conservative Catholics and Protestants are in unison in opposing abortion. "There is simply no way to predict how any one Catholic is going to vote on an issue," wrote court observer and author Marci A. Hamilton. "We live in the era of 'cafeteria Catholics,' which is to say that American Catholics pick and choose among their church's doctrines, especially when the issue is contraception, abortion or premarital sex. The Roman Catholic Church does not and cannot control how American Catholics view social issues. Thus, five Catholics will be about as predictable as any other five Americans in how they vote on hot-button issues."[36]

Into the Future: John Roberts and Samuel Alito

> The distinctly latter-day claim of sanitized separation between church and state was alien to the Founding generation's vision of the Establishment Clause. That clause was designed, above all, to protect religious liberty, not to expunge religion from the nation's official life.
>
> —John Roberts and Kenneth Starr, in amicus, *Lee v. Weisman* (1992)

Since *Lynch* teaches that display of a crèche is not per se unconstitutional, and *Allegheny County* teaches that the same is true of a menorah, it is hard to accept the proposition that the Establishment Clause is violated when these two symbols are displayed together as part of a holiday display that includes secular symbols and is dedicated to the celebration of a municipality's cultural diversity.

— Samuel Alito, delivering the opinion in *ACLU v. Schundler*
(U.S. Court of Appeals, Third Circuit, 1999)

John Roberts and Samuel Alito have not yet had a chance build extensive portfolios on religious liberty cases on the High Court, but each has given clear hints of his philosophy from lower-court rulings.

Roberts has indicated he does not take a strict "separationist" view of the First Amendment in Establishment cases. As deputy solicitor general in the Department of Justice, Roberts co-authored an amicus brief in *Lee v. Weisman* (1992). Roberts, along with then-Solicitor General Kenneth Starr, argued that a non-sectarian benediction at high school graduations does not violate the Establishment Clause. In fashioning the argument, the solicitors take a historical view of the Constitution, reminiscent of Rehnquist's opinions. The solicitors' brief traces the practices of the Founders and various branches of government over time with respect to prayer at public ceremonies, and they conclude that such practices do not violate the Establishment Clause.

"Ceremonial acknowledgments [of a deity] were so pervasive among the three branches that it is fair to say they constituted a regular practice of our early government," the solicitors wrote. "It would be modern-day arrogance in the extreme to dismiss that practice as the result of unthinking prejudice or political expedience on the part of the Founding generation. To the contrary, the Framers' approval of acknowledgments of the country's religious heritage was the product of deliberate reflection on the relation between religion and civic life."[37]

The solicitors take square aim at the *Lemon* test as a distorting factor in Establishment cases, and they advocate scrapping it. "The problem is *Lemon*. That is, rigorous application of *Lemon*'s tripartite test would invalidate ceremonial acknowledgments of religion," they wrote.

The solicitors also note that the First Amendment cannot conceivably shield people from all the forms of religious speech and symbolism that pervade society. "Under the Free Exercise and Free Speech Clauses, citizens are inevitably exposed to a volley of views that may give offense and that they may choose to ignore," they wrote. "The Framers' acceptance of ceremonial acknowledgments presupposed some minimal degree of individual tolerance that should govern modern assessments of religious acknowledgments."

As a judge on the Third U.S. Circuit Court of Appeals, Alito reached a similar conclusion in a case involving school graduation prayer. In *ACLU of New Jersey v. Black Horse Pike Regional Board of Education* (1995), he took the dissenting view that students should be allowed to vote on whether or not to conduct prayers at graduation ceremonies, and select a student to lead the prayer. The majority of the court took the contrary view—that even a student-arranged graduation prayer violates the First Amendment.[38] During his Senate confirmation hearings, Alito said the student-elected prayer in *Pike* constituted free exercise of both religion and speech upon which the government should not impinge. Speaking about the case during his confirmation hearings, Alito told Senator Dick Durban (D–Illinois), "the government itself cannot speak on religious matters, but the government also can't discriminate against private religious speech."[39]

In Establishment cases, Alito, like Roberts, has advocated a somewhat lower "wall of separation." In *ACLU v. Schundler,* Alito, as a judge in the Third Circuit Court of Appeals, upheld the constitutionality of holiday displays in Jersey City. Writing for the majority of the court, he said the displays were "indistinguishable in any constitutionally significant respect" from the displays upheld by the Supreme Court in *Lynch v. Donnelly* and *Allegheny v. ACLU.* "Holiday displays featuring a menorah, crèche and other religious and cultural symbols did not violate the Constitution. Reasonably viewed, none of these displays conveyed a message of government endorsement of Christianity, Judaism, or of religion in general but instead sent a message of pluralism and freedom to choose one's own beliefs," Alito wrote.[40]

In an interesting twist, a lower court had sided with Jersey City regarding its modified holiday display, which included not only a crèche, a menorah, and a Christmas tree, but also large plastic figures of Santa Claus, Frosty the Snowman, a red sled, and Kwanzaa symbols—which the court said "sufficiently demystified the holy, desanctified sacred symbols, and sufficiently deconsecrated the sacred," thus removing any problem with state involvement in religion. Alito, although ultimately reaching the same conclusion in allowing the display, made a point of debunking "desanctification " reasoning: "Demystification, desanctification, and deconsecration suggest a process of profanation, something that the Establishment Clause neither demands nor tolerates," he wrote.

In free exercise cases, Alito has taken an expansive view, favoring religious minorities. As a federal judge on the Third Circuit Court of Appeals, he ruled in favor of two Muslim policemen who challenged the Newark Police Department's policy requiring all officers to be clean shaven. Alito said the department's "no-beard" policy unfairly singled out the Muslim officers because of their religion and inhibited their free exercise. "If it is the Department's thinking . . . that Sunni Muslim officers who share the plaintiffs' religious beliefs are prohibited from wearing beards precisely for the purpose of obscuring the fact that they hold those beliefs, and that they differ in this respect from most of the other members of the force . . . we have before us a policy the very purpose of which is to suppress manifestations of the religious diversity that the First Amendment safeguards," Alito wrote for the majority of the court.[41]

Alito distinguished the *Newark* case from the *Employment Division v. Smith* ruling, in which the Supreme Court said "no" to peyote in religious rituals. In *Smith*, the Oregon law prohibiting peyote use made no individual exemptions—religious or otherwise. But in *Newark*, the Newark Police Department provided an exemption from the "no-beard" policy for medical reasons. Therefore, the department could not deny an exemption for religious reasons, Alito reasoned. "If a state creates a mechanism for exemptions, its refusal to extend an exemption to an instance of religious hardship suggests a discriminatory intent," he wrote, quoting from the 1986 Supreme Court case *Bowen v. Roy*. Thus, the Newark policy "tends to exhibit hostility, not neutrality, toward religion."

As deputy solicitor general, Roberts has also ruled in favor of free exercise rights. In *Lamb's Chapel v. Center Moriches Union School District* (1993), he co-authored an amicus brief in a case involving a school district that had barred after-school access to a church group that wanted to air a film series on child-rearing by radio-evangelist Dr. James Dobson. "The exclusion of petitioners' proposed lecture series constitutes unjustified viewpoint-based discrimination and violates the First Amendment," he wrote, again with then-Solicitor General Kenneth Starr. "A local school district . . . may not permit a general type of speech, such as lectures on matters of public concern, but exclude a particular speaker on such a topic because he advances a religious point of view."[42] The Supreme Court agreed, ruling unanimously that the school district had impermissibly discriminated against the church because of its religious viewpoint.[43]

Roberts, born in 1955, and Alito, born in 1950, are the two youngest members of the court and will likely have the opportunity to weigh in on many future cases.

Beyond the Wall

> The highways of church and state relationships are not likely to be one-way streets, and the Constitution's authors sought to protect religious worship from the pervasive power of government. The history of many countries attests to the hazards of religion's intruding into the political arena or of political power intruding into the legitimate and free exercise of religious belief.
>
> —Chief Justice Warren Burger, *Lemon v. Kurtzman* (1971)

> A secular state, it must be remembered, is not the same as an atheistic or antireligious state. A secular state establishes neither atheism nor religion as its official creed.
>
> —Justice Harry Blackmun, *Allegheny v. ACLU* (1989)

The Supreme Court has the responsibility to apply reason regarding an issue that transcends human reasoning: religion, and the preservation of its free exercise. And the Court has to apply coherency "respecting" an issue—the non-establishment of religion—that is so complex it often defies the structure of jurisprudence. The Court attempts to establish various "tests," metaphors, and other criteria for judging the First Amendment, but they all tend to cave in and get replaced by still newer criteria.

The battles on the Court mirror the "culture wars" raging in the broader society over the role of religion in public life, and the passions are just as strong. Even members of the nation's highest court aren't above the emotion of the issue. Some of the resulting snipes, retorts, and quips can be quite entertaining: Said Scalia, in his *Lee v. Weisman* dissent, "Unfortunately, the Court has replaced *Lemon* with its psycho-coercion test, which suffers the double disability of having no roots whatever in our people's historic practice and being as infinitely expandable as the reasons for psychotherapy itself. . . . Whatever the merit of our school prayer cases (*Engel* and *Schempp*), they do not support, much less compel, the Court's psycho-journey." Justice Burger mused at the Court's occasional acrobatics of logic. "This is not to suggest, however, that we are to engage in a legalistic minuet in which precise rules and forms must govern. A true minuet is a matter of pure form and style, the observance of which is itself the substantive end. Here we examine the form of the relationship for the light that it casts on the substance," he wrote in *Lemon*.

The battle within the Court also parallels the wars in Congress over judicial appointments. The stakes are high. The nine individuals on the Supreme Court have enormous power—some believe too much power—to shape the role of religion in public life. Some fear the Court will bury religion, and others fear the Court will establish it. Conservatives often decry "activist judges" who have overstepped the constitutional boundaries of the judiciary. "Judicial restraint" is what is needed, they say. Others point to the activism on the Court that led to desegregation and the expansion of civil rights. If the Court had not taken an activist stance, the nation would be far behind where it now is in equal rights.[44]

How can the pros and cons of judicial activism and restraint be weighed? And how can these terms be properly understood?

Judicial activism and judicial restraint can be elusive labels. And High Court justices can be hard to pinpoint. In the landmark 1947 case *Everson v. Board of Education,* Justice Felix Frankfurter voted against allowing public funds to be used for the transportation of students to parochial schools. The *Everson* case is viewed by many as the beginning of judicial activism on the Court and where it began to go wrong. But in two earlier cases, Frankfurter held fast to judicial restraint in deference to the state's civil authority to compel flag salutes in public schools. In *Minersville School District v. Gobitis* (1940) and *West Virginia State Board of Education v. Barnette* (1943), Frankfurter ruled against Jehovah's Witnesses who refused to salute the flag.[45]

More recently, Justice Antonin Scalia came out in favor of benedictions at school graduations in *Lee v. Weisman* (1992), but against sacramental peyote use in *Employment Division v. Smith* (1990). By the standards of the Frankfurter court, a ruling in favor of public school benedictions would represent judicial restraint, and Scalia's ruling against sacramental peyote use would also follow the 1940s standard of judicial restraint. On the other hand, by the standards of 2005, a reversal to put benedictions back in graduation ceremonies might be seen as judicial activism. Similarly, free exercise advocates assail Scalia's *Smith* decision as an activist destruction of religious rights. So like the terms "liberal" and "conservative," judicial "activism" and "restraint" are moving targets.

Some say what is needed is a "strict constructionist" or "literalist" view to counter years of a liberal activist Court. But Justice Thomas's view that the Establishment Clause does not apply to the states through the Fourteenth Amendment, while part of the strict constructionist vein, is, in fact, a radical proposition by modern standards. The last state to have an established church was Massachusetts, which did away with its Congregationalist establishment in 1833. Today, with Roman Catholics representing the majority of the state's population, it would be highly ironic to suggest that this former bastion of Protestantism adopt Catholicism as its official religion, or even something "respecting" that end. A tendency toward establishment is clearly not what Madison had in mind when he led his state of Virginia away from establishment in 1786 before drafting the First Amendment three years later. The movement at the time of the founding was clearly away from religious establishment and in favor of separation. Justice Hugo Black quickly summed up the philosophy behind this movement: "A union of government and religion tends to destroy government and to degrade religion."[46]

Is the alternative, then, Black's impregnable "wall" of separation, a purely secular state with nothing "respecting" religion? This is clearly not an idea most Americans would agree with, nor would it be possible. As Justice Burger observed, "No significant segment of our society and no institution within it can exist in a vacuum or in total or absolute isolation from all the other parts, much less from government."[47]

So what lies in the huge space between the two polar ideals of an absolute secular state and a theocracy? And how does the Court plot out a location where religion can make a soft landing in the public square? This is the great challenge of the Court, and it is the challenge of all Americans. "It is difficult for a citizen to keep clearly in his or her head that what the Court is doing is not straightforwardly setting public policy; but rather, a much more restricted task: interpreting the constitutional limits on the work of elected public officials. And it is not determining the wisdom or even the abstract justice of the actions of these officials, but only whether they are allowable under the Constitution. . . . The Court's role is supposed to be a limited one. It is difficult for a citizen to comprehend that. Sometimes it may be hard for judges, too," writes historian William Lee Miller.[48]

Is it possible to predict where the Court is headed in its judicial journey? Given its continually evolving positions—and the individual justices' revisions of their own ideas—it is safe to say only that the Court will continue to change and revise its philosophy and applications of the law. National standards will change, as do the meanings of what is "activist" and what is judicial "restraint."

"The 'finding' of constitutional law is not done simply out of historical judgments," Miller notes. "The question is then where exactly does it come from? The answer is that it comes from a living constitution, expanding and developing in response to the changing life of an actual people. . . . The Court should not decide what America 'is,' nor what religion 'is' either, or any of the points in a cultural dispute. Leave that to the people's continuing decision, free argument and debate."[49]

Notes

Note: Supreme Court decisions are available on the Internet at:
http://straylight.law.cornell.edu/supct/ and http://caselaw.lp.findlaw.com/.

Chapter 1. From Revival to Religious Liberty

1. John McCormick, "When the Press Misses a Story," *Chicago Tribune*, Nov. 9, 2004.

2. CNN.com Election 2004, exit poll: http://www.cnn.com/ELECTION/2004/pages/results/states/US/P/oo/epolls.o.html.
Also see Mark Silk, "Analyzing Religion, Politics and the Christian Right in the 21st Century" (lecture presented by the Walter H. Capps Center for the Study of Ethics, Religion, and Public Life, Dec. 7–8, 2005, University of California, Santa Barbara), http://www.facsnet.org/issues/faith/silk.php.

3. Ron Elving, "Moral Values and the Next 'Big Story," National Public Radio, Nov. 9, 2004.

4. CNN.com Election 2004, exit poll.

5. CNN.com Election 2006, exit poll: http://www.cnn.com/ELECTION/2006/pages/results/states/US/H/oo/epolls.o.html.

6. CNN.com Transcripts, reporting a speech by U.S. Sen. John McCain (R–Ariz.) Feb. 28, 2000, Virginia Beach, Va. http://transcripts.cnn.com/TRANSCRIPTS/0002/28/se.01.html.

7. Martin E. Marty with Jonathan Moore, *Education, Religion, and the Common Good: Advancing a Distinctively American Conversation about Religion's Role in Our Shared Life* (San Francisco: Jossey-Bass, 2000), 23.

8. William Lee Miller, *The First Liberty: Religion and the American Republic* (New York: Paragon House, 1985), 119–128, and Miller, *The First Liberty: America's Foundation in Religious Freedom, Expanded and Updated* (Washington, D.C.: Georgetown University Press, 2003), 113–124.

9. Robert Bellah, *Beyond Belief: Essays on Religion in a Post–Traditionalist World* (Berkeley: University of California Press, 1970), 41.

10. Charles C. Haynes, "Church and State and the First Amendment" (lecture presented at the FACS/Pew Journalism, Religion & Public Life seminar, "One Nation Under God: Political and Religious Dimensions of America," Sept. 23, 2002, at the *Indianapolis Star*). Haynes is quoted throughout this chapter, drawing from this lecture.

11. The Pew Research Center for the People and the Press, "Faith-Based Funding Backed, But Church-State Doubts Abound," Section IV: "Religion in American Life" (2001): http://people-press.org/reports/display.php3?PageID=115.

12. Ibid.

13. The Pew Research Center for the People and the Press, "Among Wealthy Nations, U.S. Stands Alone in Its Embrace of Religion" (2002): http://people-press.org/reports/display.php3?ReportID=167.

14. Ram A. Cnaan, "The Invisible Hand: An Overview of Religion and Social Welfare" (lecture presented at the FACS/Pew Journalism, Religion & Public Life seminar, "Church & State: The Future of Faith-Based Initiatives," Feb. 3, 2003, at the *Orlando Sentinel*, Orlando, Fla.). Also see Marty, *Education, Religion, and the Common Good*, 95

15. Rowland A. Sherrill, "Understanding People of Faith" (lecture presented at the FACS/Pew Journalism, Religion & Public Life seminar, "Understanding Faith and Terrorism," Dec. 4, 2001, at the Scripps Howard Newspapers corporate headquarters, Cincinnati, Ohio).

16. Haynes, "Church and State and the First Amendment." Also see Marty, *Education, Religion, and the Common Good*, 44.

17. Adam B. Seligman, professor of religion at Boston University, in discussion with the author, May 26, 2003.

18. Ibid.

19. Jacques Maritain, *Reflections on America* (University of Notre Dame, Jacques Maritain Center, 1956), chap. 11. http://www2.nd.edu/Departments/Maritain/etext/reflect2.html#XI.

20. Marty, *Pilgrims in Their Own Land: 500 Years of Religion in America* (New York: Penguin Books, 1988), 429–431.

21. Ibid., 58–62; also see Miller, *The First Liberty*, rev. ed., 136.

22. Marty, *Pilgrims*, ix.

23. Ibid., 108–109. Also see Miller, *The First Liberty*, 1st ed., 250–267.

24. Philip Goff, "Historical Connections between God & Country" (lecture presented at the FACS/Pew Journalism, Religion & Public Life seminar, "One Nation Under God: Political and Religious Dimensions of America," Sept. 23, 2002, at the *Indianapolis Star*). Goff is quoted throughout this chapter, drawing from this lecture. Also see Marty, *Pilgrims*, 114–120.

25. Miller, *The First Liberty*, rev. ed., 15, 180.

26. Marty, *Pilgrims*, 108–109.

27. Goff, "Historical Connections between God & Country." See Perry Miller, "From the Covenant to the Revival," in *The Shaping of American Religion*, ed. James Ward Smith and A. Leland Jamison (Princeton: Princeton University Press, 1961), 343: "The ministers did not have to 'sell' the Revolution to a public sluggish to 'buy.' They were spelling out what both they and the people sincerely believed." Also see Marty, *Pilgrims*, 131.

28. Marty, *Pilgrims*, 169–187, 196, 410–413.

29. Ibid., 477.

30. Goff, "Historical Connections between God & Country."

31. Ibid. Also see Miller, *The First Liberty*, rev. ed., 104–105.

32. Miller, *The First Liberty*, rev. ed., 13, 21, 42–43.

33. Marty, *Pilgrims*, 75.

34. Miller, *The First Liberty*, rev. ed., 36.

35. Marty, *Pilgrims*, 86.

36. Miller, *The First Liberty*, 1st ed., 270–271. Also see Marty, *Pilgrims*, 82.

37. Marty, *Pilgrims*, 69.

38. Miller, *The First Liberty*, 1st ed., 231–232.

39. Haynes, "Church and State and the First Amendment."

40. Virginia Const., art. 1, section 16, "Free exercise of religion; no establishment of religion," adopted 1786. http://legis.state.va.us/Laws/search/Constitution.htm#1S16
Also see Miller, *The First Liberty*, rev. ed., 61.

41. Miller, *The First Liberty*, rev. ed., 24, 42–43. Also see Marty, *Pilgrims*, 163.

42. Miller, *The First Liberty*, rev. ed, 4.

43. U.S. Department of State, International Religious Freedom Report, 2003, http://www.state.gov/g/drl/rls/irf/2003/24410.htm.

44. Miller, *The First Liberty*, 1st ed., 98, "In Remonstrance, one can find the full expression of the views of the Father of the Constitution and the author, more or less, of the First Amendment." Also see rev. ed., 79–88.

45. James Madison, "A Memorial and Remonstrance Against Religious Assessments," written to the General Assembly of the Commonwealth of Virginia, 1785. Available on the University of Virginia's online library, http://religiousfreedom.lib.virginia.edu/sacred/madison_m&r_1785.html.

46. Goff, "Historical Connections between God & Country." Also see Miller, *The First Liberty*, 1st ed., 103.

47. Miller, *The First Liberty*, rev. ed., 27.

48. George Washington, Farewell Address, 1796. Available on the Yale Law School's Avalon Project website: http://www.yale.edu/lawweb/avalon/washing.htm.
Also see Miller, *The First Liberty*, 1st ed., 244–245.

49. James Madison, "Monopolies, Perpetuities, Corporations, Ecclesiastical Endowments," 1819, *The Selected Works of James Madison*, The Constitution Society, http://www.constitution.org/jm/18191213_monopolies.htm.

50. Thomas Jefferson, preamble to the Virginia Act for Establishing Religious Freedom, 1779, available on the University of Virginia's online library, http://religiousfreedom.lib.virginia.edu/sacred/vaact.html.
Also see Miller, *The First Liberty*, rev. ed., 40–41, 53.

51. Miller, *The First Liberty*, 1st ed., 28–29. Also see rev. ed., 28, 43, and 97.

52. Miller, *The First Liberty*, rev. ed., 4.

53. Miller, *The First Liberty*, 1st ed., 121; and rev. ed., 119.

54. Miller, *The First Liberty*, 1st ed., 122–123: "If conscience should be taken to mean not only belief but also principled moral conviction, and not only religious but also nonreligious belief and conviction, then Madison's proposal would have been an advance over even what twentieth-century courts have come to hold. . . . If Madison's phrase had been placed in the supreme law of the land, and the word's meaning and the society's understanding had changed as they have done, then the twentieth-century result would certainly have been yet another bonanza for lawyers."

55. Miller, *The First Liberty*, rev. ed., 6.

56. Marty, *Pilgrims*, 163.

57. Miller, *The First Liberty*, rev. ed., 7, 85, 120.

58. Ibid., 41, 67.

59. Ibid., 123.

60. Charles C. Haynes and Oliver Thomas, *Finding Common Ground: A Guide to Religious Liberty in Public Schools* (Nashville, Tenn: The First Amendment Center, 2001), 41.

61. Justice Harry Blackmun, *County of Allegheny v. American Civil Liberties Union* 492 U.S. 573 (1989): "To be sure, in a pluralistic society, there may be some would-be theocrats who wish that their religion were an established creed, and some of them perhaps may be even audacious enough to claim that the lack of established religion discriminates against their preferences. But this claim gets no relief, for it contradicts the fundamental premise of the Establishment Clause itself." Also see Miller, *The First Liberty*, rev. ed., 196.

62. West Virginia State Board of Education v. Barnette 319 U.S. 624 (1943). Also see Miller, *The First Liberty*, rev. ed., 217.

63. The Williamsburg Charter, "A Reaffirmation of the First Amendment," 1988, signed by former presidents Jimmy Carter, Gerald Ford, former Supreme Court Justices William Rehnquist and Warren Burger. See a complete listing of the signers and the drafting committee here: http://www.firstamendmentcenter.org/PDF/FCGappendixB .PDF.

64. Miller, *The First Liberty*, rev. ed., 44, 99–100.

65. Charles Haynes, "History of Religious Liberty in America" (1991), the First AmendmentCenter,http://www.firstamendmentcenter.org/rel_liberty/history/overview .aspx.

66. Miller, *The First Liberty*, 1st ed., 253, 124: "If the Establishment Clause of First Amendment had been understood to mean complete separation of church and state, there surely would not have been any hope the amendment would be ratified by the states, several of which still had in some degree or another religious establishments."

67. Miller, *The First Liberty*, rev. ed., 190–195.

68. Miller, *The First Liberty*, 1st ed., 62.

69. Ibid., 294–297, 318; and rev. ed., 192–193.

70. Justice Clarence Thomas, concurring in *Elk Grove Unified School District v. Michael Newdow*, 542 U.S. 1 (2004).

71. Madison, "A Memorial and Remonstrance," 1785.

72. Miller, *The First Liberty*, 1st ed., 112–116, 136.

73. Miller, *The First Liberty*, rev. ed., 104. Also see Marty, *Pilgrims*, 164.

74. James Madison, *The Federalist No. 51*, "The Structure of the Government Must Furnish the Proper Checks and Balances Between the Different Departments," *Independent Journal* (Feb. 6, 1788). Available on the Constitution Society website: http://www .constitution.org/fed/federa51.htm.
Also see Miller, *The First Liberty*, rev. ed., 105–106; and Marty, *Pilgrims*, 164.

75. Miller, *The First Liberty*, 1st ed., 116.

76. Ibid., 69–70. Also see rev. ed., 242.

77. Miller, *The First Liberty*, 1st ed., 327, 349.

78. Ibid., 251; and rev. ed. 239.

79. Miller, *The First Liberty*, 1st ed., 259.

80. Marty, *Pilgrims*, 271–294. Also see Miller, *The First Liberty*, 1st ed., 270–272.

81. Goff, "Historical Connections between God & Country." Also see Miller, *The First Liberty*, 1st ed., 233, 272, 280; and rev. ed., 243–45.

82. Miller, *The First Liberty*, 1st ed., 340. And see p. 269, "The point still stands that the picture of religion in America has a form, a history, a tradition, and is not a totally random scatter of individual preferences—a pluralism of the more the merrier. The United States came out of the religious history of Europe, in particular of England, and has been adding its own chapters." Also see rev. ed., 228.

83. Haynes, "Church and State and the First Amendment," as quoted throughout the rest of this section.

Chapter 2. Understanding People of Faith

1. Rowland A. Sherrill, "Understanding People of Faith" (lecture presented at the FACS/Pew Journalism, Religion & Public Life seminar, entitled "Understanding Faith and Terrorism," Dec. 4, 2001, at the Scripps Howard Newspapers Board Room, Cincinnati, Ohio). Dr. Sherrill is quoted and paraphrased throughout this chapter, drawing from this lecture.

2. Also see Robert Bellah, *Beyond Belief: Essays on Religion in a Post-Traditionalist World* (Berkeley: University of California Press, 1970), 238, 249.

3. Ibid., 265–272, 43, 25, 21. Bellah discusses religion, in biological terms, as an evolutionary advance: "Animals or prereligious men could only passively endure suffering or other limitations imposed by the conditions of their existence, but religious man can to some extend transcend and dominate them through his capacity for symbolization and thus can attain a degree of freedom relative to his environment that was not previously possible." Also see Ram A. Cnaan with Robert J. Wineburg and Stephanie C. Boddie, *The Newer Deal: Social Work and Religion in Partnership* (New York: Columbia University Press, 1999), 133. In summarizing a point by theologian C. S. Lewis, Cnaan writes, "Belief in God and in a divine order that is beyond us is the key to overcoming stress and adversity. . . . There is a purpose to suffering that is beyond our human understanding, and we must be willing to submit to God's will. Some psychologists theorize that religious belief protects people from taking adversity personally and blaming themselves when things happen."

4. Martin E. Marty with Jonathan Moore, *Education, Religion, and the Common Good: Advancing a Distinctively American Conversation about Religion's Role in Our Shared Life* (San Francisco: Jossey-Bass, 2000), 9–11.

5. See Paul Tillich, "Our Ultimate Concern," in *The New Being* (New York: Charles Scribner's Sons, 1955): "There are innumerable concerns in our lives and in human life generally which demand attention, devotion, passion. But they do not demand infinite attention, unconditional devotion, ultimate passion. They are important, often very important for you and for me and for the whole of mankind. But they are not ultimately important. . . . The one thing needed—this is the first and in some sense the last answer I can give—is to be concerned ultimately, unconditionally, infinitely." Available online, http://www.religion-online.org/showchapter.asp?title=375&C=33.

6. Marty, *Education, Religion, and the Common Good*, 11. Also see Bellah, *Beyond Belief*, 261: "With respect to the human personality, the deepest ordering of impulse is cultural, religious, and occurs in myth and ritual. . . . Human action is almost by definition symbolic action, which is another way of saying that it always involves culture."

7. Bellah, *Beyond Belief*, 4–8.

8. Clifford Geertz, "Religion as a Cultural System," in *Anthropological Approaches to the Study of Religion*, ed. Michael Banton, A.S.A. Monographs, vol. 3 (London: Tavistock Press, 1966), 4. Quoted in Bellah, *Beyond Belief*, 12.

9. Bellah, *Beyond Belief*, 253–245.

10. Marty, *Education, Religion, and the Common Good*, 10.

11. Martin E. Marty, *Pilgrims in Their Own Land: 500 Years of Religion in America*, (New York: Penguin Books, 1988), 154, 160, 208.

12. Glenmary Research Center, "Religious Congregations & Membership: 2000," http://www.glenmary.org/grc/RCMS_2000/findings.htm.

13. Walter Russell Mead, "God's Country?" *Foreign Affairs* (September/October 2006) http://www.foreignaffairs.org/20060901faessay85504/walter-russell-mead/god-s-country.html.

Mead is quoted and paraphrased throughout this chapter, drawing from this article.

14. John Calvin, "Every Thing Proceeding From the Corrupt Nature of Man Damnable," in *Institutes of the Christian Religion*, Book 2, chap. 3, trans. Henry Beveridge, Esq. (London: Arnold Hatfield and Bonham Norton, 1599): "Our Saviour's words simply mean, that when separated from him, we are nothing but dry, useless wood, because, when so separated, we have no power to do good." Available online at the Center for Reformed Theology and Apologetics: http://www.reformed.org/master/index.html?mainframe=/books/institutes/.

15. Paul Tillich, "Zwingli, Luther, Calvin, Predestination and Providence," from *A History of Christian Thought*, ed. C. E. Braaten (New York: Simon and Schuster, 1972).

Also see William Lee Miller, *The First Liberty: Religion and the American Republic* (New York: Paragon House, 1985), 249, 263; and Bellah, *Beyond Belief*, 38–39.

16. Mead, "God's Country?" Also see Calvin, "Of the Eternal Election by which God Has Predestined Some," in *Institutes*, Book 3, chap. 21: "The predestination by which God adopts some to the hope of life, and adjudges others to eternal death, no man who would be thought pious ventures simply to deny."

17. Marty, *Pilgrims*, 450–458.

18. Robert N. Bellah, Richard Madsen, William M. Sullivan, Ann Swidler and Steven M. Tipton, *Habits of the Heart: Individualism and Commitment in American Life* (Berkeley: University of California Press, 1985), 219–249, quote on 219.

19. R. Drew Smith, "Following the Streams of African-American Religion" (lecture presented at the FACS/Pew Journalism, Religion & Public Life seminar, "The African-American Church in the Community," Aug. 2, 2004, at the *Charlotte Observer* in Charlotte, N.C.): http://www.facsnet.org/issues/faith/streams.php.

20. Bellah, *Habits of the Heart*, 227, 229, 237, 243. Also see Miller, *The First Liberty*, 1st ed., 278.

21. Philip Goff, "Historical Connections between God & Country" (lecture presented at the FACS/Pew Journalism, Religion & Public Life seminar, "One Nation Under God: Political and Religious Dimensions of America," Sept. 23, 2002, at the *Indianapolis Star*).

22. Bellah, *Beyond Belief*, 43; and *Habits of the Heart*, 233, 246. Also see Marty, *Pilgrims*, 246.

23. Bellah, *Habits of the Heart*, 235, 242.

24. Walt Whitman, "Song of Myself," from *Leaves of Grass* (1871) in *The Norton Anthology of American Literature*, shorter ed. (New York: W. W. Norton, 1980), 719.

25. Bellah, *Habits of the Heart*, 231.

26. Mark Silk, "Analyzing Religion, Politics and the Christian Right in the 21st century" (lecture presented by the Walter H. Capps Center for the Study of Ethics, Religion, and Public Life, Dec. 7–8, 2005, University of California, Santa Barbara), http://www.facsnet.org/issues/faith/silk.php.

27. Cnaan, *The Newer Deal*, 38.

28. William Lee Miller, *The First Liberty: America's Foundation in Religious Freedom, Expanded and Updated* (Washington, D.C.: Georgetown University Press, 2003), 27–28; 44–48. Also see Marty, *Pilgrims*, 208.

29. Calvin, *Institutes*, Book 3, chap. 21: "By predestination we mean the eternal decree of God, by which he determined with himself whatever he wished to happen with regard to every man. All are not created on equal terms, but some are preordained to eternal life, others to eternal damnation; and, accordingly, as each has been created for one or other of these ends, we say that he has been predestinated to life or to death."

30. Mead, "God's Country?" Also see Calvin, *Institutes*, Book 3, chap. 25: "For since Adam by his fall destroyed the proper order of nature, the creatures groan under the servitude to which they have been subjected through his sin; not that they are at all endued with sense, but that they naturally long for the state of perfection from which they have fallen. . . . As Christ was once offered for sins, so he shall again appear without sin unto salvation."

31. Ronald Cole-Turner, "Religious Responses to Cloning: Where Science and Theology Intersect" (lecture presented at the FACS/Pew Journalism, Religion & Public Life seminar, entitled "God and Science: Understanding the Human Cloning Story," Feb. 12, 2002, at the *Philadelphia Inquirer*): http://facsnet.org/issues/faith/cole-turner.php.

32. Alexis de Tocqueville, *Democracy in America*, Book 2, chap. 12 (1835). Available on the University of Virginia online library: http://xroads.virginia.edu/%7EHYPER/DETOC/1_ch18.htm.

33. Bellah, *Beyond Belief*, 44, 261, 282–287.

34. Ibid, 284.

35. Cnaan, *The Newer Deal*, 156: "Negative side effects of organized religions range from authoritarianism and dogmatism to support of nationalistic crusades. The preponderance of the evidence, however, suggests that religion is modestly helpful in the areas of prosocial behavior, personal and social adjustment, life satisfaction and well-being, and physical symptomatology."

36. "Taliban Show Off Remains of Ancient Buddha Statues," *National Geographic*, March 27, 2001.

37. Bellah, *Beyond Belief*, 261.

38. Ibid.

39. James Madison, "A Memorial and Remonstrance Against Religious Assessments," written to the General Assembly of the Commonwealth of Virginia, 1785. Available on the University of Virginia's online library, http://religiousfreedom.lib.virginia.edu/sacred/madison_m&r_1785.html.

40. See entry for Alfred North Whitehead on the Stanford online Encyclopedia of Philosophy: http://plato.stanford.edu/entries/whitehead/.

41. The Williamsburg Charter, "A Reaffirmation of the First Amendment," 1988, http://religiousfreedom.lib.virginia.edu/const/Willburg.html.

42. Also see Bellah in *Beyond Belief*, 223, 253: "The conclusion grows ever stronger that religion is a part of the species life of man, as central to his self-definition as speech. . . . Since religious symbolization and religious experience are inherent in the structure of human existence, all reductionism must be abandoned." See also Marty, *Education, Religion, and the Common Good*, 105.

43. Marty, *Education, Religion, and the Common Good*, 15–16.

Chapter 3. With "God on Our Side"?: American Civil Religion

1. Wilfred McClay, "The Soul of a Nation," *The Public Interest*, no. 155 (Spring, 2004), 2.

2. Rowland A. Sherrill, "Religion, Civil Society and Community" (lecture presented at the FACS/Pew Journalism, Religion & Public Life seminar, "One Nation Under God: Political and Religious Dimensions of America," Sept. 23, 2002, at the *Indianapolis Star*). Dr. Sherrill is quoted and paraphrased throughout this chapter from this lecture.

3. "Lawmakers Blast Pledge Ruling," CNN.com, June 27, 2002, http://archives.cnn.com/2002/LAW/06/26/pledge.allegiance/.

4. "Bush Criticizes Spanish U.S. Anthem," BBC News, April 28, 2006, http://news.bbc.co.uk/2/hi/entertainment/4955360.stm.

5. Arnold Schwarzenegger, "Next Step for Immigration," *Los Angeles Times*, March 28, 2006.

6. Martin E. Marty, *Pilgrims in Their Own Land: 500 Years of Religion in America* (New York: Penguin Books, 1988), 155–156, 220–221, 404.

7. Alexis de Tocqueville, *Democracy in America*, Book I, chap. 18 (1835). Available on the University of Virginia online library: http://xroads.virginia.edu/%7EHYPER/DETOC/1_ch18.htm.

8. The Pew Research Center for the People and the Press, "Americans Struggle with Religion's Role at Home and Abroad" (2002), part 1, "Religion in America": http://people-press.org/reports/display.php3?PageID=386.

9. William Lee Miller, *The First Liberty: America's Foundation in Religious Freedom*, Expanded and Updated (Washington, D.C.: Georgetown University Press, 2003), 253.

10. Bob Dylan, "With God on Our Side," ((c) 1963, Special Rider Music), from *The Times They Are A-Changin'* (Columbia Records, 1964), http://www.bobdylan.com/songs/withgod.html.

11. Robert Bellah, "Civil Religion in America," *Daedalus* 96, no.1 (1967). Republished in *Beyond Belief: Essays on Religion in a Post-Traditionalist World* (Berkeley: University of California Press, 1991), 168–189.

12. Angeliki Kanavou, Assistant Professor of Political Science and Peace Studies, Chapman University, in discussion with the author, February 2005.

13. Jean Jacques Rousseau, *The Social Contract, or Principles of Political Right* (1762), Book IV: "That the General Will is Indestructible,"

14. Bellah, *Beyond Belief*, 171.

15. Robert N. Bellah, *The Broken Covenant: American Civil Religion in Time of Trial* (Chicago: University of Chicago Press, 1992), 164–165.

16. John Winthrop, "A Model of Christian Charity," sermon delivered in 1630 on board the ship *Arbella*. Available on the University of Virginia's online library: http://religiousfreedom.lib.virginia.edu/sacred/charity.html.

17. Sherrill, "Religion, Civil Society and Community." Also see Bellah, *The Broken Covenant*, 1–35; Miller, *The First Liberty*, 180–182; and Marty, *Pilgrims*, 58–62, 63–66; 475–477.

18. Matthew 5:15.

19. Charles C. Haynes, "Church and State and the First Amendment" (lecture presented at the FACS/Pew Journalism, Religion & Public Life seminar, "One Nation Under God: Political and Religious Dimensions of America," Sept. 23, 2002, at the *Indianapolis Star*).

20. Bellah, *The Broken Covenant*, 173–180.

21. William Lee Miller, *The First Liberty: Religion and the American Republic* (New York: Paragon House, 1985), 62–64, 238; and rev. ed., 92. Also see Bellah, *The Broken Covenant*, 44.

22. Marty, *Pilgrims*, 156.

23. Benjamin Franklin, "Proposals Relating to the Education of Youth in Pennsylvania" (1749), http://www.historycarper.com/resources/twobf2/educate.htm.

Also see Marty, *Pilgrims*, 155–158, and Miller, *The First Liberty*, 1st ed., 240.

24. B. L. Rayner, "Diffusion of Knowledge," in *The Life of Thomas Jefferson* (Boston: Lilly, Wait, Colman, & Holden, 1834). Available on the University of Virginia website: http://etext.virginia.edu/jefferson/biog/lj13.htm.

25. Thomas Jefferson, "Religion," in *Notes on the State of Virginia* (1781), available on the University of Virginia Library's Electronic Text Center: http://etext.lib.virginia.edu/toc/modeng/public/JefVirg.html.

26. Miller, *The First Liberty*, 1st ed., 259, "America in its formative days developed out of those [religious] enthusiasms a kind of seminationalist religion and a semireligious nationalism with some of the results of which we are living still, with which the world is coping still."

27. Bruce Springsteen, "Chords for Change," *New York Times*, Aug. 5, 2004.

28. George Washington, First Inaugural Address, April 30, 1789, http://www.yale.edu/lawweb/avalon/presiden/inaug/wash1.htm.

29. Thomas Jefferson, First Inaugural Address, March 4, 1801, http://www.yale.edu/lawweb/avalon/presiden/inaug/jefinau1.htm.

30. James Monroe, Second Inaugural Address, March 5, 1821, http://www.yale.edu/lawweb/avalon/presiden/inaug/monroe2.htm.

31. John F. Kennedy, Inaugural Address, Jan. 20, 1961, http://www.yale.edu/lawweb/avalon/presiden/inaug/kennedy.htm.

32. Bellah, "Civil Religion in America," http://hirr.hartsem.edu/Bellah/articles_5.htm.

33. Ibid.

34. Martin E. Marty with Jonathan Moore, *Education, Religion, and the Common Good: Advancing a Distinctively American Conversation about Religion's Role in Our Shared Life,* (San Francisco: Jossey-Bass, 2000), 138. Also see Bellah, *The Broken Covenant*, 175.

35. *Elk Grove Unified School District v. Michael Newdow*, 02–1624 S. Ct. 542 (2004).

36. Bellah, *The Broken Covenant*, 169.

37. Winthrop, "A Model of Christian Charity," http://religiousfreedom.lib.virginia .edu/sacred/charity.html.

38. Bellah, *The Broken Covenant*, 25.

39. John Calvin, "Of Civil Government," in *Institutes of the Christian Religion*, Book 4, chap. 20, trans. Henry Beveridge (London: Arnold Hatfield and Bonham Norton, 1599): "But he who knows to distinguish between the body and the soul, between the present fleeting life and that which is future and eternal, will have no difficulty in understanding that the spiritual kingdom of Christ and civil government are things very widely separated." Available online at the Center for Reformed Theology and Apologetics: http://www.reformed.org/master/index.html?mainframe=/books/institutes/.

Also see Bellah, *The Broken Covenant*, 17, and Richard Hooker, "Discovery and Reformation" (Pullman: Washington State University, 1996), http://www.wsu.edu/%7 Edee/REFORM/.

40. Bellah, *The Broken Covenant*, 168. Also see Bellah, *Beyond Belief*, 67–68.

41. Robert N. Bellah, Richard Madsen, William M. Sullivan, Ann Swidler, and Steven M. Tipton, *Habits of the Heart: Individualism and Commitment in American Life* (Berkeley: University of California Press, 1985), 254; and Bellah, *The Broken Covenant*, 21–27.

Also see Miller, *The First Liberty*, 1st ed., 343–353, and rev. ed., 27, 44–48, 92.

42. Charles-Louis de Montesquieu, *The Spirit of Laws* (1748), Book V, http://www .constitution.org/cm/sol_05.htm#002.

43. Thomas Jefferson, "A Bill for the More General Diffusion of Knowledge," submitted to the Virginia assembly in 1779. Available on the Electronic Text Center, University of Virginia Library, http://etext.lib.virginia.edu/etcbin/toccer-new2?id=JefPapr .sgm&images=images/modeng&data=/texts/english/modeng/parsed&tag=public&part =5&division=div1.

44. Paul Tillich, "Zwingli, Luther, Calvin, Predestination and Providence," in *A History of Christian Thought*, ed. C. E. Braaten (New York: Simon and Schuster, 1972). Also see Miller, *The First Liberty*, 1st ed., 249.

45. George Washington, Farewell Address, 1796, http://www.yale.edu/lawweb/ avalon/washing.htm.

Also see Miller, *The First Liberty*, 1st ed., 244–245.

46. Adam Smith, *An Inquiry into the Nature and Causes of the Wealth of Nations* (1776), available on the Adam Smith Institute website: http://www.adamsmith.org/ smith/won-b4-c2.htm.

47. Bellah, *The Broken Covenant*, 62. Also see Bellah, *Beyond Belief*, 15, and Marty, *Pilgrims*, 310, 412.

48. Mark Skousen, "The Making of Modern Economics" (Armonk, N.Y.: M. E. Sharpe, 2000).

49. Cotton Mather, A Christian At His Calling, available on the American Colonist's Library, http://home.wi.rr.com/rickgardiner/primarysources.htm.

50. Tillich, "Zwingli, Luther, Calvin, Predestination and Providence," in *A History of Christian Thought* http://www.religion-online.org/showchapter.asp?title=2310&C=2308.

Also see Bellah, *Beyond Belief*, 38–39, and Marty, *Pilgrims*, 309.

51. Bellah, *The Broken Covenant*, 62.

52. Ibid., 64. Also see Marty, *Pilgrims,* 60.

53. Marty, *Pilgrims,* 307–310.

54. Andrew Carnegie, "Dunfermline and America," from *Autobiography* (1920), chap. 2, http://www.wordowner.com/carnegie/chapter2.htm.

55. Andrew Carnegie, "Wealth," 1889, available on the Swarthmore College website, http://www.swarthmore.edu/SocSci/rbannis1/AIH19th/Carnegie.html.

56. Bellah, *The Broken Covenant,* 85,143.

57. Carnegie, *Autobiography,* chap. 11, http://www.wordowner.com/carnegie/chapter11.htm.

58. Tocqueville, *Democracy in America,* Book I, chap. 18.

59. Marty, *Pilgrims,* 169–187, 309. Also see Bellah, *The Broken Covenant,* 36–60, and Bellah, *Beyond Belief,* 182.

60. Marty, *Pilgrims,* 243–244.

61. Bellah, *The Broken Covenant,* 43. Also see University of Delaware, "Notable People," http://www.udel.edu/Archives/Archives/NotablePeople/alison.html.

62. Abraham Lincoln, speaking in Gettysburg, Pa., Nov. 19, 1863 http://www.yale.edu/lawweb/avalon/gettyb.htm.

63. Bellah, *Beyond Belief,* 178.

64. Robert N. Bellah, "Habits of the Heart:: Implications for Religion," lecture delivered at St. Mark's Catholic Church, Isla Vista, Calif., Feb. 21, 1986, http://www.robertbellah.com/lectures_5.htm.

65. President Woodrow Wilson, speaking to a joint session of Congress, April 2, 1917 http://www.firstworldwar.com/source/usawardeclaration.htm.
Also see Marty, *Pilgrims,* 361–364.

66. Franklin D. Roosevelt, State of the Union Address, Jan. 6, 1942, http://www.presidency.ucsb.edu/ws/index.php?pid=16253.
Also see Miller, *The First Liberty,* 1st ed., 275.

67. George W. Bush, 2005 Inaugural Address, http://www.whitehouse.gov/news/releases/2005/01/20050120-1.html.

68. Bellah, "Religion and the Legitimation of the American Republic" in *Varieties of Civil Religion,* ed. Robert Bellah and Phillip E. Hammond (New York: Harper & Row, 1980).

69. "No casualties? White House Disputes Robertson Comment," CNN.com, Oct. 21, 2004, http://www.cnn.com/2004/ALLPOLITICS/10/19/robertson.bush.iraq/.

70. Bellah, *Beyond Belief,* 176–179. Also see Marty, *Pilgrims,* 220–224.

71. Abraham Lincoln, Second Inaugural Address, March 4, 1865, http://www.yale.edu/lawweb/avalon/presiden/inaug/lincoln2.htm. Also see Marty, *Pilgrims,* 224.

72. Abraham Lincoln, at a speech in Chicago, Sept. 13, 1862; quoted by Jerald C. Brauer in *Protestantism in America: A Narrative History* (Philadelphia: Westminster Press, 1965), http://www.religion-online.org/showchapter.asp?title=1663&C=1666.

73. Marty, *Pilgrims,* 224.

74. Bellah, *The Broken Covenant,* 36–60.

75. Charles Haynes, "Understanding the Roots of Religious Liberty" (lecture presented at the FACS/Pew Journalism, Religion & Public Life seminar, "Reporting on Religious Liberty in America Today," Sept. 9, 2004, at the Freedom Forum headquarters, Arlington, Va.).

76. Bellah, *The Broken Covenant*, 139. Also see Marty, *Pilgrims*, 262.

77. Bellah, "Salvation and Success in America," in *The Broken Covenant*, 61-86.

78. Marty, *Pilgrims*, 258, 440. Also see Bellah, "The American Taboo on Socialism" in *The Broken Covenant*.

79. Martin Luther King Jr., "I Have a Dream" speech, Aug. 28, 1963, Washington, D.C. http://www.americanrhetoric.com/speeches/mlkihaveadream.htm.

80. David Howard-Pitney, "To Form a More Perfect Union: African Americans and American Civil Religion," in *New Day Begun: African American Churches and Civic Culture in Post-Civil Rights America*, ed. R. Drew Smith (Durham: Duke University Press, 2003), 89–112.

81. Barak Obama, *The Audacity of Hope: Thoughts on Reclaiming the American Dream* (New York: Random House, 2006), excerpted in *Time* magazine, Oct. 23, 2006, 56–60.

82. Marty, *Pilgrims*, 445–450.

83. See Samuel P. Huntington, "The Hispanic Challenge," *Foreign Policy* (March/April, 2004): "As their numbers increase, Mexican Americans feel increasingly comfortable with their own culture and often contemptuous of American culture. The persistence of Mexican immigration into the United States reduces the incentives for cultural assimilation. Mexican Americans no longer think of themselves as members of a small minority who must accommodate the dominant group and adopt its culture. As their numbers increase, they become more committed to their own ethnic identity and culture. Sustained numerical expansion promotes cultural consolidation and leads Mexican Americans not to minimize but to glory in the differences between their culture and U.S. culture."

84. Judy Gans, "The Economics of Immigration" (lecture presented at a Communications Institute journalism seminar, June 22, 2006, at the *Arizona Daily Star* in Tucson, Ariz.): http://analysisonline.org/immigration/gans.html.

Gans notes that many of the things being said about Latinos today were said at the turn of the last century about Italians—"that they were culturally and politically too different than traditional sources of American society. And today we have Judge Samuel Alito being criticized as one more white guy on the Supreme Court. . . . I think we've been here as a country before, and we don't have anything to worry about. There is more concern about immigrant incorporation than there needs to be."

85. Theodore Roosevelt, "The Square Deal in Americanism" in *The Great Adventure, The Works of Theodore Roosevelt. Memorial Edition*, vol. 21 (New York: Charles Scribner's Sons, 1923–26), 329. Also see Bellah, *The Broken Covenant*, 41.

86. Roosevelt, "The German Horror," in *The Great Adventure*, 329.

87. Gordon Hanson, "Examining the Economic Impacts of Immigration" (lecture presented at The National Symposium on Immigration, sponsored by The Communications Institute, Nov. 16, 2006, at the Arizona State Capitol): http://analysisonline.org/immigration/hanson.html.

88. Gans, "The Economics of Immigration."

89. Huntington, "The Hispanic Challenge," *Foreign Policy* (March/April, 2004), http://www.foreignpolicy.com/story/cms.php?story_id=2495&page=0.

Also see Miller, *The First Liberty*, 1st ed., 290.

90. Luis D. León, "César Chávez and Mexican American Civil Religion," in *Latino*

Religions and Civic Activism in the United States, ed. Gastón Espinosa, Virgilio Elizondo, and Jesse Miranda (New York: Oxford University Press, 2005), 53–63.

91. Gustavo Arellano, "The Protests of Allegiance," *Los Angeles Times*, March 28, 2006.

92. Bellah, *The Broken Covenant*, 104–105.

93. Susan Sontag, "What's Happening in America," *Partisan Review* (Winter 1967), 57. Also see Bellah in *The Broken Covenant*, 93, quoting Harold Cruse: "America is an unfinished nation—the product of a badly bungled process of inter-group cultural fusion. America is a nation that lies to itself about who and what it is. It is a nation of minorities ruled by a minority of one—it thinks and acts as if it were a nation of white Anglo-Saxon Protestants."

94. Bellah, *The Broken Covenant*, 104, 107. He continues, "For 50 years and more America's most established intellectuals, artists, and writers have been subjecting the narrower version of American character and values to devastating criticism. . . . In the last ten years or so this criticism has begun to disaffect a whole generation. Students in many American universities have begun not only to believe what many of their professors have long been saying but to act on that belief with a single-minded rigor that has often appalled their teachers. They have frequently displayed a moralistic self-righteousness and a personal vulgarity that makes one wonder whether they are criticizing American character or exemplifying it at its worst." Also see Marty on "Anglo-Saxons" in *Pilgrims*, 338–339, 391, 425, 435.

95. Theodore Roosevelt, to President of the American Defense Society, Jan. 3, 1919, in *The Works of Theodore Roosevelt, Memorial Edition*, vol. 24: 554. Roosevelt's full quote in context: "There can be no divided allegiance here. We have room for but one language here, and that is the English language, for we intend to see that the crucible turns our people out as Americans, of American nationality, and not as dwellers in a polyglot boarding-house; and we have room for but one soul loyalty, and that is loyalty to the American people."

96. Roosevelt, *The Great Adventure*, 326.

97. Huntington, "The Hispanic Challenge."

98. Yehudah Mirsky, "Civil Religion and the Establishment Clause," *Yale Law Journal* 95 (May 1986), 1252.

99. Justice Anthony Kennedy, writing for the Court in *Lee v. Weisman*, 505 U.S.. 577 (1992).

100. Ibid.

101. Justice Sandra Day O'Connor, concurring in *Elk Grove Unified School Dist. v. Newdow*, 542 U.S. 1 (2004).

102. David Limbaugh, *Persecution: How Liberals Are Waging War against Christianity* (Washington, D.C.: Regnery, 2003), 235.

103. *Newdow v. U.S. Congress*, first amended complaint (filed in the U.S. District Court, Eastern District of California, April, 2005) 145, http://www.restorethepledge .com/.

104. Louis C. Rabaut, statement in sponsorship of a resolution to amend the Pledge of Allegiance, *100 Cong. Rec. 17*, appendix (April 1, 1954), A2515–16.

105. Thomas A. Burke, in support of a resolution to amend the Pledge of Allegiance, 83rd Congress, 2nd sess, *100 Cong. Rec. 7* (June 22, 1954), 8,563.

106. Rabaut, *100 Cong. Rec. 17*, appendix (April 1, 1954), A2515–16.

107. *Newdow v. U.S. Congress*, 115.

108. Brief filed on behalf of defendants in *Roechild and Jan Roe v. Rio Union School District*, U.S. Court of Appeals, Ninth Circuit (June 1, 2006), 25.

109. "Battle over God in U.S. History Class," *San Francisco Chronicle*, Dec. 8, 2004.

110. Mirsky, "Civil Religion and the Establishment Clause," 1257.

111. Justice Potter Stewart concurring in *Jacobellis v. Ohio*, 378 U.S. 184 (1964).

112. Tocqueville, *Democracy in America*, Book I, chap. 18.

113. Bellah, "Habits of the Heart: Implications for Religion."

114. John Landis, "The Sprawling California Dream" (lecture, May 18, 2001, Santa Rosa, Calif.): http://www.facsnet.org/tools/env_luse/landis.php.

115. Mirsky, "Civil Religion and the Establishment Clause," 1237.

116. Ryan J. Dowd, "In a Monotheistic Non-Sectarian Civic Deity We Trust: The Establishment Clause of the First Amendment and Governmentally Created American Civil Religion," *Journal of the DuPage County Bar Assn.* (2002), http://www.dcba.org/brief/novissue/2002/art41102.htm.

117. C. Welton Gaddy, "God Talk in the Public Square," in *Quoting God: How Media Shape Ideas about Religion and Culture*, ed. Claire H. Badaracco (Waco: Baylor University Press, 2005), 50.

118. Ibid., 56.

119. Ibid., 43.

120. George W. Bush, State of the Union Address, Jan. 29, 2002, http://www.whitehouse.gov/news/releases/2002/01/20020129-11.html.

121. George W. Bush, speaking to U.S. troops, Feb. 16, 2002, in Anchorage, Alaska, http://www.whitehouse.gov/news/releases/2002/02/20020216-1.html.

122. George W. Bush, speaking at the National Prayer Breakfast, Feb. 7, 2002, Washington, D.C., http://www.whitehouse.gov/news/releases/2002/02/20020207-1.html.

123. George W. Bush, speaking at the 20th anniversary of the National Endowment for Democracy, Nov. 6, 2003, at the United States Chamber of Commerce, Washington, D.C. http://www.whitehouse.gov/news/releases/2003/11/20031106-2.html.

124. Michael Gerson, "Religion, Rhetoric, and the Presidency" (lecture presented at the Ethics and Public Policy Center semi-annual conference on religion and public life, Dec. 6, 2004, at the Pier House in Key West, Fla.), http://www.eppc.org/publications/pubID.2237/pub_detail.asp.

125. Bellah, *The Broken Covenant*, 172, 183–184. He further states: "America [at its founding] was not simply a neutral legal state within which the individual could rationally pursue his self-interest. . . . Among the majority population self-interest was intertwined with idealism in deep and complex ways. . . . But the meaning of the American experience will remain forever opaque to those who, once they see through the most simple-minded version of American idealism, can find only violence and self-interest in its stead."

126. Edward Gibbon, *The History of the Decline and Fall of the Roman Empire* (1776), vol. 1, chap. 1, http://www.ccel.org/g/gibbon/decline/volume1/chap1.htm#INT.

Gibbon continues, "The fidelity of the citizens to each other and to the state was confirmed by the habits of education and the prejudices of religion. Honour, as well as virtue, was the principle of the republic; the ambitious citizens laboured to deserve the solemn glories of a triumph; and the ardour of the Roman youth was kindled into active emulation as often as they beheld the domestic images of their ancestors."

127. Bellah, *The Broken Covenant*, 22, 23

128. John Winthrop, "A Model of Christian Charity." The quote in the text is condensed and paraphrased from this passage, "If we shall deal falsely with our God in this work we have undertaken, and so cause Him to withdraw His present help from us, we shall be made a story and a by-word through the world. We shall open the mouths of enemies to speak evil of the ways of God, and all professors for God's sake. We shall shame the faces of many of God's worthy servants, and cause their prayers to be turned into curses upon us till we be consumed out of the good land whither we are going."

129. Bellah, "Nativism and Cultural Pluralism in America," in *The Broken Covenant*.

130. Bellah, *The Broken Covenant*, 151, 153, 162.

Chapter 4. Finding the Common Threads of Religious Liberty

1. Charles C. Haynes, "The Foundations of Religious Liberty" (lecture presented at the FACS/Pew Journalism, Religion & Public Life seminar, "One Nation Under God: Political and Religious Dimensions of America," Sept. 4, 2003, Crowne Plaza Hotel, Seattle, Wash.); and, Charles Haynes, "Understanding the Roots of Religious Liberty" (lecture presented at the FACS/Pew Journalism, Religion & Public Life seminar, "Reporting on Religious Liberty in America Today," Sept. 9, 2004, at the Freedom Forum headquarters, Arlington, Va.). Dr. Haynes is quoted and paraphrased throughout this chapter, drawing from these two lectures on the same topic.

2. William Lee Miller, *The First Liberty: America's Foundation in Religious Freedom, Expanded and Updated* (Washington, D.C.: Georgetown University Press, 2003), 130–137. Also see Martin E. Marty, *Pilgrims in Their Own Land: 500 Years of Religion in America* (New York: Penguin Books, 1984), 75–89.

3. Robert N. Bellah, *The Broken Covenant: American Civil Religion in Time of Trial* (Chicago: University of Chicago Press, 1992), 13–16. Also see Miller, *The First Liberty*, rev. ed., 135.

4. John Winthrop, "A Model of Christian Charity," sermon delivered in 1630 on board the ship *Arbella*. Available via the Hanover College Historical Texts Project, http://history.hanover.edu/texts/winthmod.html.

5. Bellah, *The Broken Covenant*, 1–35.

6. Paul Tillich, "Zwingli, Luther, Calvin, Predestination and Providence," in *A History of Christian Thought*, ed. C. E. Braaten (New York: Simon and Schuster, 1972). Also see Marty, *Pilgrims*, 111.

7. John Calvin, "The Righteousness of Works Improperly Inferred from Rewards," *Institutes of the Christian Religion*, Book 3, chap. 18, translated by Henry Beveridge, Esq. (London: Arnold Hatfield and Bonham Norton, 1599): "But though it is by mercy alone that God admits his people to life, yet as he leads them into possession of it by the course of good works, that he may complete his work in them in the order which he has destined." Available online at the Center for Reformed Theology and Apologetics website: http://www.reformed.org/master/index.html?mainframe=/books/institutes/.

8. Calvin, "Of the Last Resurrection," in *Institutes*, Book 3, chap. 25: "We who have

received the first-fruits of the Spirit may be ashamed to grovel in our corruption, instead of at least imitating the inanimate elements which are bearing the punishment of another's sin."

9. Marty, *Pilgrims*, 75–78. Also see Miller, *The First Liberty*, rev. ed., 133.

10. William Lee Miller, *The First Liberty: Religion and the American Republic* (Paragon House, 1985), 280; and rev. ed., 134–135.

11. Also see Miller, *The First Liberty*, rev. ed., 158.

12. Edward Gibbon, *The History of the Decline and Fall of the Roman Empire* (1776), vol. 2, chap. 21, Part I: "The Edict of Milan, the great charter of toleration, had confirmed to each individual of the Roman world the privilege of choosing and professing his own religion. But this inestimable privilege was soon violated; with the knowledge of truth, the emperor imbibed the maxims of persecution; and the sects which dissented from the Catholic Church were afflicted and oppressed by the triumph of Christianity." http://www.worldwideschool.org/library/books/hst/roman/TheDeclineandFallofThe RomanEmpire-2/chap26.html.

13. Also see Marty, *Pilgrims*, 75–89; and Miller, *The First Liberty*, rev. ed., 145–147, 162.

14. Miller, *The First Liberty*, rev. ed., 139.

15. Roger Williams, "The Bloody Tenant of Persecution" (1644), http://www.constitution.org/bcp/religlib.htm#001.

16. Miller, *The First Liberty*, rev. ed., 155–156, 141.

17. Miller, *The First Liberty*, 1st ed., 272–280.

18. Ibid., 153, 165, 167–168.

19. Also see Miller, *The First Liberty*, rev. ed., 137, 161.

20. Ibid., 147, 158.

21. Marty, *Pilgrims*, 78.

22. Miller, *The First Liberty*, 1st ed., 156.

23. Marty, *Pilgrims*, 77. Also see Miller, *The First Liberty*, rev. ed., 148, 175.

24. Miller, *The First Liberty*, rev. ed., 58, 175–180. Also see Marty, *Pilgrims*, 150–154.

25. Thomas Jefferson, *Virginia Statute of Religious Freedom* (1786), http://religious freedom.lib.virginia.edu/sacred/vaact.html.

26. Miller, *The First Liberty*, rev. ed., 51, 56.

27. Ibid., 129.

28. George W. Bush, State of the Union Address, Feb. 2, 2005, http://www.white house.gov/news/releases/2005/02/20050202-11.html.

Bill Clinton, acceptance speech at the Democratic National Convention, July 16 1992, http://www.presidency.ucsb.edu/shownomination.php?convid=7.

Ronald Reagan, Farewell Address to the Nation, Jan. 11, 1989, http://www.ronald reagan.com/sp_21.html.

29. Bellah, *The Broken Covenant*, 87–111.

30. Bellah, "Imperialism, American Style," *Christian Century* (March 8, 2003), 20–25.

31. Miller, *The First Liberty*, rev. ed., 180–182.

32. Marty, *Pilgrims*, 160, 181, 293.

33. Miller, *The First Liberty*, rev. ed., 182.

34. *Famous American Trials: Salem Witchcraft Trials, 1692*, University of Missouri–

Kansas City School of Law: http://www.law.umkc.edu/faculty/projects/ftrials/salem/
SALEM.HTM.

35. Increase Mather, "Cases of Conscience Concerning Evil Spirits Personat-
ing Men" (Boston: Benjamin Harris, 1693), available on the University of Virginia
Documentary Archive and Transcription Project: http://etext.lib.virginia.edu/salem/
witchcraft/speccol/mather/.

36. Miller, *The First Liberty*, rev. ed., 129.

37. Also see Calvin, "Every Thing Proceeding from the Corrupt Nature of Man
Damnable," in *Institutes*, Book 2, chap. 3: "You see that he [the Apostle Paul] places
unlawful and depraved desires not in the sensual part merely, but in the mind itself,
and therefore requires that it should be renewed. Indeed, he had a little before drawn a
picture of human nature, which shows that there is no part in which it is not perverted
and corrupted."

38. Sydney E. Ahlstrom, "Theology in America: A Historical Survey," in *The Shaping of American Religion*, ed. James Ward Smith and A. Leland Jamison (Princeton:
Princeton University Press, 1961), 279: "Their [Puritans'] principles were to become
long-lasting emphases in American church-life and theology not only because they
were so effectively institutionalized in a region destined to wield major influence in a
growing nation; but because, in a somewhat modified form, they were also perpetuated
by contemporary Anglicans, Presbyterians, Baptists, and even Quakers. They would
become part of the westward-surging Methodist tide and make their way, as well, into
many communions of continental heritage."

39. Marty, *Pilgrims*, 84, 140–146, 272–273. Also see Miller, *The First Liberty*, 1st ed.,
276, 281–291.

40. "Falwell: I Blew It," CBS News, Sept. 18, 2001, http://www.cbsnews.com/stories/
2001/09/18/archive/main311660.shtml.

41. Bellah, *The Broken Covenant*, 52–55.

42. *Newdow v. U.S. Congress*, first amended complaint (filed in the U.S. District
Court, Eastern District of California, April, 2005). Available on Michael Newdow's website: http://www.restorethepledge.com/.

43. Roy Moore, transcript of speech at dedication of monument, 2001, WSFA TV,
Montgomery, Ala. http://www.wsfa.com/Global/story.asp?S=1056322.

44. George Washington, Farewell Address, 1796, available on Yale Law School's
Avalon Project site, http://www.yale.edu/lawweb/avalon/washing.htm.

45. The Foundation for Moral Law site provides transcriptions of the monument:
http://www.morallaw.org/Monument.htm.

46. Miller, *The First Liberty*, 1st ed., 234–246.

47. Ibid., 236.

48. Ibid., 227. Also see rev. ed., 141, 145, 150.

49. Marty, *Pilgrims*, 77. Also see Miller, *The First Liberty*, rev. ed., 137.

50. Marty, *Pilgrims*, 69, 146–148. Also see Miller, *The First Liberty*, 1st ed., 275; and
rev. ed., 165–167.

51. Miller, *The First Liberty*, 1st ed., 274–279. Also see Marty, *Pilgrims*, 185, 287.

52. Miller, *The First Liberty*, rev. ed., 170–171.

53. Lord Kinross, *The Ottoman Centuries: The Rise and Fall of the Turkish Empire*
(New York: William Morrow, 1977), 346.

54. John Locke, "A Letter Concerning Toleration," (1689), http://www.constitution
.org/jl/tolerati.htm.
Also see Miller, *The First Liberty*, rev. ed., 171.

55. "Lawmaker Won't Apologize for 'Islamophobic' Letter," CNN.com, Dec. 21, 2006,
http://www.cnn.com/2006/POLITICS/12/20/lawmaker.koran/.

56. "Dubai Firm to Sell U.S. Port Operations," *Washington Post*, March 10, 2006.

57. "UAE Company Seeks to Avert Conflict with Congress," CNN.com, Feb. 26,
2006, http://www.cnn.com/2006/POLITICS/02/26/ports.dubai/index.html.

58. "Baker Road Residents Take up Sides on Proposed Mosque," *Katy Times*, March
14, 2007, http://www.katytimes.com/articles/2006/12/04/news/01news.txt.

59. Miller, *The First Liberty*, rev. ed., 253. Also see Robert Bellah, "Islamic Tradition and the Problems of Modernization," in *Beyond Belief: Essays on Religion in a Post-
Traditionalist World* (Berkeley: University of California Press, 1970), 146–166.

60. Robert N. Bellah, Richard Madsen, William M. Sullivan, Ann Swidler, and
Steven M. Tipton, *Habits of the Heart: Individualism and Commitment in American Life*
(Berkeley: University of California Press, 1985), 32–33. Also see Miller, *The First Liberty*,
1st ed., 236–244.

61. Bellah, *The Broken Covenant*, 104, 107. Also see Martin E. Marty with Jonathan
Moore, *Education, Religion, and the Common Good: Advancing a Distinctively American
Conversation about Religion's Role in Our Shared Life* (San Francisco: Jossey-Bass, 2000),
103, 134, and Joseph G. Kronick, "Writing American: Between Canon and Literature,"
New Centennial Review 1, no. 3 (Winter 2001): 37–66.

62. See University of California, Santa Barbara's American History and Institutions
Requirement: http://www.advising.ltsc.ucsb.edu/graduation/ahireq.php; http://www
.advising.ltsc.ucsb.edu/graduation/ahir.php; and the "Ethnicity Requirement" and "European Traditions": http://www.advising.ltsc.ucsb.edu/graduation/ge.php.

63. Miller, *The First Liberty*, 1st ed., 347–348: "And just who was this Thomas
Jefferson to talk about Truth being mighty and prevailing and all of that? A Virginia
aristocrat. An owner of slaves. A *white Anglo-Saxon male* with a big house on a hill and
acres and acres of Virginia land. A strictly eighteenth century mind. Truth, said to be
sufficient against all the winds of doctrine, becomes another breeze among them, and,
after all, how to you know which is which? And above all, who is to say?"

Chapter 5. Religious Liberty in Public Schools

1. *Zelman v. Simmons-Harris*, 536 U.S. 639 (2002).

2. *Good News Club v. Milford Central School*, 533 U.S. 98 (2001. *Board of Education of
Westside Community Schools v. Mergens*, (1990) 496 U.S. 226. Also see *Prince v. Jacoby*,
No. 99–35490 (U.S. District Court for the Western District of Washington, 2002): http://
www.ca9.uscourts.gov/ca9/newopinions.nsf/8407B7C60D0F634D88256C2F005AB250/
$file/9935490.pdf?openelement.

3. *Santa Fe Independent School District v. Doe*, 530 U.S. 290 (2000).

4. *Lee v. Weisman*, 505 U.S. 577 (1992).

5. *Edwards v. Aguillard*, 482 U.S. 578 (1987).

6. Martin E. Marty with Jonathan Moore, *Education, Religion, and the Common*

Good: Advancing a Distinctively American Conversation about Religion's Role in Our Shared Life (San Francisco: Jossey-Bass, 2000), 23.

7. *School District of Abington Township, Pennsylvania v. Schempp*, 374 U.S. 203 (1963).

8. Charles C. Haynes, "Church and State and the First Amendment" (lecture presented at the FACS/Pew Journalism, Religion & Public Life seminar, "One Nation Under God: Political and Religious Dimensions of America," Sept. 23, 2002, at the *Indianapolis Star*), http://www.facsnet.org/issues/faith/haynes_indy.php#public.

Also see Charles C. Haynes and Oliver Thomas, *Finding Common Ground: A Guide to Religious Liberty in Public Schools* (Nashville, Tenn.: The First Amendment Center, 2001), 5, 34.

9. Marty, *Education, Religion, and the Common Good*, 43–44.

10. *Lemon v. Kurtzman*, 403 U.S. 602 (1971).

11. Oliver Thomas, "Church and State: The Legal Framework" (lecture presented at a FACS/Pew Journalism, Religion & Public Life seminar entitled, "Church and State: Religious Liberty and Public Schools," Oct. 15, 2002, at the *Pittsburgh Post-Gazette*, Pittsburgh, Pa.), http://www.facsnet.org/issues/faith/thomas.php.

12. Justice Sandra Day O'Connor, concurring in *County of Allegheny v. American Civil Liberties Union*, 492 U.S. 573 (1989).

13. Justice Anthony Kennedy, writing for the Court in *Lee v. Weisman*, 505 U.S. 577 (1992).

14. *Engel v. Vitale*, 370 U.S. 421 (1962). *School District of Abington Township, Pennsylvania v. Schempp* (1963).

15. Marty, *Education, Religion, and the Common Good*, 38.

16. Charles Haynes, "Religious Liberty and Public Schools" (lecture presented at a FACS/Pew Journalism, Religion & Public Life seminar entitled, "Church and State: Religious Liberty and Public Schools," Oct. 15, 2002, at the *Pittsburgh Post-Gazette*, Pittsburgh, Pa.) http://www.facsnet.org/issues/faith/haynes_pittsburgh.php#modern.

17. William Lee Miller, *The First Liberty: America's Foundation in Religious Freedom, Expanded and Updated* (Washington, D.C.: Georgetown University Press, 2003), 199.

18. Justice Hugo Black, writing the opinion of the Court in *McCollum v. Board of Education*, 333 U.S. 203 (1948).

19. *West Virginia State Board of Education v. Barnette*, 319 U.S. 624 (1943). Also see Miller, *The First Liberty*, 213.

20. Haynes, "Church and State and the First Amendment."

21. Haynes and Thomas, *Finding Common Ground*, 34–35.

22. *Tinker v. Des Moines Independent Community School District*, 393 U.S. 503 (1969).

23. Charles C. Haynes, Sam Chaltain, John E. Ferguson Jr., David L. Hudson Jr., and Oliver Thomas, *The First Amendment in Schools* (Nashville: The First Amendment Center, 2003), 59–68, 92–104. http://www.firstamendmentschools.org/resources/publications.aspx.

Also see Haynes and Thomas, *Finding Common Ground*, 49–58, 81–82.

24. *Board of Education of Westside Community Schools v. Mergens*, 496 U.S. 226 (1990). Also see Haynes et al., *The First Amendment in Schools*, 87–89.

25. Samuel Alito, dissenting in *C.H. v. Oliva*, No. 98–5061 (U.S. Court of Ap-

peals for the Third Circuit, 2000), http://caselaw.lp.findlaw.com/cgi-bin/getcase.pl?
court=3rd&navby=case&no=985061.

26. *West's Encyclopedia of American Law* defines Strict Scrutiny as follows: "A standard of judicial review for a challenged policy in which the court presumes the policy to be invalid unless the government can demonstrate a compelling interest to justify the policy. . . . Once a court determines that strict scrutiny must be applied, it is presumed that the law or policy is unconstitutional. The government has the burden of proving that its challenged policy is constitutional. To withstand strict scrutiny, the government must show that its policy is necessary to achieve a compelling state interest. If this is proved, the state must then demonstrate that the legislation is narrowly tailored to achieve the intended result." http://www.answers.com/topic/strict-scrutiny.

27. Haynes and Thomas, *Finding Common Ground*, 50. Also see Haynes et al., *The First Amendment in Schools*, 37, 42.

28. Haynes et al., *The First Amendment in Schools*, 42, 70.

29. Alito, *C.H. v. Oliva*. Also see *Settle v. Dickson County School Board*, 53 F.3d 152 (6th Cir. 1995): "Federal courts should exercise particular restraint in classroom conflicts between student and teacher over matters falling within the ordinary authority over curriculum and course content." Summary: http://www.firstamendmentschools .org/freedoms/case.aspx?id=1678.

30. *DeNooyer v. Livonia Public Schools*, U.S. App. LEXIS 30084 (6th Cir. 1993). Summary: http://www.firstamendmentschools.org/freedoms/case.aspx?id=1677.

31. Haynes et al., *The First Amendment in Schools*, 47–49.

32. *Everson v. Board of Education of the Township of Ewing*, 330 U.S. 1 (1947). Also see Miller, *The First Liberty*, 192–197.

33. Quoted in Fielding Buck, "A Backgrounder on School Vouchers," Oct. 30, 2002, FACSNET, http://www.facsnet.org/issues/faith/vouchers_pittsburgh.php.

34. Ibid.

35. Haynes, "Church and State and the First Amendment."

36. "Tennessee v. John Scopes: The Monkey Trial (1927)," from *Famous Trials in American History*, University of Missouri–Kansas City School of Law, http://www.law .umkc.edu/faculty/projects/ftrials/scopes/scopes.htm.

37. "Judge Rejects Teaching Intelligent Design," *New York Times*, Dec. 21, 2005.

38. "Judge Nixes Evolution Textbook Stickers: Disclaimer Questioning Theory Ruled Unconstitutional," Associated Press, Jan. 13, 2005, http://www.msnbc.msn.com/id/ 6822028/.

39. "Kansas School Board Redefines Science," Nov. 8, 2005, CNN.com, http://www .cnn.com/2005/EDUCATION/11/08/evolution.debate.ap/.

40. Judge John E. Jones III, *Tammy Kitzmiller v. Dover Area School District*, 04cv2688 (U.S. District Court for the Middle District of Pennsylvania, 2005), http://www.pamd .uscourts.gov/kitzmiller/kitzmiller_342.pdf.

41. Kansas Science Education Standards, approved Nov. 8, 2005: http://www.ksde .org/LinkClick.aspx?link=Standards%20Documents/Science/sciencestd.pdf&tabid=144 and http://www.ksde.org/Default.aspx?tabid=144.

42. Kansas State Board of Education Meeting Minutes, Nov. 8, 2005: http://www .ksde.org/LinkClick.aspx?fileticket=WP1mkErsRxY%3d&tabid=63&mid=405.

43. Kansas Science Education Standards, revised Jan. 22, 2007: http://www.ksde

.org/LinkClick.aspx?fileticket=djOUn3F9d9k%3D&tabid=144 and http://www.ksde.org/ LinkClick.aspx?fileticket=gSI1ztoxcRc%3D&tabid=144.

44. Kansas State Board of Education Meeting Minutes, Feb. 13, 2007: http://www .ksde.org/LinkClick.aspx?fileticket=Zu6QQxNfHzo%3d&tabid=63&mid=405.

45. *Wallace v. Jaffree*, 472 U.S. 38 (1985).Also see Haynes et al., *The First Amendment in Schools*, 44, 132.

46. Haynes and Thomas, *Finding Common Ground*, 55. Also see Haynes et al., *The First Amendment in Schools*, 67–68, 126–127, and Justice Abe Fortas, writing for the Court in *Tinker v. Des Moines Independent Community School District*.

47. Haynes et al., *The First Amendment in Schools*, 75–78.

48. Marty, *Education, Religion, and the Common Good*, 61, 136.

49. Charles Haynes, "Religious Liberty and Public Schools," http://www.facsnet.org/ issues/faith/haynes_pittsburgh.php#modern.

50. Marty, *Education, Religion, and the Common Good*, 28, 45–46.

51. Ibid., 139.

52. Ibid., 23, 27. Also see Haynes and Thomas, *Finding Common Ground*, 6–8.

53. Miller, *The First Liberty*, 202.

54. "Battle over God in U.S. History Class," *San Francisco Chronicle*, Dec. 8, 2004.

55. Marty, *Education, Religion, and the Common Good*, 46.

56. Haynes and Thomas, *Finding Common Ground*, 90.

Chapter 6. Transforming Lives and Transforming Government: Faith-Based Initiatives

1. The White House, "Fact Sheet: Compassion in Action: Producing Real Results for Americans Most in Need," March 1, 2005, http://www.whitehouse.gov/news/releases/ 2005/03/20050301–1.html.

2. Ram A. Cnaan, "The Invisible Caring Hand: An Overview of Religion and Social Welfare" (lecture presented at the FACS/Pew Journalism, Religion & Public Life seminar, entitled "Church & State: The Future of Faith-Based Initiatives," Feb. 3, 2003, at the *Orlando Sentinel* in Orlando, Fla.). Dr. Cnaan is quoted and paraphrased throughout this chapter, drawing from this lecture.

3. The White House, "President Discusses Compassionate Conservative Agenda in Dallas," Aug. 3, 2004, http://www.whitehouse.gov/news/releases/2004/08/20040803–11 .html.

4. Anne Farris, Richard P. Nathan, and David J. Wright, "The Expanding Administrative Presidency: George W. Bush and the Faith-Based Initiative," the Roundtable on Religion and Social Welfare Policy, 2004, http://www.religionandsocialpolicy.org/publi cations/publication.cfm?id=64.

5. Alexis de Tocqueville, "How the Americans Combat Individualism by the Principle of Self-Interest Rightly Understood," in *Democracy in America* (1835), Book 2, chap. 8. Available on the University of Virginia online library: http://xroads.virginia .edu/%7EHYPER/DETOC/1_ch18.htm.

6. Ram A. Cnaan with Robert J. Wineburg and Stephanie C. Boddie, *The Newer Deal: Social Work and Religion in Partnership* (New York: Columbia University Press, 1999), 158.

7. *Nonprofit Almanac 2007*, National Center for Charitable Statistics at the Urban Institute, http://www.urban.org/UploadedPDF/311373_nonprofit_sector.pdf.

8. Jim Castelli and John D. McCarthy, "Religion-Sponsored Social Services: The Not-So-Independent Sector," Aspen Institute Nonprofit Sector Research Fund, March 1998.

http://members.aol.com/jimcast/id6.htm.

Also see Cnaan, *The Newer Deal*, 12, 181.

9. *The New Nonprofit Almanac 2001: Facts and Figures on the Independent Sector* (Washington, D.C.: The Independent Sector, 2001), http://www.independentsector.org/PDFs/inbrief.pdf.

Also see Cnaan, *The Newer Deal*, 158–159.

10. Robert V. Kemper and Julie Adkins, *The World as It Should Be: Faith-Based Community Development in America* (Santa Fe, N.M.: School of American Research Press, 2005), http://faculty.smu.edu/rkemper/Faith-based_community_development.htm.

11. "Faith and Philanthropy: The Connection between Charitable Behavior and Giving to Religion" (Washington, D.C.: The Independent Sector, 2002), http://www.independentsector.org/PDFs/faithphil.pdf.

12. Mark Chaves, *Congregations in America* (Cambridge: Harvard University Press, 2004), chap. 3.

13. Cnaan, *The Newer Deal*, 301, "More than 50 percent of the budgets of Catholic Charities, Jewish Family and Children's Services and Lutheran Social Ministries, to name just a few agencies, comes from public coffers."

14. The White House, "Executive Order: Establishment of White House Office of Faith-Based and Community Initiatives," Jan. 29, 2001, http://www.whitehouse.gov/news/releases/2001/01/20010129-2.html.

15. The White House, "Unlevel Playing Field: Barriers to Participation by Faith-Based and Community Organizations in Federal Social Service Programs," August, 2001, http://www.whitehouse.gov/news/releases/2001/08/20010816-3-report.pdf.

16. Also see Cnaan, *The Newer Deal*, 19, 281, 291, and 308: "If voluntary organizations are pressured by the government, either directly or indirectly, to do something beyond their missions, then these organizations are no longer voluntary."

17. The White House "Executive Orders Issued by President George W. Bush," http://www.whitehouse.gov/news/orders/.

18. Anne Farris, "The Tale of Two HR 7s," The Roundtable on Religion and Social Welfare Policy, Oct. 7, 2003, http://www.religionandsocialpolicy.org/news/article.cfm?id=952.

19. The White House, "President's Remarks at Faith-Based and Community Initiatives Conference, Los Angeles Convention Center," March 3, 2004, http://www.whitehouse.gov/news/releases/2004/03/20040303-13.html.

20. Farris, Nathan, and Wright, "The Expanding Administrative Presidency."

21. The White House, "Charitable Choice: The Facts," http://www.whitehouse.gov/government/fbci/guidance/charitable.html.

22. The White House, "President Discusses Faith-Based Initiative at Power Center Celebration," Sept. 12, 2003, Houston, Tex., http://www.whitehouse.gov/news/releases/2003/09/20030912-14.html.

23. Substance Abuse & Mental Health Services Administration (SAMHSA), "The

Matrix Priority Programs: Addressing Unmet and Emerging Needs," http://www
.samhsa.gov/Matrix/brochure.aspx.

24. SoberRecovery, "Alcoholism Addiction and Mental Health Help Addiction
Treatment Information and Support, Faith-Based Treatment," http://www.soberrecovery
.com/links/faithbasedtreatment.html.

25. Robert J. Wineburg, *A Limited Partnership: The Politics of Religion, Welfare, and
Social Service* (New York: Columbia University Press, 2001), 76–77.

26. The Association of Gospel Rescue Missions, "Substance Abuse and Welfare Reform," http://www.agrm.org/welfare/drugs.html.

27. Ray Davies, "20th Century Man" (Davray Music Ltd., 1971): "I was born in a
welfare state/ Ruled by bureaucracy/ Controlled by civil servants/ And people dressed
in grey/ Got no privacy, got no liberty/ 'Cos the twentieth century people/ Took it all
away from me." http://kinks.it.rit.edu/discography/showsong.php?song=415.

28. Cnaan *The Newer Deal*, 10, 297.

29. Marvin Olasky, *The Tragedy of American Compassion* (Washington, D.C.:
Regnery, 1992), chap. 12. Also see Cnaan *The Newer Deal*, 9.

30. Farris, Nathan, and Wright, "The Expanding Administrative Presidency," 6.

31. Steven Rathgeb Smith, John P. Bartkowski, and Susan Grettenberger, *Comparative Views on the Role and Effect of Faith in Social Services* (The Roundtable on Religion
and Social Welfare Policy, 2006), 6: "Overall, our findings run counter to the prevailing
image employed in many discussions of faith-based and secular organizations—an image
of two types of organizations operating in distinctly separate organizational fields. . . . In
sometimes surprising ways, faith-based organizations with quite different levels of faith
integration share important commonalities with secular service agencies."
http://www.religionandsocialpolicy.org/publications/publication.cfm?id=85.

32. Cnaan, "The Invisible Caring Hand: An Overview of Religion and Social Welfare," http://www.facsnet.org/issues/faith/faith-based1.htm#lives.
Also see Cnaan *The Newer Deal*, 160.

33. The White House, "Executive Order: Equal Protection of the Laws for Faith-
based and Community Organizations," Dec. 12, 2002, http://www.whitehouse.gov/news/
releases/2002/12/20021212-6.html.

34. Ira C. Lupu and Robert W. Tuttle, "Developments in the Faith-Based and Community Initiatives: Comments on Notices of Proposed Rulemaking and Guidance Document," Jan. 9, 2003, The Roundtable on Religion and Social Welfare Policy, http://www
.religionandsocialpolicy.org/publications/publication.cfm?id=24.
This report is quoted throughout the rest of this section.

35. *American Jewish Congress v. Corporation for National and Community Service*, 04–
5817 (D.C. Cir, 2005), http://pacer.cadc.uscourts.gov/docs/common/opinions/200503/
04-5317a.pdf.

36. "Supreme Court Rejects Appeal: Ruling Stands Allowing Use of Public
Funds for Teachers in Religious Schools," The Roundtable on Religion and Social
Welfare Policy, Jan.10, 2006, http://www.religionandsocialpolicy.org/news/article.cfm?
id=3720&sublevel=3.

37. The White House, "Executive Order: Equal Protection of the Laws for Faith-
based and Community Organizations," Dec. 12, 2002.

38. Cnaan *The Newer Deal*, 10, 300.

39. See the Roundtable on Religion and Social Welfare Policy legal publications index: http://www.religionandsocialpolicy.org/publications/index.cfm?PubCat=2

40. *Americans United for Separation of Church & State v. Prison Fellowship Ministries*, 4:03-cv-90074 (U.S. Southern District Iowa, 2006): http://www.iasd.uscourts.gov/iasd/opinions.nsf/55fa4cbb8063b06c862568620076059d/f0e6eb32c02590a786257184006464d5/$FILE/Americans%206-2-06.pdf.

41. Ira C. Lupu and Robert W. Tuttle, *State of the Law 2006: Legal Developments Affecting Government Partnerships with Faith-Based Organizations* (Albany, N.Y.: The Roundtable on Religion and Social Welfare Policy, 2006), 12.

42. *Jay F. Hein, White House Office of Faith-Based and Community Initiatives v. Freedom From Religion Foundation* (Sup. Ct., No. 06-157), 2007. This case was originally filed as *Freedom from Religion Foundation v. Jim Towey, Director of White House Office of Faith-Based and Community Initiatives* (U.S. District Court, Western District of Wisconsin, June, 2004). See excerpt from the original complaint: "The preferences for and endorsements of faith-based organizations by the defendants, as preferred providers of social services funded with federal taxpayer appropriations, belie the claim that defendants are trying to level the playing field for access to federal funds by faith-based organizations. Defendants' actions include the funded support of national and regional conferences, at which faith-based organizations are singled out as particularly worthy of federal funding because of their religious orientation, and the belief in God is extolled as distinguishing the claimed effectiveness of faith-based social services." http://ffrf.org/legal/faithbased_complaint.html.

43. U.S. Const. art. III, s. 2, cl. 1 defines the parties subject to the jurisdiction of the federal judiciary as limited "to controversies to which the United States shall be a party; to controversies between two or more states, between a state and Citizens of another state, between Citizens of different states, between Citizens of the same state, claiming lands under grants of different states, and between a state, or the Citizens thereof, and foreign states, Citizens or subjects." See the full article on the Yale Law School website, http://www.yale.edu/lawweb/avalon/art3.htm.

44. Souter continued, "The importance of . . . injuries alleged in Establishment Clause challenges to federal spending . . . has deep historical roots going back to the ideal of religious liberty in James Madison's 'Memorial and Remonstrance Against Religious Assessments,' that the government of a free society may not 'force a citizen to contribute three pence only of his property for the support of any one establishment' of religion." See the full text of Madison's "Memorial and Remonstrance": http://religiousfreedom.lib.virginia.edu/sacred/madison_m&r_1785.html.

45. "U.S. Not Winning War in Iraq, Bush Says for First Time," *Washington Post*, Dec. 20, 2006.

46. *American Jewish Congress v. Corporation for National and Community Service*, No. 04-5315 (U.S. Court of Appeals, D.C. Cir. 2005): http://pacer.cadc.uscourts.gov/docs/common/opinions/200503/04-5317a.pdf; http://www.usdoj.gov/osg/briefs/2005/oresponses/2005-0282.resp.html; http://www.socialpolicyandreligion.org/legal/legal_update_display.cfm?id=34.

47. *Lown v. Salvation Army*, 04 Civ. 1562 (U.S. Southern Dist. N.Y., 2005), http://www.socialpolicyandreligion.org/legal/legal_update_display.cfm?id=38; http://www.social

policyandreligion.org/legal/legal_update_display.cfm?id=27; http://www.whitehouse
.gov/news/releases/2006/03/20060309-3.html.

48. Judge Robert W. Pratt, *Americans United for Separation of Church & State v.
Prison Fellowship Ministries*, 4:03-cv-90074 (U.S. Southern District Iowa, 2006), 125.

49. *Locke v. Davey*, 540 U.S. 712 (2004).

50. See these websites for more information on Blaine amendments: http://www
.blaineamendments.org/Intro/whatis.html;http://churchstatelaw.com/historicalmaterials/
8_11.asp.

51. Lupu and Tuttle, *State of the Law 2004: Partnerships between Government and
Faith-Based Organizations*, Roundtable on Religion and Social Welfare Policy, Dec. 9,
2004, http://www.religionandsocialpolicy.org/publications/publication.cfm?id=51.

52. Ibid., 9.

53. Peter Wallsten, Tom Hamburger, and Nicholas Riccardi, "Bush Rewarded by
Black Pastors' Faith: His stands, backed by funding of ministries, redefined the GOP's
image with some clergy." *Los Angeles Times*, Jan. 18, 2005.

54. Farris, Nathan, and Wright, "The Expanding Administrative Presidency," 16.

55. U.S. Rep. Elijah E. Cummings (D–Maryland), "For God Hath Not Given Us the
Spirit of Fear," Feb. 18, 2001, Greater Bethel AME Church, Charlotte, N.C.

56. Pat Robertson, "Faith-Based Initiatives Pose Some Problems" (no posting date),
http://www.patrobertson.com/NewsCommentary/FaithBasedInitiatives.asp.

57. William Lee Miller, *The First Liberty: America's Foundation in Religious Freedom,
Expanded and Updated* (Washington, D.C.: Georgetown University Press, 2003), 158.

58. James Madison, "Monopolies Perpetuities Corporations and Ecclesiastical Endowments" from papers written in retirement, 1819, http://www.constitution.org/jm/
18191213_monopolies.htm.

59. *Zelman v. Simmons-Harris*, 536 U.S. 639 (2002). Although this quote is excerpted
from a dissenting opinion, Breyer's point on this issue summarizes the general position
of the court for the past sixty years.

60. The White House, "President Discusses Faith-Based Initiative at Power Center
Celebration," Sept. 12, 2003, Houston, Tex., http://www.whitehouse.gov/news/releases/
2003/09/20030912-14.html.

61. Lupu and Tuttle, *State of the Law 2004*, 1.

62. Farris, Nathan, and Wright, "The Expanding Administrative Presidency," 2–3.

63. Cnaan, *The Newer Deal*, 292.

64. Ibid., 20, 279.

65. Richard P. Nathan, "Gaining Perspective on Faith-Based Issues" (lecture pre-
sented at the FACS/Pew Journalism, Religion & Public Life seminar, entitled, "Church
& State: The Future of Faith-Based Initiatives," Feb. 3, 2003, at the *Orlando Sentinel* in
Orlando, Fla.), http://facsnet.org/issues/faith/nathan.php.

66. Cnaan, *The Newer Deal*, 113–132.

67. Cotton Mather, "Bonifacius: An Essay Upon the Good, that is Devised and Designed by Those who Desire the Great End of Life and to Do Good While They Live,"
(1710): http://ksghome.harvard.edu/%7Ephall/08.%20Mather.pdf.
Also see Cnaan, *The Newer Deal*, 115.

68. Cnaan, *The Newer Deal*, 114.

69. Martin E. Marty, *Pilgrims in Their Own Land: 500 Years of Religion in America* (New York: Penguin Books, 1988), 347–355. Also see Sydney E. Ahlstrom, "Theology in America: A Historical Survey," in *The Shaping of American Religion*, ed. James Ward Smith and A. Leland Jamison (Princeton: Princeton University Press, 1961), 294–298.

70. Cnaan, *The Newer Deal*, 122.

71. Ibid., 119.

72. Ibid., 280.

73. Lupu and Tuttle, *State of the Law 2004*, 65.

74. Cnaan, *The Newer Deal*, 10 and 279.

75. Ronald Reagan, Remarks on Private Sector Initiatives at a White House Luncheon for National Religious Leaders, April 13, 1982, http://www.presidency.ucsb.edu/ws/index.php?pid=42386.

Reagan invokes Luke 10:25–37.

76. William J. Clinton, Acceptance Speech to the Democratic National Convention, July 16, 1992, New York, http://www.presidency.ucsb.edu/shownomination.php?convid=7.

77. Cnaan, *The Newer Deal*, 280–283.

78. The White House, "Unlevel Playing Field: Barriers to Participation by Faith-Based and Community Organizations in Federal Social Service Programs," August 2001, http://www.whitehouse.gov/news/releases/2001/08/20010816-3-report.pdf.

79. Cnaan, "The Invisible Caring Hand."

Chapter 7. Beyond the "Wall of Separation":
The Supreme Court and the First Amendment

1. William Lee Miller, *The First Liberty: Religion and the American Republic* (New York: Paragon House, 1985), 228, and Miller, *The First Liberty: America's Foundation in Religious Freedom, Expanded and Updated* (Washington, D.C.: Georgetown University Press, 2003), 192–193.

2. Thomas Jefferson, Letter to the Danbury Baptist Association (Jan. 1, 1802). Available on the University of Virginia online library: http://etext.lib.virginia.edu/toc/modeng/public/JefDanb.html.

Also see Miller, *The First Liberty*, rev. ed., 197.

3. Justice Hugo Black, delivering the opinion of the Court in *Everson v. Board of Education of the Township of Ewing*, 330 U.S. 1 (1947).

4. Chief Justice Warren Burger, delivering the opinion of the Court in *Lemon v. Kurtzman*, 403 U.S. 602 (1971).

5. *Wallace v. Jaffree*, 472 U.S. 38 (1985).

6. Justice Anthony Kennedy, concurring and dissenting, *County of Allegheny v. American Civil Liberties Union*, 492 U.S. 573 (1989).

7. Miller, *The First Liberty*, 1st ed., 330. Also see rev. ed., 160.

8. *Sherbert v. Verner*, 374 U.S. 398 (1963).

9. *Employment Division, Department of Human Resources of Oregon v. Smith*, 494 U.S. 872 (1990). Also see Miller, *The First Liberty*, rev. ed., 218.

10. *Employment Division v. Smith*, U.S. 660 (1988), certiorari to the Supreme Court of Oregon.

11. U.S. Code, Title 42, Chapter 21B, Religious Freedom Restoration, http://www4 .law.cornell.edu/uscode/html/uscode42/usc_sup_01_42_10_21B.html.

12. Justice Anthony Kennedy, delivering the opinion of the Court in *City of Boerne v. Flores*, 95–2074 (1997).

13. Miller, *The First Liberty*, rev. ed., 220.

14. See "State Religious Freedom Restoration Acts" on the RJ&L Religious Liberty Archive, http://www.churchstatelaw.com/statestatutes/religiousfreedom.asp

15. *Cutter v. Wilkinson*, 544 U.S. 709, (2005).

16. *Gonzales v. O Centro Espirita Beneficente Uniao Do Vegetal*, 04–1084 (2006).

17. *Lynch v. Donnelly*, 465 U.S. 668 (1984).

18. Justice Clarence Thomas, concurring in *Elk Grove Unified School District v. Michael Newdow*, 542 U.S. 1 (2004).

19. Justice Antonin Scalia, dissenting in *Lee v. Weisman*, 505 U.S. 577 (1991).

20. "Case Study of *Gonzales v. O Centro Espirita Beneficente Uniao Do Vegetal*, Herbal Tea Case: A Government Loss?" First Amendment Center, Nov. 1, 2005, http://www .firstamendmentcenter.org/faclibrary/casesummary.aspx?case=Gonzales_v_O_Centro_ Espirita_Beneficiente_Uniao_Do_Vegetal.

21. Miller, *The First Liberty*, rev. ed., 160, 190–191.

22. *Reynolds v. United States*, 98 U.S. 145 (1878).

23. Miller, *The First Liberty*, rev. ed., 119.

24. Miller, *The First Liberty*, 1st ed., 333–343.

25. Harlan Fiske Stone, "The Conscientious Objector," *Columbia University Quarterly* (October 1919), http://fp.okstate.edu/vestal/polsci4983/Articles/Chief_Justice_ Stone.htm.

26. Justice Tom Clark, writing for the Court in *School District of Abington Township, Pennsylvania v. Schempp*, 374 U.S. 203 (1963).

27. Miller, *The First Liberty*, 1st ed., 334. Also see rev. ed., 7, 222–227.

28. Justice Charles Evans Hughes, dissenting in *U.S. v. MacIntosh*, 283 U.S. 605 (1931).

29. *United States v. Seeger*, 380 U.S. 163 (1965).

30. Miller, *The First Liberty*, rev. ed., 196.

31. "Transcript: Day Two of the Roberts Confirmation Hearings," Sept. 13, 2005, *Washington Post*, http://www.washingtonpost.com/wp-dyn/content/article/2005/09/13/ AR2005091300876.html.

Also see Miller, *The First Liberty*, 1st ed., 284–286; and rev. ed., 250.

32. "Transcript: U.S. Senate Judiciary Committee Hearing on Judge Samuel Alito's Nomination to the Supreme Court," Jan. 10, 2006, *Washington Post*, http://www.wash ingtonpost.com/wp-dyn/content/article/2005/09/13/AR2005091300876.html.

33. *Gonzales v. Carhart*, 550, U.S. 05–380 (2007), http://www.supremecourtus.gov/ opinions/06pdf/05-380.pdf.

34. Pope John Paul II, "Statements on the Death Penalty by the Holy Father," available on the United States Conference of Catholic Bishops website: http://www.usccb .org/sdwp/national/deathpenalty/holyfather.shtml.

35. Schriro v. Landrigan, 550, U.S. 05–1575 (2007), http://www.supremecourtus.gov/ opinions/06pdf/05-1575.pdf.

36. Marci A. Hamilton, "Is the Court Catholic?" *Los Angeles Times*, Dec. 18, 2005.

37. Office of the Solicitor General, in amicus, Lee v. Weisman, No. 90–1014 (1990), http://www.usdoj.gov/osg/briefs/1990/sg900105.txt.

38. *ACLU of New Jersey v. Black Horse Pike Regional Board of Education*, No. 94–5233 (3rd Cir. 1995), http://www.ca3.uscourts.gov/opinarch/95a1109p.txt.

39. "Religion Clauses Protect Nonbelief, Alito Testifies," First Amendment Center, Jan. 13, 2006, http://www.firstamendmentcenter.org/news.aspx?id=16313.

40. *ACLU v. Schundler*, No. 98–5021 (3rd Cir. 1999), http://www.ca3.uscourts.gov/opinarch/985021.txt.

41. *Fraternal Order of Police, Newark Lodge No. 12; Faruq Abdul-Aziz and Shakoor Mustafa v. City of Newark*, No. 97–5542 (3d Cir. 1999), http://www.becketfund.org/litigate/newarkopinion.html.

42. Office of the Solicitor General, *Lamb's Chapel v. Center Moriches Union School District*, No. 91–2024, to S. Ct. (1992).

43. *Lamb's Chapel v. Center Moriches Union Free School District*, 508 U.S. 384 (1993).

44. Miller, *The First Liberty*, 1st ed., 326.

45. Miller, *The First Liberty*, 1st ed., 325–330. Also see rev. ed., 213–215.

46. Justice Hugo Black, delivering the opinion of the Court, *Engel v. Vitale*, 370 U.S. 421 (1962).

47. Chief Justice Warren Burger, delivering the opinion of the Court, *Lynch v. Donnelly* (1984).

48. Miller, *The First Liberty*, 1st ed., 319.

49. Ibid., 323.

Index

Education, 95, 104, 140; evolving models of, 99; fear of discussing religion in, 3, 6, 94; free exercise of religion in, 100–103; Jefferson on moral and civic instruction in, 49, 52; *Lamb's Chapel v. Center Moriches Union School District,* 167; Pennsylvania legal case regarding teaching intelligent design in, xiii–xiv, 105; in Protestant de facto establishment, 19; religious liberty in, 94–111; Supreme Court decisions on religion in, 94; teaching about religion in, 95–96, 108–11; unsettled religious liberty issues in, 106–8

Puritans, 7–8; assimilation of, 87; Calvinism of, 29, 33, 51, 52, 79; Franklin and, 93; influence on colonial America, 8, 29; legacy of, 86–87, 187n.38; paradox of, 79; predestination accepted by, 29, 33, 79; for religious liberty only for themselves, 85; Salem witch trials, 86; stereotypes of, 87; unfavorable view of, 86; Williams's criticism of, 80; Winthrop as leader of, 7–8, 46–47, 78–80; work valued by, 53

Quakers: exclusion from mainstream, xiii; as "Old Light," 8; as peace church, 157; in Pennsylvania, 10; Puritan influence on, 187n.38; Rhode Island as haven for, 90; Williams on toleration of, 82, 90; Williams's view of, 82, 90

"Queries of the Highest Consideration" (Williams), 80–81

Quoting God (Gaddy), 73

Rabaut, Louis C., 68
"rags to riches" dream, 54
rationalist view of religion, 26
Rauschenbusch, Walter, 135, 136
Reagan, Ronald, xiv, 20, 41, 47, 55, 71, 84, 137
reductionism, 39, 178n.42
Reformed Christianity, 51
Regas, George, xii
Rehnquist, William: on Establishment Clause decisions, 141, 161; on *Lemon v. Kurtzman,* 143–44; on *Locke v. Davey,* 128; on modern interpretations of First Amendment, 17; Roberts compared with, 165; on *Wallace v. Jaffree,* 141, 161; on *Zelman v. Simmons-Harris,* 104

religion: academic approach to, 110, 111; as affecting all news beats and humanities, 6; America's religious identification, 4; defining, 25–27; deism, 48, 50, 67, 68, 165; and family values, 134; fear of discussing in public schools, 3, 6, 94; as flourishing without government, 18–20; Freud's view of, 25; and identity, xiii; as irritating to outsiders, 24, 32–35; in lives of Americans, 3–5; number of congregations in U.S., 116; number of religious groups in U.S., 10; as "opiate of the masses," 25, 26; and philanthropy, 115–17, 133–34; in politics, 1–3; psychological characteristics associated with, 34–35, 177n.35; public versus private, 30–32, 109; rationalist and non-rationalist views of, 26; reducing acrimony in debates over, 38–40; relationships with culture, 36; republican, 43, 49; September, 11, 2001, attacks and awareness of importance of, 6, 27; stereotypes of religious people, 24–25, 32; teaching about in public schools, 95–96, 108–11; understanding people of faith, 24–40; varieties of American, 27–30. *See also* atheism; Bible, the; Christianity; civil religion; established churches; God; Islam; Jews and Judaism; prayer; religious liberty; religious strife; religious symbols; separation of church and state

Religious Freedom Restoration Act of 1993, 147–48, 155

Religious Land Use and Institutionalized Persons Act of 2000, 148

religious liberty: and Calvin's Geneva, 52; common threads of, 77–93; current issues in debate over, xii; diversity as basis of, 17–18; freedom of conscience concept underlies, 13; in public schools, 94–111; in Rhode Island, xii, 10, 90; state religious freedom restoration acts, 148; Virginia Statute for Religious Freedom, 11–12; Roger Williams as advocate of, 78. *See also* freedom of conscience; free exercise of religion; Religious Liberty Clauses

Religious Liberty Clauses: conscience not mentioned in, 13, 156; freedom of conscience concept underlies, 13; language of, 14; for maintaining unity in state of plurality, 100; as neither clear-cut nor absolute, 140; neutrality required by, 95–97; statement of, xii; strict constructionists on modern